Women in Song
and Yuan China

Women in Song and Yuan China

Bret Hinsch

宋元

ROWMAN & LITTLEFIELD
Lanham • Boulder • New York • London

Published by Rowman & Littlefield
An imprint of The Rowman & Littlefield Publishing Group, Inc.
4501 Forbes Boulevard, Suite 200, Lanham, Maryland 20706
www.rowman.com

6 Tinworth Street, London SE11 5AL, United Kingdom

British Library Cataloguing in Publication Information Available

Library of Congress Cataloging-in-Publication Data

Names: Hinsch, Bret, author.
Title: Women in Song and Yuan China / Bret Hinsch.
Description: Lanham : Rowman & Littlefield, [2021] | Includes bibliographical
    references and index.
Identifiers: LCCN 2020033387 (print) | LCCN 2020033388 (ebook) | ISBN
    9781538144916 (cloth) | ISBN 9781538144923 (epub)
    ISBN 9781538171165 (pbk)
Subjects: LCSH: Women—China—History—To 1500. | Women—China—Social
    conditions. | Sex role—China—History—To 1500. | China—History—Song dynasty,
    960–1279. | China—History—Yuan dynasty, 1260–1368.
Classification: LCC HQ1767 .H58 2021 (print) | LCC HQ1767 (ebook) | DDC
    305.420951—dc23
LC record available at https://lccn.loc.gov/2020033387
LC ebook record available at https://lccn.loc.gov/2020033388

Contents

Chronology of Dynasties and Eras

Introduction

Chinese women have always lived out their lives amid the currents of national affairs, subject to both abrupt upheavals and gradual shifts.[1] In the course of China's long history, several eras stand out as transformational. In antiquity, the invention of basic technologies such as agriculture, metallurgy, and writing allowed a sophisticated civilization to emerge. National unification in 221 BCE, concurrent with the establishment of the emperor system, set down a political arrangement that endured for more than two millennia. And the fall of the Han dynasty in the third century CE initiated a long interlude of division and chaos that only came to an end when the Sui dynasty reunited the realm in 589.

This book covers the changes that resulted from the next great period of transition, when a far more prosperous and dynamic society rose up to replace the aristocratic caste system. The era following the fall of the Eastern Han dynasty is often referred to as medieval. At that time, power, wealth, and prestige became closely tied to genealogy. A person's obligations and opportunities were usually predetermined at birth. Although the uppermost elite usually lacked noble title, historians nevertheless refer to them as aristocrats because they inherited their privileged status.[2] Aristocratic families intermarried for generations, creating an exclusive caste. Though small in number, they dominated politics, the economy, and culture. This social framework endured until the end of the Tang dynasty.

As the rulers of the Tang dynasty steadily lost control of China's periphery, the dynasty went into a long decline. Finally in 907 a warlord deposed the last Tang emperor, bringing the dynasty to a close. As the state collapsed, bandits pillaged the main cities, targeting the aristocracy in particular. The elite had congregated around the capital city of Chang'an, as many of them served in the central government. By gathering together in such a small area, they made themselves extremely vulnerable. When bandits captured the capital, they massacred the nobility and looted their property. Those who survived found themselves impoverished.

Historians point to the transition from Tang to Song as one of the most important turning points in Chinese history. Most famously, Naitō Konan (1866–1934), the driving force behind the influential Kyoto school of historiography, argued that the shift from aristocratic Tang society to the far more meritocratic Song system marked a major rupture.[3] Thereafter the elite could no longer rely on hereditary privilege to dominate society. Education, government service, and influential connections became new strategies for success. China's economy, social structure, and culture altered as well. Women and men had to respond to these fundamental changes, and they adjusted their behavior, values, and expectations to suit new circumstances.[4]

In the year 960 a military leader under the short-lived Later Zhou dynasty (951–960) staged a coup d'état. He declared himself Emperor Taizu (r. 960–976) and established a new dynasty that he called Song, which would endure for more than three centuries. Taizu was a talented general. He and his successor, Emperor Taizong (r. 976–997), reunified the realm and established a workable system of government. Notably, Taizu passed the throne to his younger brother instead of a son, as had been customary in previous dynasties. He probably did so to help stabilize the state, as his brother was mature and experienced. Whatever Taizu's motivations, he muddied the line of succession. Due to this early precedent, the Song imperial line lacked primogeniture. The emperor did not have to be the eldest son of the previous monarch. This ambiguity sometimes allowed empresses dowager to have a say in choosing the ruler.

With the realm reunited and stabilized, Emperor Taizong devoted himself to establishing a comprehensive administrative framework. The Song system differed from that of the Tang in some key respects. Whereas the central government had previously been fairly weak, Song rulers consolidated authority and created a strong central government. They understood how empowering local leaders had previously led to civil unrest, so they did not invest provincial officials with too much authority. And while Tang emperors made decisions after casually discussing matters with leading officials, Song court procedures were far more formal, bureaucratic, and professional.

The type of men serving in government also changed. The most important aristocratic families of the Tang had been exterminated, so emperors could no longer select high ministers from the traditional hereditary elite. Instead they relied on demanding civil service examinations to identify intelligent and educated candidates for office. This meritocratic system opened up opportunities to men of talent throughout the nation. Henceforth, those who aspired to serve in office had to spend years preparing for grueling examinations that tested their familiarity with the classical canon and ability to compose fluent essays. This learning may have been unrelated to the mechanics of administration, but it proved diligence, the capacity to master large amounts of information, and an ability to write bureaucratic documents in the proper style. During Taizong's reign alone, more than five thousand men obtained degrees. The examination system produced a new social stratum of literati officials who staked their prestige on their educational credentials and mastery of high culture, not the length of their genealogy.

The founding rulers Taizu and Taizong had to devote themselves to warfare, which honed their talents. But their successors grew up in the effete environs of the palace, so they were far less vigorous. Even so, some rulers continued to refine the workings of administration. In particular, Emperor Zhenzong (r. 997–1022) established offices and regulations appropriate for all levels of government, bringing the bureaucratic system to maturity. Among all of China's dynasties, the Song came closest to the Confucian ideal of rule by talented men who had been shaped by classical learning.

During the reign of Emperor Zhenzong in the early eleventh century, nomadic peoples began to pose a serious threat. The neighboring Liao kingdom to the northeast, ruled by Khitan conquerors, periodically raided China's border regions. Although Zhenzong lacked a martial demeanor, he nevertheless aggressively counterattacked and forced Liao to negotiate. Both sides agreed to a nonaggression pact. However, to obtain this agreement, Zhenzong had to treat the ruler of Liao as his equal. This compromise enraged hawkish officials who demanded that China hold itself above neighboring countries.

Factionalism, slanders, and intrigues plagued the Liao court, gradually weakening that state. In 1121, Jurchen nomads allied with China, and the two armies simultaneously invaded Liao. This two-pronged attack brought down the Liao state, and the Khitans fled to central Asia. Ominously for China, although Chinese troops had little success in battle, the Jurchens readily overcame their foes. Everyone realized that the victory had been achieved by Jurchens, not Chinese. After destroying Liao, the Jurchens established a state called Jin, which imitated Chinese administration in many respects.

Although the Chinese and Khitans had been adversaries, the destruction of Liao presaged future challenges for China. The triumph over Liao emboldened the Jurchens, and they set their sights on their giant neighbor to the south. Unfortunately for China, at this critical time an idiosyncratic and incompetent ruler happened to occupy the throne. Emperor Huizong (r. 1082–1135) dedicated himself to aesthetic pursuits and squandered the government's budget on palaces, gardens, and artworks. Huizong may have been a talented artist and tasteful connoisseur, but this hedonistic ruler had little interest in boring meetings and documents. He let corrupt minions make key decisions, and they sidelined competent officials. Largely due to Huizong's chronic mismanagement, when Jurchen horsemen invaded in 1125, China's government could not muster an effective response. The Jurchen army defeated China's armies and carried off Huizong and his court to a humiliating captivity where they lived in poverty and tilled the land. During this invasion, hordes of terrified Chinese fled south. Remnants of China's government reestablished an attenuated state known as the Southern Song, making the prosperous commercial city Hangzhou their new capital. In the aftermath of this conflict, China ended up divided between the Jin dynasty in the north and the Southern Song in the south.

Figure I.1. Empress Cao (Wikimedia Commons)

When the Jurchens settled in China, they found themselves vastly out-numbered by their Chinese subjects. To administer this huge realm and win over a hostile populace, they adopted many aspects of Chinese culture. The Jurchen nobility confiscated large landholdings and enjoyed immense wealth. But their followers, accustomed to a nomadic way of life, struggled to adapt to sedentary existence. Many failed to thrive in their strange new surround-ings. Given the incompatibility of nomadic Jurchen customs with settled life, Jin rulers relied heavily on established Chinese institutions and Confucian ideology to rule.

The Jin emperors realized that they lacked the resources to conquer the Southern Song state, so they accepted coexistence. And while some Chinese patriots agitated for an invasion of the north, the Song remnants made only token efforts to reunify the realm. Most southerners accepted the inevitability of national division. In fact, northern émigrés came to appreciate life in the south. At first they felt alienated by the unfamiliar landscape and customs, and they longed to return home. But over time they embraced the lush environment and sophisticated culture. The sudden influx of talented and industrious northern refugees boosted the southern economy and elevated scholarship and the arts.

Eventually, a powerful army gathered along China's northern frontier, threatening both the Jin and the Southern Song dynasties. In prior decades, Chinggis (Genghis) Khan (1162–1227) had led Mongol tribesmen out of their isolated homeland and conquered an immense empire that stretched across Eurasia. The Mongols looked to China as their next target. In 1211 they invaded Jurchen territory, annihilated Jin, and annexed northern China. Then in the 1250s they commenced hostilities against the Southern Song. The decayed dynasty could not resist this onslaught, and the Mongols decisively defeated China's army in 1279.

Wang Qinghui (fl. 1270), consort of the last ruler of the Southern Song, wrote a poem lamenting her country's defeat. She described the psychological effects of this cataclysmic event from the perspective of a palace lady, mourn-ing China's downfall as the sad termination of an age of beauty and glory.[5]

> The lotus of Taiyi Pond
> Has nothing of the color she displayed in the past.
> Still she remembers
> The imperial favor that fell like rain and dew
> In jade towers and golden pavilions.
> Her fame spread, an orchid hairpin among the imperial consorts,
> A radiant blush suffused her lotus face as she accompanied the emperor.
> Suddenly one day
> War drums approached across the heavens,
> Splendor came to an end.

Mongol conquerors used Chinese-style administration to stabilize and rule their subjugated territory, establishing a dynasty called Yuan. But, even though the Yuan government maintained many Chinese practices, the Mongol khans nevertheless differed considerably from traditional Chinese emperors. They came from a pastoral culture with values and institutions unsuited to sedentary agricultural society. The Mongols' stunning success in conquering a vast empire that stretched from eastern Europe to Korea made them overconfident, and they blithely cast aside the norms that had underpinned effective Chinese government for centuries. The Mongols had little patience for bureaucracy. Yuan rulers and officials made many decisions in an ad hoc manner, throwing the state into confusion.

Kublai Khan (r. 1271–1294), grandson of Chinggis, established the capital of the Yuan dynasty at Dadu (Beijing). The Mongol invasion had been unusually savage. The invading horde massacred ordinary Chinese indiscriminately, earning the hatred of the conquered.[6] Kublai tried to reassure his hostile new subjects and win their support. Nevertheless, the Mongols faced formidable challenges, and their traditional methods of rule did not suit such a large and complex nation. Only the support of efficient Han officials allowed the Yuan dynasty to endure as long as it did. Eventually a series of natural disasters and famines pushed the peasantry into rebellion. The rebel commander Zhu Yuanzhang declared the advent of a new dynasty that he called Ming and led an army against the hated foreign overlords. He eventually expelled the Mongols from China, bringing the Yuan to an end in 1368 after less than a century of rule.

Sometimes the historian gets so caught up in the dramatic narrative of emperors and wars that far more significant facts end up overlooked. Above all, China's Song dynasty stands out as the most advanced civilization that humanity had ever constructed up to that point. When compared to Song emperors, Western monarchs of the time seem shabby, ignorant, and barbarous. While Europeans eked out a living in a poor feudalistic society not far above the subsistence level, the Chinese were building large and opulent cities. Artisans created splendid craftworks, and merchants sold a dazzling array of consumer goods. During the twelfth and thirteenth centuries, European kings and nobles had a rudimentary education, if any. In contrast, contemporary Chinese rulers and officials had to master a demanding curriculum covering history, literature, and philosophy.

Economic historians regard the transition between Tang and Song as a major turning point in Chinese history.[7] During the Tang dynasty, China had about sixty million people. By the twelfth century, this had risen to one hundred million.[8] Moreover, as millions of people drifted south, the population of southern China increased. Fecund southern paddies supplanted the dry northern plains as China's economic heartland, raising agricultural output. Rich rice harvests sparked an explosion of economic activity.

Population increases also spurred the growth of cities, a trend that transformed Chinese society and culture. Urban centers not only became larger and more numerous, but they also had an unprecedented atmosphere. Tang dynasty cities were semirural by modern standards. Most of the alleged inhabitants were in fact peasants living in nearby villages. In contrast, Song cities would have seemed familiar to modern eyes.

The Tang had restricted commerce to designated market areas controlled by officials, but Song authorities loosened government oversight, allowing commerce to flourish. Productivity, organizational efficiency, and technology all advanced rapidly, providing a wider range of goods and services at lower prices than ever before. Shops selling every imaginable product lined the main streets, creating a culture of consumption. Restaurants, teahouses, and bordellos catered to every budget, and ordinary people could search for pleasures amid a sophisticated milieu. However, not everyone could freely participate in this exciting new society. Women were largely confined to the home. They may have been able to enjoy new consumer goods coming in from outside, but only men could take full advantage of the fun and exciting new urban spaces.

During the Song, the relations among people were reconfigured along new lines. As the commercial economy flourished, society became far more complex than before.[9] The Tang had ended with the sudden extermination of the dominant aristocratic class, so a new elite emerged.[10] Links between genealogy, wealth, and power broke down, and social mobility no longer seemed exceptional. Amid these new circumstances, respected families declined from wealth to poverty, and newcomers rose to take their place.[11] Savvy merchants could become extremely rich. These nouveaux riches flaunted their wealth and aped the lifestyles of the literati. They wore silk garments, resided in luxurious mansions, drank fine tea, assembled impressive gardens, and collected antiques. Even though most people had a stable position in society, the possibility that someone might either rise or fall in station confronted people with novel possibilities that they found both exciting and disturbing.

While social mobility benefited merchants, it posed challenges for the landowning gentry. Status had become increasingly linked to wealth, so they could no longer depend on a lengthy genealogy to sustain them. However, the gentry despised most types of productive work, limiting themselves to agriculture, teaching, and the civil service. Because of these self-imposed economic limitations, a gentry family periodically had to produce someone capable of serving in the bureaucracy to bring in a fresh infusion of wealth.

An influx of capital from government service allowed a family to maintain their status for a few more generations. To survive, the gentry had to focus their attentions on passing the examinations used to recruit officials. Coincidentally, rising educational attainments allowed them to undertake highly refined cultural pursuits. In this way, the gentry became literati, embracing high culture as an essential component of their privileged status.

Song culture also stands out as a time of great creativity. Growing prosperity roused cultural effervescence. Simultaneously, stiffly competitive examinations elevated educational standards and polished taste and manners. Technological changes also fostered cultural change. Printing became widespread, making books affordable. For the first time, books became ordinary objects, and readers could easily assemble private libraries. This explosion in written material presents a precious gift to the historian. Sources from this period are more copious and varied than in previous eras, when texts had to be laboriously transcribed by hand.

The new atmosphere of cultivation spurred scholarship and gave birth to new ideas. Compared to the educated people of medieval times, the Song intellectual elite were far less interested in religion. The Confucian revival that had begun in the Tang came to fruition during the Song, encouraging the literati to devote their time to classical learning and cultivated amusements. Scholars did not just study past ideas but also reinterpreted ancient texts, giving rise to the Neo-Confucian movement. Initial reactions to Neo-Confucianism varied. During the Song dynasty, most people considered Neo-Confucian thinkers excessively strict, so they initially had limited influence. However, Song Neo-Confucianism found an enthusiastic audience in subsequent eras. These teachings eventually enjoyed government sponsorship and became the official ideology of the Chinese state.

Song writings show more fluency and self-confidence than before. While Tang prose was often ornate and pretentious, Song authors wrote in a far more engaging manner. Song authors used a supple new prose style to offer authentic insights into their society, providing higher-quality sources for the historian. The new mode of writing affected the content of commemorative eulogies, a major source for women's history.[12] Tang eulogies had often employed florid turns of phrase and arcane classical allusions. Although these texts look impressive, they do not seem very convincing. Tang authors depicted the deceased as a bland social archetype, not a distinct individual. In contrast, Song epitaphs seem much more realistic. Writers included unique personal details and revealing anecdotes that provide an interesting and more faithful portrait of the deceased.

Readers can be forgiven for questioning the time frame of this book. Usually a historical study covers a period that constitutes a coherent unity. Admittedly, the Song and Yuan dynasties differed in fundamental ways and often seem to present more differences than similarities. In this case, however, comparing these two periods side by side serves a valuable function. It allows scholars to address one of the most contested issues in the history of Chinese women. Historians have frequently observed that restrictions on women's lives generally intensified over the course of Chinese imperial history. The Six Dynasties, Sui, and Tang are often described as relatively "open" eras when women enjoyed considerable autonomy.[13] Yet by the Ming dynasty, the scope of permissible action for women had contracted notably.[14] The law discriminated against female interests. Footbinding had become extremely common, making it physically impossible for women to engage in many activities outside the home. And social norms encouraged strict fidelity and reclusion.

At some point between the Tang and Ming eras, women's lives underwent substantial changes. However, the timing of this disjunction remains disputed. Early twentieth-century intellectuals such as Hu Shi and Lin Yutang singled out the Song as a time when the Chinese became increasingly close-minded.[15] During the Republican era, it became common to blame Buddhism for fostering torpid conservatism.[16] At that time, thinkers such as Qian Mu saw Buddhism as an agent of Indian culture, which they considered backward, superstitious, and enervating. Others pointed to the rise of Neo-Confucianism, together with the Song obsession with classicism and ritual orthodoxy, as making Chinese society more restrictive. More recent scholarship has also argued that the Song represents a major turning point in Chinese women's history. These historians claim that reactionary social, legal, and cultural trends began in the Song and culminated in the Ming and Qing.[17]

Recently, however, other historians have begun to contest this point of view. The revisionist interpretation points to the numerous similarities between Tang and Song society and contends that women's general social position was fairly similar in these two eras. These scholars believe that the main transformations in gender ideals occurred not during the Song but under the rule of three conquest states: the Liao dynasty of the Khitans, the Jin dynasty established by the Jurchens, and the Mongols' Yuan dynasty. These alien regimes differed fundamentally from both Tang and Song in key respects. Recent investigations of the kinship customs, laws, edicts, and administrative regulations under these alien regimes suggest that many of their policies and customs had a negative impact on the lives of Chinese women.

Historians have yet to come to a consensus regarding the impact that the conquest regimes had on China. The Yuan stands out as perhaps the most controversial dynasty in China's long history. Chinese historians traditionally had a virulently hostile view of Mongols and the Yuan, to the point that they denied the dynasty's legitimacy and were loath to admit any long-term influence on Chinese institutions or culture. Since the 1980s, however, opinions have shifted somewhat.[18] The Chinese government considers the Mongols an ethnic minority, so instead of viewing the Yuan as a conquest regime they have rebranded it as a legitimate dynasty ruled by a Chinese ethnic minority. Yet in spite of this change in the official viewpoint, Chinese academia maintains a negative view of the Yuan and the Chinese public considers the Mongol conquest a terrible catastrophe.

Scholars in other regions have also condemned Mongol rule. Historians in Russia and the countries of Central and West Asia conventionally portrayed the Mongols as cruel and destructive.[19] And many Muslim historians consider the Mongol sack of Baghdad a crushing blow to Islam. Until fairly recently, Western academics took a similarly negative view of the Mongol Empire. However, revisionists have recently pressed for a reassessment of the place that nomads hold in world history. They argue that instead of seeing nomads solely from the standpoint of the sedentary peoples they affected, they should be understood on their own terms. This reimagining of nomadic culture portrays it as sophisticated and worthy of respect.[20] A sympathetic approach to nomadism has led some historians in the West to reassess the Yuan dynasty. They note that most Chinese came to consider the Yuan legitimate and emphasize the impact of certain Yuan institutions on Chinese administration and culture.[21]

The purpose of this book is not to understand the Mongols from the standpoint of Inner Asian history but to assess their impact on China. Given this goal, they should be seen from the Chinese standpoint. Chinese sources overwhelmingly describe the Mongols as cruel conquerors and incompetent administrators. Their reign began as an orgy of needless destruction, resulting in the deaths of untold millions. Thereafter the Mongols instituted a poorly designed administrative system that hobbled ministers in the central government. Paralysis at the center devolved power down to local officials, wealthy gentry, and hooligans, who then tore the realm apart. Ineffective institutions doomed the Yuan to steady disintegration. After decades of misrule, the Mongol regime finally collapsed from the crushing weight of its own ineptitude.

The bulk of this book describes the Song, which had a far longer history than the regimes established by foreign invaders. A coda then examines the society and administration of the Liao, Jin, and Yuan dynasties from the standpoint of the condition of women. Juxtaposing the Song with succeeding conquest dynasties helps to clarify the fraught question of how the conquest dynasties affected female status, and which era should be considered the time of greatest transition in Chinese women's history.

Chapter 1

Family

The transition from the stratified aristocratic society of the Tang dynasty to the far more dynamic Song system challenged the ways that people thought about kinship and family. Because women spent most of their time within the domestic sphere, these changes had a particularly large impact on female identity and experience. Many aspects of Song family life remained unchanged. The state continued to uphold basic Tang regulations regarding kinship. Marriage between people of divergent social backgrounds was still prohibited so as to maintain the reputation of the elite.[1] And, as before, the government prohibited polyandry (the marriage of one woman to two or more men), a pragmatic measure sometimes used by the poor to reduce the cost of marriage.[2]

Regardless of this overarching continuity, some regulations regarding family life nevertheless altered appreciably. Compared to earlier eras, Song authorities put far more emphasis on the domestic models set down in classical ritual and ethics. Ancient authorities believed that women should stay at home most of the time. As the government took actions to enforce these strictures, women found themselves increasingly confined to the domestic realm. The revival of classical standards also diminished women's overall standing in the eyes of society and the state. The justice system sometimes treated women and men very differently. Whereas a man convicted of a serious crime might be sentenced to exile, a woman found guilty of the same offense would be consigned to the custody of her family.[3] Authorities believed that sending a woman away from her kin would contravene family ethics, so they modified punishments to bind female convicts even more tightly to the home. Jurists believed that even a woman who committed a crime ought to spend her entire life embedded within a family, where she would presumably be under the firm control of either parents or husband.

Following the collapse of the Eastern Han dynasty in the third century, many ethnic Chinese intermarried with nomadic peoples and assimilated foreign kinship practices. Song officials despised steppe customs and tried to extirpate behaviors that departed from ancient norms. Laws enforced ancient ritual rules that prohibited inappropriate marriage partners, such as people of the same surname or of different generations.[4] Most importantly, unlike the medieval dynasties, which tolerated considerable ethnic mixing, the Song state prohibited marriages between ethnic Han and nomadic peoples.[5] This policy reversed the long-standing practice of allowing unions between people of different ethnic groups.

Although thinkers and officials reconceptualized family organization along classical lines, ideas about kinship remained inconsistent. The Song elite conceived of the family in contradictory ways.[6] Sometimes they referenced the ancient classics and described the family in idealized terms. Nonetheless, they also recognized that current social conditions differed considerably from those of antiquity and ignored inapplicable traditions. Although they esteemed ancient norms, even the gentry often behaved pragmatically. Ordinary people conceived of the family in economic terms, regarding it as a group of kin holding wealth in common. These competing visions, based on either the ancient classics or economic reality, gave rise to conflicting priorities. Whereas ritual obligations enforced hierarchy, economic and social necessity encouraged tolerance and flexibility.

The conflict between ideals and pragmatism can be seen in how people dealt with the question of who should lead the family. The rites strengthened the integrity of the male line of descent and demanded a thoroughly patriarchal family system. Yet sometimes a woman had to serve as the de facto head of a household. Administrative documents mention the existence of so-called female households (*nühu*).[7] This term did not refer to a household composed only of women but to a group of coresidents headed by a woman termed a "female head" (*nüzhu*). Song law followed Tang precedent in granting a widow who lacked an adult son authority over the household. Sometimes a female head of household served temporarily until her son reached maturity, at which time he took over this duty. If a childless widow did not remarry, she managed her deceased husband's property for the rest of her life. She was expected to appoint one of his kinsmen as a legal heir who would inherit the estate when she died. Sometimes a woman would bring in a new husband to live in her former spouse's home, using matrilocal residence to maintain the continuity of the household. The government allowed women to serve as head of household out of necessity. A household had to have a designated manager because the government wanted to invest a specific individual with responsibility for paying taxes on behalf of the entire family.

Later the government of the Ming dynasty strictly regulated the actions of female heads of household. But during the Song, women serving in this role enjoyed considerable autonomy.

Over the course of the dynasty, family structure came under increasing stress. Faced with the vicissitudes of war and chaos, people had to be pragmatic, so they behaved in ways that their forebears would have regarded with dismay.[8] Many families fragmented. Brothers divided up family land while a parent remained alive. The average size of households decreased, infanticide became common, and some parents with multiple sons sent a child away to be raised in a Daoist or Buddhist institution. In response to the widening gap between contemporary customs and classical ideals, Neo-Confucian thinkers called for the restoration of ancient standards of family propriety. They demanded that families regroup as large joint households and even lineages. Yet, given the pressures that families faced, even ethical purists found it challenging to maintain a multigenerational household whose members held property in common.

When a large family split up, women often took the blame. Since ancient times, men had regarded wives as outsiders to the core patrilineal family and assumed that female interests contravened those of men. In some respects, the interests of female and male family members did indeed differ. Male seniors could maximize their power by holding a large household together, as this arrangement kept more people under their direct control. In contrast, a woman who convinced her husband to establish a separate household would have fewer male superiors in the home and thus gain more autonomy.

Although Confucian rhetoric blamed selfish women for family breakups, in fact the rules of inheritance usually triggered fragmentation.[9] When a society practices primogeniture, it is in the economic interests of younger brothers to live with the eldest sibling who controls the family's wealth. But China had partitive inheritance. Because each son received a share of family land, in the long run there was no reason for brothers to continue residing together after the death of their parents, and they usually established separate households as soon as possible.

Contrary to the image of women as home wreckers bent on separating husbands from their kinsmen, in reality they did not seek to bring down the male-dominated kinship system.[10] Women usually tried to enforce domestic rules and customs, as breaking the rules and flouting ethical norms earned them contempt. If a married woman worked within the prevailing framework and strengthened her family, she could win the respect of her husband's kin and raise her own standing among them.

The average size of families fluctuated considerably over the centuries, altering family dynamics with each change. Song families tended to be smaller than those of the Tang, which had six or more members on average.[11] During the Song era, sons usually left home and established an independent household when they married, so the size of families shrank. The conventional family consisted of wife and husband, their unmarried children, and perhaps one of the husband's parents.[12] Small households had practical advantages. They could more easily escape the attentions of the authorities, and members might sometimes avoid taxes and corvée duty. Moreover, during the Southern Song, the amount of land held by the average family decreased.[13] A smaller field could not sustain as many people, so family size contracted.

The story collection *Extensive Records of the Taiping Era* (*Taiping guangji*), completed at the beginning of the Song in 978, describes numerous fictional families. According to these accounts, family size was closely related to general social standing. The families of wealthy landowners in the narratives have 5.6 members on average, while commoner families consist of only 3.9 people.[14] Family size continued to contract over time. Those described in the thirteenth-century story collection *Records of Yi Jian* (*Yi Jian zhi*) are even smaller. In these tales, wealthy families have 4.7 members, while those of commoners have four people.[15]

Although smaller families had become the norm during the Song, sometimes two or more nuclear families lived side by side, shared a cooking stove, and held property in common. In doing so, they created a large communal family.[16] Expanding the size of the kinship group benefited members by enlarging the pool of available resources. Uniting families could also help overcome the steady fragmentation of property holdings that resulted from generation after generation of partitive inheritance. Because each son received a share of the family landholdings, the average size of their fields inevitably decreased over time. Coming together as a large extended household could reunite a family's divided fields.

Because large kinship groupings offered benefits, it made sense to encourage them by valorizing extended families. Neo-Confucians praised large families as a moral antidote to individual selfishness. Yet, even as people employed Neo-Confucian ideas to legitimize larger kinship organizations, they borrowed concrete organizational techniques from Buddhism. Communal families often copied the management practices of Buddhist monasteries, which presented a clear blueprint for harmonious communal life. Monks or nuns shared common property, submitted to an orderly leadership structure, and kept meticulous records. By copying Buddhist monastic management, extended families could remain stable even as they expanded in size.

Because kin found it convenient to gather together for mutual benefit, lineages and clans regained importance.[17] People once again put great emphasis on ancestral ties. Qingming, one of the most important annual festivals, was dedicated to the veneration of ancestors. And a bride performed rites to honor her new husband's ancestors to signal her entry into his family. Given the stress that people put on their forebears, descendants of a common ancestor found it convenient to come together and cooperate.[18] Large kinship units took several forms: extended households, communal families, lineages, and clans. A lineage consisted of a group of extended relatives who traced their descent back to a common ancestor. If a group of alleged kin owned property or other assets in common, they constituted a clan. Given the utility of these groupings, sometimes people created fictional kinship bonds. Neighbors who shared a surname might declare themselves to be related, even if they had no proof of kinship.

Although medieval Chinese society also had clans, these organizations took on new functions during the Song era. Due to the weak and fragmented medieval administrative system, earlier clans often played important political, administrative, and military roles in their communities. They helped stabilize and even govern local society in times of chaos. But with the rise of efficient bureaucratic government, officials no longer allowed clans to handle local administration. Clan leaders redirected their attentions toward managing their members' collective wealth and conducting rituals.

As the population grew and land ownership became increasingly unequal, many families ended up scratching out a living on plots of land that were too small. People pushed to the economic margins often turned to their extended kin for aid. The inequality of landholdings helps account for the rising importance of large kinship organizations. When numerous families formed a clan, even if most of the members were poor, they could raise their collective standard of living by pooling resources. Literati aided clan formation by collating detailed genealogies used to demarcate membership. And as lineages and clans established ancestral halls in imitation of the great literati families, they could appear dignified and raise their collective status. Moreover, scions of the minor gentry could bolster their reputation and gain authority by becoming clan leaders.[19] People in Guangdong and Fujian enthusiastically embraced clan ideals. These groupings became important in the south, even as they remained relatively uncommon in much of the north.

Because women were largely confined to the domestic realm, shifts in kinship organization had a particularly large impact on their lives. In general, as the size of a family increases, the overall status of its female members tends to decline. In smaller families, women often control many household resources, whereas in large families senior men dominate assets and regulate the behavior of members, restricting female agency.[20] During the Song, some thinkers tried to redefine women's kinship position by stressing their membership in lineages. People had traditionally considered women primarily as members of a family. However, the Neo-Confucian thinker Cheng Yi (1033–1107) reconceptualized female identity by emphasizing that women belong to a lineage as well.[21] While this might seem like a trivial distinction, in fact this shift carried significant implications. Women traditionally had important roles in the family. However, they had a minor place in the lineage system, where their duties were largely ceremonial. Shifting the focus of women's identity from family to lineage thus decreased their overall importance within the kinship system.

Although Cheng Yi seems to have seen the lineage as a tool for containing women, in fact the relationship between female agency and the size of kinship units was far from straightforward.[22] The formation of lineages and clans extended the scope of the domestic realm, presenting women with new opportunities. Because women already had important roles within the family, sometimes they took on leadership positions in a lineage organization. Moreover, pooling common property could also benefit women. Lineages sometimes deployed their resources to support chaste widows, so the rise of lineages expanded the range of options and allowed some widows to avoid having to remarry out of economic necessity.

Due to the changing social structure, relations between affines differed somewhat from before. Although families still used the male line to reckon descent, men had increasingly close ties with the families of their wives and mothers.[23] This shift in kinship relations resulted from more general changes in social structure during the Tang–Song transition. The aristocratic society of the Tang had stressed genealogy as the paramount factor determining social status. Families with exalted ancestry attracted the best marriage partners. During the Song, however, elite families selected sons-in-law according to different criteria. As the administrative system became more meritocratic, family background no longer predicted a young man's potential for a successful career. He had to succeed at the civil service examinations to gain office, and an impressive genealogy did not guarantee that he would obtain a degree. Faced with these changes, instead of looking for a son-in-law with the most prestigious lineage, elite families searched for a man who had already passed the examinations or at least seemed likely to eventually pass.[24]

Aligning with a degreed in-law could help a family's men gain connections, sponsors, and allies. Passing the civil service examinations also served as a prestigious social marker. The gentry realized that they could no longer maintain high position simply by intermarrying with established counterparts. They had to match a daughter with whichever man had the best career prospects, even if he came from a somewhat lower background.[25] If a promising son-in-law became a successful official as expected, his wife's family would benefit from his reputation, connections, and wealth. The son-in-law of a high official might often even reside with his wife's family for a time, as a close relationship could be advantageous to both sides in the long run.[26] The increasing desirability of degree holders did not end intermarriage among the elite, as the men who succeeded at the exams usually came from gentry backgrounds.[27] However, the criteria used to judge the appeal of particular elite men as marriage partners had shifted significantly from genealogy to merit.

The number of degree holders was limited, so elite families with daughters had to compete for their attentions. As families vied with one another to attract the best sons-in-law, they offered increasingly large dowries to attract a suitable groom. The fathers of brides were willing to pay out a large dowry in return for possible future rewards. Even wealthy merchants sometimes paid out an expensive dowry to marry their daughters into respected literati families as a way to elevate their own standing.[28] Dowries had already begun to increase during the Tang era. As competition to marry one's daughter to a degree candidate intensified during the Song, dowries came to exceed betrothal gifts in value.[29]

A family's status affected the geographic range of its marriage partners. The lower gentry usually intermarried with counterparts of comparable standing living nearby.[30] Those higher up had to search farther away if they wanted to find an appropriate match. Generally speaking, the higher a family's status, the more distant its marriage partners.[31] Savvy families sought alliances both with those already in power as well as with men who might become important in the future. Some elite families practiced even more diversified strategies by intermarrying with the imperial line and high officials.[32] Even so, people hoped to find a spouse from the same general region who spoke the same dialect for the sake of compatibility.

The Wu family of Pucheng in Fujian exemplifies the marriage practices of the upper elite.[33] This talented family produced examination graduates for generations and became extremely prominent in the early Song. They selected their marriage partners very carefully and allied themselves with nationally prominent figures, including Wang Anshi. However, their ambitions eventually proved dangerous, as some of their powerful in-laws belonged to factions that eventually fell from favor. Links to disgraced affines contributed to the eventual decline of the Wu, who lost prominence during the Southern Song.

The female poet Zheng Yunduan (ca. 1327–1356) summed up the potential drawbacks of marriage with an important official family.[34]

When planting flowers, don't plant them by the official highway,
And when marrying daughters, don't marry them to noble princes.
Flowers planted by the official road get plucked by passers-by,
Daughters married to noble princes do not enjoy long unions.

⊶⫤⊷

Writers of popular fiction used their works to explore the changing forms of marriage. At this time, stories about the "talented man and beautiful woman" became an important genre. According to this new romantic ideal, a desirable woman should be matched with a gifted young man who shows good career potential. Yuan dynasty dramas about a man taking an examination often featured a female character who sacrifices herself for the sake of her loved one's advancement.[35] In a typical script, a woman married to an aspiring student selflessly encourages him to go to the capital to take an examination, even though this requires them to spend time apart. They look on this separation as a terrible hardship, but in the end he earns a degree, so her unselfish devotion pays off.

As the hereditary aristocracy lost their stranglehold on high office, marriage increasingly devolved into a financial transaction between two families. As the economy grew, elite families had more money, wealth became increasingly fluid, and social mobility increased. Faced with these circumstances, people increasingly relied on marriage finance to better their prospects.[36] While the parents of brides sought a son-in-law with a degree or office, grooms sought a wife with a large dowry. In effect, the groom was selling himself to his in-laws, and the bride's family was buying a well-placed kinsman. Some dowries were very substantial and might include large tracts of land. As a contemporary writer described the customs of the time, "for sickness they are addicted to shamans. For funerals they are addicted to Buddhism. And for marriage they are addicted to wealth."[37]

Some authorities criticized the blatant commercialization of marriage. The conservative Neo-Confucian thinker Sima Guang (1019–1086) believed that a wedding is above all a union of two surnames, so it should take place in the ancestral temple and be marked by solemn ceremonies.[38] He complained that greed had degraded marriage, and the families of brides and grooms haggled as if they were buying and selling slaves. In spite of criticism, in-laws exchanged increasing amounts of wealth to cement their relationship.

The rising expense of marriage caused problems.[39] Concern about the implications of financial marriages sparked moral panic, with critics warning that this unseemly practice would erode ethical standards. They feared that respectable families might accept an unseemly match simply for profit. But aside from concerns over the propriety of financial marriage, rising costs raised real-world complications as well. As dowries expanded, it became increasingly difficult for families to accumulate such a large sum, so some young women had to delay marriage. Moreover, financial marriage could complicate domestic life. If spouses came from extremely different social backgrounds, domestic friction became more likely.

The new dynamics of marriage gave rise to novel strategies. It became extremely common for a teacher to select a son-in-law from among his students.[40] Men preparing for the civil service examinations were often taught by a senior relative, usually a maternal uncle, and cross-cousin marriage was not uncommon.[41] Some people even considered this an optimal match and encouraged it. To circumvent incest taboos, a man would usually marry a cousin from his mother's side. A maternal relative serving as a young man's teacher would be in the best position to assess his potential. If he thought that his student had a bright future, he might propose a match with his own daughter. Because these men were already kinsmen and lived in the same region, this sort of marriage was particularly convenient. The teacher would devote his full attention to his son-in-law cum student, increasing the chance that the young man would pass the examinations and assume office.

Families without sons sometimes resorted to matrilocal residence, the wife bringing in a husband to live with her parents.[42] Although grooms considered this arrangement embarrassing, they sometimes consented to it to raise their standard of living. Matrilocal husbands were usually men with poor prospects. If a man had several brothers, he could not expect to inherit much land. His family might not even be able to afford a decent betrothal gift. Although the escalation of dowry has garnered the most attention from historians, during the Song and Yuan the price of betrothal gifts increased as well, pushing up the cost of marriage for both sides.[43] A man who lacked enough funds to make a good match might consent to marry a woman who lacked brothers and move into her home in lieu of a betrothal gift. By means of this arrangement, her family gained his labor, and he enjoyed a higher standard of living. However, Song inheritance law strictly prohibited a matrilocal son-in-law from inheriting the estate of his wife's parents, as he remained outside the patrilineal line of descent. The estate would skip a generation and devolve to the couple's son. Although matrilocal marriage emerged among the peasantry, sometimes literati families brought in a son-in-law as well. If a wealthy man was extremely fond of his daughter and did not want to lose her, he could invite his son-in-law to live with his family, thereby keeping his beloved daughter at home. A young man from a somewhat lower background would see this unconventional arrangement as a step up the social ladder. If he was still a student, her kinsmen could help him prepare for the exams.

Although the Song system was relatively meritocratic, family background still mattered. Information gleaned from epitaphs attests that literati families commonly intermarried, as they continued to value ties with counterparts of comparable social standing.[44] In some cases, brothers from one family married the sisters from another, forming a closed marriage circle between two families of similar prestige.[45] Sometimes interlocking marriages produced bonds so intricate that agnates and affines blurred together into one large kinship conglomeration.[46] This strategy guaranteed that a son-in-law would come from a respectable family, kept kinsmen together in the same locale, and excluded outsiders from breaking into their exclusive social group. Sometimes this practice developed into hereditary cross-cousin marriage.[47] Although theoretically prohibited by law, this sort of union was nevertheless still fairly common among the elite. However, if families rose or fell in status, the quality of their marriage partners would have to be readjusted. Hereditary cross-cousin marriage could only endure as long as two families maintained a similar position in society.

The age of brides increased over the course of the Tang dynasty, so when the Song began, the marriage age was higher than the historic average.[48] This anomaly sparked a discussion of the ideal age of marriage. Both Sima Guang (1019–1986) and Zhu Xi (1130–1200) believed that a man should wed between the ages of sixteen and thirty, and a woman between fourteen and twenty.[49] Song law sought to regulate marriage age, fixing fifteen *sui* for men and thirteen for women as ideal.[50] However, families relied on custom and expediency to decide when their offspring should wed. A girl could marry any time after the pinning ceremony (*jili*), when she changed her hairstyle to mark the formal onset of adulthood. During the Song period, this ceremony might occur any time from age fifteen to twenty-four. A girl would normally be pinned at fifteen, although she would undergo the ceremony earlier if her parents wanted to marry her off at a younger age, or later if her marriage had to be delayed.[51]

Most studies put the average age of Song brides at seventeen or eighteen.[52] The women documented in a sample of eighty-two epitaphs married at an average age of 18.41.[53] Another study of one hundred epitaphs found that these women married at age 17.89 on average. The oldest wed at twenty-three and the youngest at fourteen.[54] Both of these numbers are higher than the average for the early Tang, showing a general rise in the age of brides from elite families. A comprehensive study of the marriage ages of 418 women showed that the ages of brides varied over time. Most married in their late teens, but the age of marriage rose somewhat over the course of the Song.[55]

Table 1.1. Average Age of
Marriage for Women with Epitaphs

Era	Average Marriage Age (in sui)
1006–1040	19.91
1071–1100	17.99
1161–1190	19.37
1191–1120	20.48
1121–1250	21.16
1251–1279	22.4

Table 1.2. Percentages for Each
Marriage Age of Women with Epitaphs

Age (in sui)	Percentage
16	10.0
17	15.8
18	17.0
19	14.4
20	8.9
21	5.5

Tables 1.1 and 1.2 show that the most common marriage age for Song women was eighteen followed by sixteen. Of the women in this sample of epitaphs, 66 percent wed between ages sixteen and twenty, and 24.6 percent married after twenty. The average age of marriage for these women was 19.04. A study of marriages under the Jin dynasty found that northern women in this era wed between ages thirteen and twenty-three, with most marrying between eighteen and twenty-three.[56] In other words, like the Song, the age of Jin brides was also relatively high.

Men's marriage ages varied more than those of women. The average groom was 23.07 years old, but some men put off marriage until they were in their thirties.[57] A man from a wealthy family might take a concubine to start a family while young. He would marry later, after he had established his career and could attract a woman with a lavish dowry. As before, a groom was typically older than his bride, most often by about four years. In many marriages, however, the age difference was far more extreme.[58]

The comparatively high age of marriage for women at this time likely had several causes.[59] Most importantly, economic pressure drove the age of marriage higher than previous norms. Both dowry and betrothal gifts rose in value, making it difficult for families of brides and grooms to save up enough money to finance marriages. In particular, a gentry family might have to delay their daughter's engagement until they had a large enough dowry to attract a desirable son-in-law. In addition, due to the revival of classic rites, people took mourning more seriously than before. Some parents postponed a daughter's marriage until the mourning period for a deceased kinsman had been completed. War and chaos also caused families to defer weddings during times of hardship. And an obsession with education and the civil service examinations often led men from gentry families to postpone marriage until they had passed this hurdle and could demonstrate good prospects.[60]

In previous eras, the influence of classical ritual had gone into eclipse, so custom largely determined how people conducted weddings and thought about marriage. Moreover, during the medieval period, nomadic conquerors exerted a major influence on wedding customs, so these became raucous affairs involving tents and horses. Confucian thinkers looked upon these alien innovations with dismay. They considered boisterous celebrations an inappropriate way to formalize such an important undertaking.

More generally, Song literati sought to renovate society's major institutions, including marriage, by reordering life according to the dictates of classical ritual.[61] They naively looked back to ancient society as a utopian archetype. Confucian moralists hoped that by reviving ancient standards, they could recreate a model community in the present. However, this idealistic project encountered difficulties. Some ancient rites had not been recorded, making them impossible to resurrect. The ceremonies that survived often seemed antiquated or odd. Moreover, Buddhist or Daoist ceremonies had become deeply rooted.

Faced with these challenges, some of the most important minds of the time, including Sima Guang, Zhu Xi, and Cheng Yi, sought to determine which rituals were proper and practicable. As part of this project, conservative Confucians promoted dignified weddings. They wanted families to forgo music, as this contravened ancient practices. They also wanted to purge vulgar revelry and remake the wedding as a dignified ceremony solemnized in the groom's ancestral temple.[62]

Although most marriages lasted until the death of one of the spouses, Song law included provisions for divorce. Women wrote poetry lamenting unhappy marriages, and broken conjugal relationships were not uncommon. However, husbands and wives had very different divorce rights. Tang authorities had codified ritual restrictions on divorce as law, and the Song maintained similar provisions. The law gave men considerable latitude to divorce their wives but strictly limited female rights.[63] Women could only bring a lawsuit to appeal for divorce if the marriage had obviously failed.[64] For example, a wife could request divorce if her husband had committed adultery, developed mental illness, or was too poor to support her. Even though female-initiated divorce was theoretically possible, it seems to have been extremely rare. Divorcees were objects of pity and had poor prospects for remarriage. A wife would be unlikely to try to end her marriage unless the situation was absolutely unendurable.

Blood relatives of the emperor were subject to unique divorce procedures.[65] An imperial clansman had to petition the throne to effect a divorce. After the ruler granted permission and the couple divorced, they would only be allowed to remarry after the potential match had been investigated and approved by the court of the imperial clan. These burdensome provisions were intended to discourage divorce among the emperor's relatives so as to maintain their collective reputation for probity.

As under Tang law, a husband had to name one of seven reasons to justify divorce: a wife's disobedience to her parents-in-law, barrenness, licentiousness, jealousy, illness, loquaciousness, or theft. He could not divorce her under three circumstances: she had no family to return to, she had mourned his parents for three years, or the couple had married while poor and subsequently become rich. Divorce almost always had a far greater impact on the wife than the husband, so legal specialists codified these provisions from the ritual code to give wives more security. Nevertheless, the permissible conditions for divorce were so vaguely worded that a husband could always find some excuse to cast out an undesirable wife. Public opinion was probably the best protection for wives. Fear of gossip dissuaded a man from divorcing his wife without good cause. Society looked on divorce as a squalid matter, and most men wanted to avoid it if possible.[66] If a couple found themselves completely incompatible or a wife could not bear children, a man with sufficient means would usually take a concubine rather than divorce his wife.

A couple could also mutually agree to separate. However, a wife could not effect divorce without her husband's agreement. To allow wives to escape from an abusive marriage, the Song maintained a mechanism from medieval law called righteous separation (*yijue*). Sometimes a government functionary could compel a couple to divorce, a practice that had been standard bureaucratic procedure for centuries.[67] If a local magistrate received word that a married woman in his district was the victim of domestic violence, he could investigate the case. If it turned out that she was being abused, he could annul the marriage in order to protect her from her husband. This sort of annulment did not require the consent of either spouse. Officials also had the authority to annul an illegal marriage, such as bigamy or incest.

Traditionally the state had refrained from intervening in most domestic affairs. During the Song dynasty, however, the government tried to manage the relationships of married couples. Grounded in Confucian ideals, Song law envisioned society as an interlocking series of hierarchies and reciprocal obligations that extended outward from the family. Government functionaries enforced hierarchy between spouses, as the inequality of this relationship constituted a basic social building block.[68] If a husband assaulted and injured his wife, he would receive two degrees of punishment less than an ordinary assault. In contrast, a woman who merely struck her husband was liable to be sentenced to a year of penal servitude.

Even though both ritual and law conceptualized marriage as an unequal relationship, people often praised companionate marriages.[69] And despite the fact that the classics enjoined a couple from displaying excessive intimacy lest they become licentious, over time marriage had taken on an increasingly emotional dimension. Spouses did not hesitate to express affection for one another. Although companionate marriages had advantages, strong conjugal feelings could also cause problems. Officials usually did not take their wives along to distant postings, so many elite women spent a great deal of time apart from their spouses. When couples were separated, the wife often felt very dissatisfied with her situation. Officials' wives frequently wrote emotionally charged poetry expressing their unhappiness at the hardship of separation from their husbands.[70] Conjugal love also became an important theme in popular fiction.[71] These romantic short stories furnished the plots for many stage dramas, transferring the theme of loving marriage to the performing arts. About a third of Yuan dynasty dramas feature characters who manage to overcome adversity and marry their beloved.[72] Audiences of both written and performance literature clearly enjoyed plots about romantic marriage.

Ongoing changes in society affected relations between spouses, giving rise to new types of conjugal relationships. The thriving commercial economy induced many people to become merchants. The merchant lifestyle differed considerably from that of most professions, such as peasants and craftsmen, and their families pioneered new forms of marriage.[73] Many merchants were itinerant, requiring husband and wife to spend much of their time apart. Due to frequent separation, spouses often became relatively independent of one another. This open arrangement contravened conventional marriage, which had traditionally been seen as an intense relationship of mutual reliance. Although the wives of officials were also separated from husbands on distant postings, these couples felt committed to Confucian propriety, so they strove to maintain conventional ties. In contrast, merchants felt far less constrained by traditional ethics, which had little relevance to their way of life. Merchant couples dealt with matters pragmatically, seeing one another when possible and adapting their relationship to suit their irregular lifestyle. They also frequently based their relationships on deeply shared sentiments, redefining the conjugal bond in terms of feeling rather than duty.

Changing funerary customs also reflected shifting attitudes toward marriage. Most people considered marriage essential. If a child died before marrying, some families would even hold a posthumous marriage ceremony to wed their offspring to another deceased person.[74] Although this practice lacked the sanction of classical ritual, it had very ancient roots. Surprisingly, Neo-Confucian thinkers rarely discussed burial customs. Since these matters lay largely beyond classical ritual, custom and expediency governed how people interred spouses. High-status couples were interred in tombs consisting of parallel chambers of equal size.[75] A passage between the two chambers was thought to allow the souls of the deceased to communicate. Because husband and wife had similar chambers and tomb goods, their burial arrangements emphasized their closeness and theoretical equality within the context of the conjugal relationship.

Given the importance of affinal relationships, wives tended to maintain close bonds with their natal kin. Early medieval kinship had put great stress on the maternal line of descent, making the kinship system a fusion of patrilineal and matrilineal elements. Even though literati emphasized the primacy of the male line, in conformity with the ancient rites, women felt intimately linked to their blood relatives, and their sons valued ties with their maternal kin as well.[76] Even Neo-Confucian ideologues recognized the importance of affinal connections. Although Zhu Xi believed that a wife's primary loyalty ought to rest with her husband and in-laws, he nevertheless assumed that she would remain attached to her natal family and they would influence her behavior.[77]

Wives kept in close touch with the family of their birth.[78] A married woman's relationship with her parents and siblings depended on the distance that separated them. She could not travel far by herself, so if her family lived at a distance, contact was limited. This is one reason the gentry often chose wives from neighboring families, as it allowed the two sides to foster a close relationship. If a woman lived in proximity to her natal family, she could return home to participate in domestic rituals and celebrate festivals. She might also spend time in the home of her birth if her blood relations needed her help to nurse the sick and elderly. If a wife lacked brothers, she might assume far more responsibilities within the family of her birth. During the Southern Song era, people believed that a married daughter without brothers could take on filial duties normally performed by men, supporting her parents and also taking on a son's role in family rituals such as funerals.[79]

The families of husband and wife could also rely on one another for mutual aid. Song writers recorded numerous instances of daughters and their blood

kinsmen supporting one another when necessary.[80] Husbands had no reason
to discourage these ties. To the contrary, a robust relationship with another
family expanded the pool of available resources. In fact, men often actively
cultivated ties with their maternal kinsmen, especially their mothers' brothers. This feeling of attachment was mutual. A maternal uncle often served as
mentor and protector of his sister's son.[81]

Although it was generally in a woman's interest to wed, marriage did not
necessarily bring immediate benefits. Moving in with unfamiliar in-laws was
sure to be disorienting, and a wife's new relations did not necessarily receive
her amicably. Even so, marriage gave a woman the opportunity to bear legitimate children and take on the honored role of mother, elevating her social
standing significantly.[82] Song literature is replete with stories of stern and
resourceful mothers. A poem by Guan Daosheng (1262–1319) gives a sense
of the confidence that motherhood bestowed on a woman.[83]

> As Spring is fair, today is also fair,
> Casually I stroll with my children under the bamboo.
> The sense of spring is recently much stronger;
> Leafy, leafy my children grow by the side of the stone.

When a son grew up and married, his mother became a mother-in-law, an
even more authoritative social role. From the point of view of the average
woman, marrying and bearing children was the best opportunity for elevating
her position in society.

Studies of Song fertility have put the average number of children at
between 5.5 and 6.5 per woman. These figures are far higher than comparable
numbers from the Sui and Tang eras. Various studies estimate the number of
children per wife in elite families at between 3.3 and 4.77.[84] It is not clear why
fertility rose in this period. Perhaps prosperity made families more confident
and optimistic, so they wanted to raise more offspring. The high rate of infant
mortality also affected attitudes toward children. Physicians recognized the
inherent weakness of newborns and considered them extremely vulnerable,
so they routinely prescribed medicines intended to strengthen babies and
increase their chance of survival. Parents bathed newborns in herbal decoc-
tions, wrapped them up to keep them warm, and used talismans and incanta-
tions to ward off illness.[85] Some families likely had more children than they
actually desired to ensure that at least one or two would survive to adulthood.

As the price of dowries escalated, it became more expensive than ever
before to raise a daughter.[86] Largely as a result of rising dowry costs, families

increasingly preferred to raise sons. In model fictional families from both the early and late Song, sons far outnumbered daughters. The rich families described in the *Records of Yi Jian* have an average of 2.1 sons but only 0.4 daughters. The strong preference for sons had a major impact on the demographics of society as a whole, as China ended up with a badly skewed sex ratio. A study of epitaphs shows a clearly unbalanced sex ratio of 60 percent boys and 40 percent girls.[87] Women made up an estimated 42.77 percent of the population.[88] Coupled with the practice of concubinage by the affluent, which took many women off the marriage market, it became very difficult for poor men to find a wife.

Even as some families had more children, others took measures to limit family size. Abortion and infanticide became extremely common, especially in regions facing intense population pressure such as Fujian.[89] Popular fiction addressed this disturbing issue. Female characters in Song stories would kill a child for a variety of reasons. Sometimes an unwed mother wanted to rid herself of an infant that society would not accept. In other stories, a widow kills the child of her first husband so that she can remarry more easily. Fiction writers criticized abortion and infanticide by concocting characters who suffer supernatural punishment for these sins. In one story, a father who forces his daughter to abort her fetus is condemned to hell. Others suffer karmic retribution and end up reborn under terrible circumstances.[90]

Although the state prohibited the murder of children, it remained common nonetheless. Thinkers and officials discussed the reasons that many people did not want to raise children.[91] They believed that these extreme acts were usually motivated by financial pressure, including poverty, high taxes, and the expense of marriage. Authorities considered motherhood the natural female condition, so for a woman to murder her child seemed inexplicable and disturbing.

Given the dangers of childbirth, the high death rate of infants, and the frequency of infanticide, society deemed the mother who successfully raised her children to maturity to have accomplished a worthy feat. In recompense for this care, children owed mothers a lifetime of respect and obedience. Filial piety had long been a key ethical principle underpinning Chinese social relations. Educational texts aimed at women sought to inculcate filial virtue, and many girls read the *Classic of Filial Piety* (*Xiaojing*) as part of their instruction.[92] During the Song dynasty, filiality became closely associated with the mother-son bond. The filial child stood out as a moral paragon, and people often cultivated a reputation for filiality to gain respect. Many biographies of prominent people emphasize their filial devotion as a way to express high character.[93] Sometimes a man took extreme measures to prove filial devotion. He might write a sutra in his own blood, offer his blood to the gods as a sacrifice on behalf of a sick parent, or cut off a piece of his body for use as medicine.

The state required children to treat their parents with respect. Song law followed Tang precedent in criminalizing disobedience to parents, and judges upheld parental authority.[94] Mothers sometimes brought lawsuits to force wayward sons to obey them.[95] And a magistrate might release a female convict so that she could care for an old or ailing parent or grandparent or a parent-in-law.[96] Women were primary caregivers within the family, so they had to take on much of the burden of filial obligation.

Because children were expected to defer to parents, the nature of the relationship between stepmothers and their husbands' children provoked discussion.[97] Within the Song mourning system, a person owed the same obligations to a stepmother as to a birth mother, so in theory the two kinship roles were equivalent. Moreover, the law regarded a stepmother as akin to a natural mother in many respects. Nevertheless, in some circumstances, stepmothers remained more distant from their stepchildren. For example, even if a man's birth mother remarried, the bond of mother and son continued to connect them, so he was still obliged to mourn her. But if a man's stepmother remarried, under Song law the tie between stepmother and stepson was broken. Moreover, if a stepmother killed her stepson, the penalty was heavier than if the same crime had been committed by a birth mother. Although jurists intended this provision to prevent domestic abuse by stepmothers, it shows that people regarded them as somewhat different from natural mothers. The law also prohibited a stepmother from expelling her stepsons from the house or denying them an inheritance after the death of their father. These regulations suggest that some stepmothers had weak bonds with their husbands' children and did not always treat them properly.

Although parents and children constituted the core of the family, the domestic realm included marginal members as well. Rising prosperity and comprehensive commercial networks facilitated the sale of women, making concubinage increasingly common.[98] Major cities had markets where brokers sold the services of concubines and other servile women. About a third of elite men took a concubine at some point. Purchasing and maintaining a concubine was expensive, making them a status symbol.

There were different types of concubines, some more highly regarded than others. The most valued concubine served as a housekeeper who took over domestic management upon the death of a wife. A man who did not want to remarry could purchase a capable woman to supervise household matters.

Other concubines gained a master's favor due to sex or romance, and they could also enjoy elevated status. However, most concubines were little more than servants, slaves, or sexual playthings. Men often rented a concubine for a period of time instead of purchasing her.[99] This arrangement was less expensive than taking on a woman long term, and it also allowed a man to return her to the broker once the sense of novelty had worn off.

Concubinage had traditionally been an informal arrangement loosely regulated by custom, but the Song government managed the relations between concubine and master much more closely than before. The law code had very specific rules regarding concubinage, and written contracts recorded the sale of these women. For the first time, authorities provided precise definitions that distinguished a concubine (*qie*) from a bond servant or slave (*bi* or *nüshi*). The son of a concubine was expected to recognize his father's official wife as his true mother. Due to this practice, the son of a concubine was in theory equal to that born to a wife. Nevertheless, people often regarded them as inferior to a wife's sons. Song thinkers debated what sort of relationship the son of a concubine ought to have with his birth mother. Zhu Xi saw this as a full mother-son bond.[100] He believed that a man born to a concubine should mourn her for three years when she died, as he would his adoptive mother. Others saw a concubine mother as akin to a wet nurse and recommended mourning her in an attenuated fashion.

As concubinage came under increased regulation, these women gained some basic rights.[101] The integration of provisions regarding concubines into the law allowed them the possibility of legal redress when wronged. Concubines occasionally sued their masters when they felt aggrieved.[102] Moreover, these women could own property. When a concubine entered her master's household, she might bring along some property as a kind of de facto dowry. This wealth belonged to her personally, and her master could not confiscate it. Sometimes a favored concubine received valuables from her master, which might include jewels or even land. Upon a man's death, his kinsmen could not take back this wealth. However, a concubine did not inherit anything from her master, and she had no right to remain in the household after he died. His sons might decide to let her stay, or they could send her away, likely with some monetary compensation.

In addition to concubines, a household might include other women who performed similar roles, even though their legal status differed. Wealthy families had numerous servants. Although the law classified them as base (*jian*) people, it nevertheless protected them against certain kinds of physical abuse.[103] Authorities also guaranteed their free status, so an employer could not enslave them. Under the law, a maid had a special relationship with her employers. The Song legal system often enforced patrimonial relationships, and jurists looked upon maids as low-ranking members of their employers' families. Sometimes an employer would initiate a sexual relationship with a female servant. If she bore a child, the law treated her as akin to a concubine. The Song code specifically addressed the inheritance rights of children born to maids, which suggests that this was not an uncommon situation.

Bond servants who performed domestic labor in wealthy households had an even lower status.[104] Although their condition resembled slavery, it was not permanent. A master could purchase a bond servant for a term of ten years, after which she could leave him. In contrast, when a man bought a concubine, her position was permanent. Because people thought of concubinage as somewhat similar to marriage, the bond never lapsed. Mourning customs attest to the marginal position of bond servants within the household. A concubine was obligated to mourn for members of her master's family, showing that people considered her a kind of kin. In contrast, bond servants had no such responsibility. Although they lived in the household, they were not part of the family.

The presence of women from lowly backgrounds in a prosperous and educated household could give rise to awkward situations.[105] Most scandals involving members of the imperial clan involved concubines and female servants.[106] Although elite men frequently took concubines, they remained very suspicious of these women. The relationship between a wealthy man and his concubine was grounded in money and sex instead of the classic rites, making it morally dubious. Moreover, these women came from much lower backgrounds than their masters, and their crude behavior could sometimes provoke quarrels and even domestic violence. Also, because a concubine did not necessarily stay with her master permanently, their transient relationship introduced an element of instability into the household, threatening family order.

Not surprisingly, the plight of concubines evoked widespread pity.[107] Officials felt sorry for ladies from ruined gentry families who ended up as concubines. Sometimes they financed a dowry for a concubine born into a respectable family so that she could enter an honorable marriage. Literature also shows that concubines evoked uneasy feelings among women of good birth.[108] When a family failed, the wife and daughters often ended up as concubines, so the presence of a concubine in the home served as an unwelcome reminder of the fragility of female social standing.

Unease and resentment toward concubines gave rise to mistreatment. Many stories describe a concubine or bond servant being abused to death or murdered outright by a jealous wife. The wronged concubine then turns into a ghost so that she can exact posthumous revenge. These disturbing tales suggest that concubines and wives often had a bad relationship with each other. Aside from jealousy and other kinds of antipathy, this tension had a financial basis as well. A concubine who bore a son would disrupt the division of the family estate, as her sons could claim a share of the family wealth. Given the generosity of inheritance law in this regard, wives feared the introduction of a concubine into the home, as she might degrade the economic standing of their own children. Although men found concubinage convenient, this practice destabilized the kinship system and complicated domestic life.

Under the conquest dynasties in northern China, people organized their families somewhat differently. Long before the Khitans established the Liao state, their tribes and clans had already fragmented into small families.[109] Originally the Khitan people were divided into eight groups who practiced reciprocal marriage relations. They were polygamous, so a man could also have minor wives and concubines in addition to his senior wife.[110] When the Khitans settled in China and established the Liao dynasty, like all foreign conquerors they found themselves far outnumbered by their Chinese subjects. To avoid being subsumed, the Khitan elite established a marriage system intended to maintain their distinct ethnic identity.[111] The rulers of Liao declined to marry ethnic Han and instead took Khitan wives. They bolstered the status of their in-laws by granting them power and honors. In this way the Khitans not only preserved their communal identity but also made ethnicity the supreme source of privilege within the Liao system. Ethnic endogamy made the descendants of nomadic conquerors a hereditary caste.

Originally the Khitans lacked surnames.[112] Each kin group had a toponym that denoted their place of residence. After settling in China, the Khitan elite took surnames and adopted aspects of the Chinese kinship system, as they considered these customs appropriate for the rulers of a Chinese dynasty. The uppermost Liao elite belonged to two clans: Yelü and Xiao. The Liao emperors were all Yelü and their wives were Xiao, so the Yelü constituted the imperial clan and the Xiao were their consort kin. Under this system, a Liao emperor married one of his mother's kinswomen. Although the Khitans practiced polygamy, a senior wife had precedence over the others. Some wealthy Khitan men also kept concubines.

The Khitans relied heavily on educated ethnic Han families to staff the bureaucracy and sustain effective administration. Privileged Han had complex marriage ties.[113] Most often, they intermarried with the other Han official families. These marriages were usually not a singular event. Instead, several elite families would form a marriage circle and intermarry repeatedly for generations, forging extremely tight bonds and creating a politically influential faction. Also, as the conquering steppe nobility had privileged status, important Han sometimes married into aristocratic Khitan, Balhae (Bohai), or Tätäbi (Xi) families. Educated Chinese did not like marrying foreigners, whom they despised as cultural inferiors. Even so, some families accepted these unions as an expedient measure to advance their fortunes under the alien regime.

Khitan men had extremely close links with their in-laws. Some marriages were even matrilocal, and it was not uncommon for a man to work for his wife's family for a period of time in lieu of bridewealth. Archaeologists have unearthed many Liao dynasty inscriptions that describe Khitan and Han families.[114] A typical Liao family consisted of a male head of household, children, grandchildren, and the wives of the family's men. Adopted children had a secondary status in the family. A slave was also a kind of family member, albeit of very low standing. Liao families varied considerably in size. Some included only kin of the same generation: a man and his spouse, or coresident brothers and their spouses. Two-generation families consisted of parents and unwed children. A three-generation family had grandparents, parents, and children.

A Liao edict of 983 declared that sons should observe filial piety and reside with their parents for as long as either remained alive.[115] This command altered the structure of Liao families, causing them to become larger and more complex. Another edict of 1074 encouraged people to maintain large households encompassing three generations.[116] These orders seem to have had an impact. Epitaphs confirm that many Liao families were fairly large and included multiple generations. The low population density in Liao allowed the average family to own more land than those in other regions, so people had sufficient resources to raise more children. One study of Liao inscriptions determined that ethnic Han had an average of 6.05 reported children while Khitans had 5.12.[117] Ethnic Han living under the Liao regime had a similar family structure. Seventy-five epitaphs record an average of 6.05 children per family, so their families were far larger than those under the Song to the south. When grandparents are taken into account, the average Liao family may have had seven or eight members, making them larger than the historic average in China.

Inscriptions record that most elite men had at least one concubine. Men also routinely remarried after the death of their wives, making families even more complex. And sometimes when a young woman died, her younger sister would marry the deceased woman's husband to replace her. The complicated families of Liao may have emerged in reaction to a high death rate. Many epitaphs mention that the deceased died from one of a number of communicable diseases, which seem to have been unusually prevalent at the time. Expanding a family's size would have helped to keep it stable when a member died.

The Jin dynasty ruled over a much larger area than Liao, and some places had much higher population density than the sparsely inhabited northeast. The Jurchens were polygynous and expected nobles to have several wives as a mark of high status. Even some ordinary Jurchen men had more than one wife due to levirate, as they routinely married the widows of brothers and other close male relatives. Whereas Chinese men traditionally took younger women as wives, Jurchen brides were often older than their grooms. Traditionally, when a poor Jurchen woman reached marriage age, she could stand by the side of the road and sing a song about herself to attract a suitor.[118] If a passerby took a liking to her, he could take her home and pay the requisite bride price to her family later. Many Jurchen families were matrilocal, the groom moving in with his wife's family.[119] As with the Khitans, these men worked in lieu of bridewealth to compensate in-laws for losing their daughter's labor. Jurchens were strictly exogamous, marrying within their tribe but outside their clan.[120] Each clan married with another designated clan, so two clans (moieties) within a tribe had reciprocal marriage relations.

The Jurchens settled in China took surnames and altered their marriage system to suit their changed circumstances.[121] They adopted Chinese surname exogamy, so they had to marry outside their tribe. This change caused tribes and clans to lose their significance, and so large kinship groupings fragmented into small families. In response to these changes, Jin emperors promoted monogamy. Most Jin women married between the ages of eighteen and twenty-three, and they lived to an average age of 59.34. Families had an average of 4.1 to 4.6 children, so the average Jin family had six or seven members.[122]

After the Jurchens settled in China, their rulers encouraged them to continue marrying one another.[123] The Jin government initially banned Jurchens from marrying Han and promoted ethnic endogamy to maintain a strong common identity. Even so, many people ignored this prohibition, and in 1191 the Jin legalized ethnic intermarriage. Jurchen rulers took Han women into the palace as consorts, so the latter Jin dynasty emperors had mixed blood. By the end of the dynasty, Jurchens and Han became increasingly equal in status, and Han men even began taking Jurchen women as concubines. Nevertheless, the most prestigious Jurchen families still maintained close-knit marriage circles.

Although Jin family size exceeded that of Song, the fertility rate remained below that of Liao. According to inscriptional evidence, Jin families had six or seven members on average.[124] Polygyny affected the birth rate. As a man took more wives, the number of children born to each woman decreased.[125] In a monogamous marriage, a wife had an average of 4.1 children, but a wife in a polygynous marriage had only two children. If a man had six wives, each of them bore only 0.3 children on average.

When the Mongols ruled China, they encouraged ethnic mixing. This attitude stemmed from their political use of marriage. After they conquered an enormous empire, they used marriage to bind the unwieldy state together. Mongol rulers married their daughters to allies and the leaders of conquered peoples, and some of these women had significant political roles in their husband's realm. When political marriage became important, the Mongol elite began to favor monogamy.[126] Polygyny builds bonds with a wider range of marriage partners, while monogamy creates more intense and exclusive affinal relationships. Over time, the Mongols came to favor the latter strategy. Political marriage also altered the relations between married women and their blood kin. Whereas a wife had previously been fully integrated into her husband's family, married women began to maintain closer links with their natal relatives, thereby making affinal connections more useful. Because the Mongol rulers relied heavily on marriage alliances, it became advantageous to intensify the ties between affines. Two groups would intermarry repeatedly through several generations, creating a preferential marriage exchange and intensifying their common bond. Levirate helped maintain kinship ties even after the death of a politically important husband. Because one son often inherited political authority while another received a larger share of family wealth, levirate could sometimes recombine these two legacies.[127]

During the Yuan dynasty, China saw an influx of foreign peoples. Because Yuan was a multiethnic state, intermarriage between different groups became an important issue. In some respects, marriage laws loosened. During the early medieval era and up through the Jin dynasty, the state had strictly banned marriage between people of extremely different backgrounds to maintain the prevailing social hierarchy. The Mongols did not enforce these prohibitions consistently.[128] Judicial authorities were faced with the problem of untangling the status of children born to parents of extremely different backgrounds, such as a free person and a slave.

Not only did the Yuan permit marriage between different ethnic groups, but in fact they saw intermarriage as a necessity.[129] The number of Mongols who settled in China, along with allied peoples classed together as Semu, was very small compared to the native population, particularly in the south. In many areas it was difficult for Mongols and Semu to find marriage partners of the same ethnicity, so they could not practice strict ethnic endogamy. The Mongols had long intermarried with conquered peoples, so they did not consider ethnic mixing problematic. At first, Mongol and Semu men took Han wives. Mongols of every background married Han women, particularly in regions with small Mongol communities. Eventually the daughters of Mongols and Semu started to marry Han men.

The Ma family of Onggud (Wanggu) typifies this process.[130] The Ma were native to central Asia and settled in China during the Yuan as part of the Semu migration. Traditionally they had married with families of similar ethnicity and background. When they set down roots in China and served as officials under the Yuan, they married with other families in the middle bureaucracy. Over time, the Ma became highly sinicized and embraced Chinese ideas of cultural orthodoxy. They began to choose their marriage partners not on the basis of ethnicity but instead sought to unite with families that exhibited a high degree of Confucian learning. Many other Mongol and Semu families replicated the trajectory of the Ma. As a result of this sort of intermarriage, the Yuan saw a high degree of cultural mixing.

During the Yuan dynasty, the number of children in each family remained close to Song levels. According to the official government figures in the *Yuan History* (*Yuanshi*), the standard account of the era, the average household had about 4.5 members, with the precise number fluctuating over time.[131] The standard Yuan dynasty family came close to the early imperial ideal of five members. However, household size varied considerably by region, as each part of China had different norms of family organization and residence. While households in Gansu had an average of 11.62 members, those in the harsh environment of Zhongshu on the Tibetan plateau had only 2.72 people. At this time, violence and uncertainty encouraged extended relatives to come together for mutual benefit, so some ethnic Han households became extremely large. In the most extreme cases, up to two hundred people might reside together. As always, the Chinese family had to adapt to the particular circumstances that prevailed in each time and place.

Chapter 2

Government

Because women were strictly excluded from public life, usually only high birth or marriage presented opportunities to accrue political power. In spite of these restrictions, a highly capable woman occasionally found a way to exploit unusual circumstances and become a leader. Yang Miaozhen (ca. 1193–1250) was the sister of a rebel leader during the violent collapse of the Jin dynasty.[1] When her brother died, Yang took over his ragtag army, enlarged it, and was leading more than ten thousand soldiers before reaching the age of twenty. Yang married one of her soldiers, and the rebel couple fought and ruled side by side, carving out a large domain in north China. Although the couple officially pledged loyalty to the Southern Song, in fact they were independent warlords and governed this territory themselves. After Yang's husband died, she threw in her lot with the Mongols, who rewarded her by making her governor of Shandong.

Yang Miaozhen's success was highly unusual. Women warriors were almost always confined to the pages of imaginative literature. Tales of female fighters fascinated Song readers, and popular fiction depicted many female knights errant (*nüxia*).[2] Like their male counterparts, these characters employed strength, valor, and cunning to perform righteous deeds and punish villains. These fictional combatants did not attract attention because they resembled real women. To the contrary, they captivated readers by casting aside the rules of female propriety in service of a higher cause, brazenly fighting alongside men.

Female poets sometimes wrote about warfare, intriguing male readers by offering a woman's perspective on a stock masculine theme. Zhang Yuniang (1250–1277) lived during the Mongol conquest and suffered terribly from the warfare and chaos around her.[3] These tribulations made her extremely apprehensive about the nation's fate. She vented her concerns by writing patriotic poetry, demanding that responsible men behave heroically. Zhang shocked the literary world by rejecting demure feminine stereotypes and writing in a forceful style. Even so, many readers felt moved that a young woman would compose such stirring verses. Zhang's originality continued to attract the attention of readers in later eras. Her forthright works inspired generations of female poets to take up similar themes. The mid-seventeenth-century female poet Chai Jingyi followed Zhang's example and wrote a moving poem about the Southern Song woman Liang Hongyu (1102–1135), who fought against the Jurchens.[4]

> Jade-white face and cloud coiffure brushed with the dust of war,
> The little "Lotus Battalion" clustered at the river's edge.
> Carrying—not well-bucket and rice mortar—but the drums of battle,
> Who would believe the hero was a fair maid?

Militaristic women may have been largely confined to the imagination, but these images of female warriors and patriots nevertheless had a deep cultural impact, inspiring numerous stories, poems, and operas.

During the chaotic Five Dynasties period that followed the fall of the Tang, nomadic khans overran much of north China. These rulers' consorts often acted as counselors, advising and manipulating their husbands in traditional steppe fashion.[5] After the Song dynasty was established, women once again faced a system designed to exclude them. Although a few women managed to gain power during rebellions, in general the only way they could affect policy was by influencing the inner circle of powerful officials surrounding the emperor. As before, the most influential women resided in the palace.

The Song palace was an immense establishment that housed between two thousand and three thousand female residents at any given time.[6] The palace environs may have been grand and luxurious, but life inside these walls was not necessarily pleasant. Within these privileged surroundings, disease was rampant. Sons of the emperors had a surprisingly short life expectancy. A third of Song princes died in their youth, and their average life expectancy was only 29.44. In contrast, members of the Song ruling class as a whole lived to about 64.47.[7] These insalubrious conditions affected women as well.

In every era, the officialdom detested large harems, both because of the vast expense and due to the enervating atmosphere. To keep the palace population in check, excess women were periodically expelled. Contrary to Tang custom, the previous emperor's consorts remained in the palace after his death. Because of incest taboos, the new ruler could not be physically intimate with his predecessor's women, so he took new concubines. In consequence, the number of palace ladies increased every time a monarch died. Besides the legion of minor consorts, the palace had also employed thousands of resident servants and workers, many of them female. Large numbers of female workers also came into the palace each day from the outside. Other female staff performed support services such as laundry and tailoring in ancillary buildings outside the palace grounds.

Large palace establishments were not new. Medieval palaces also had numerous female residents. At the time, officials set up a comprehensive administrative system to manage this unwieldy organization, and Song palace managers generally adhered to established procedures.[8] As before, empresses and other consorts had to obey extremely detailed regulations. These rules enforced discipline and also made it difficult for women to interfere in affairs of state. Officials constantly monitored palace ladies to ensure that they remained insulated from politics. They even prohibited palace women from communicating with officials in the outer court lest they try to influence the state bureaucracy.

Palace consorts were ranked in a clear hierarchy ranging from the empress down to minor concubines. The Tang had 121 grades of imperial consorts, but Song administrators found this system unwieldy and reduced the number of ranks to twenty-four.[9] These positions were fluid, and a woman could be promoted or demoted depending on her relationship with the emperor. If the ruler took an interest in a minor concubine, she would be given a higher grade. Each of these ranks was theoretically comparable to an office in the regular government bureaucracy and came with a fixed stipend. The families of high-level consorts received grants, and a woman might receive additional funds if she attracted the emperor's favor.

Numerous officials serving in various bureaus administered palace affairs. As before, many palace officials were female. In addition to dedicated female officials, educated imperial consorts also sometimes worked in the palace bureaucracy. In practice, the palace had two systems of organization.[10] A professional network of female officials and workers oversaw most tasks, together with some imperial consorts. Although these two systems were theoretically distinct, Northern Song emperors often selected harem women from among the female palace officials, so the two organizations became closely intertwined.

In addition to serving as consorts and female officials, women occupied other prestigious positions as well. The wives of high officials received honorific titles commensurate with their husbands' ranks.[11] Like their spouses, officials' wives were allowed to wear special clothing and ornaments that marked their title and grade. Even though these women did not live in the palace or serve as imperial consorts, their titles were nevertheless extensions of the palace hierarchy.

Wet nurses (*rubi*) also lived in the palace.[12] Women from wealthy families traditionally looked down on the tedious task of nursing infants, so they turned their babies over to nursemaids from the bottom rungs of society. As an infant grew older, the wet nurse often became the child's nanny. This custom had unusual consequences. Women of low birth raised the future emperor and other members of the imperial clan. Wet nurses had considerable influence over the upbringing of the emperor's children and were held responsible for raising them properly. Emperor Taizong even blamed a prince's wet nurse for his spoiled behavior and had her caned as punishment.[13]

During the Song, palace wet nurses had a status equivalent to bond servants or slaves. Yet in spite of their degraded position, they often developed an intense intimate bond with the children they raised. If one of a woman's charges later became important, she could enjoy lavish rewards and rise dramatically in status. In previous dynasties, wet nurses sometimes even became significant political actors. Under the Song system, however, officials established mechanisms that suppressed the powers of empresses and imperial concubines, and these measures also kept wet nurses in check.

With thousands of women living in a confined space and competing for one man's attention, the atmosphere in the palace could seem tense and claustrophobic. Jealousy was a basic fact of life. Even an empress feared that her position could be undermined if the emperor became enamored of a pretty rival. Empress Yang (1162–1233) used poetry to vent her sense of insecurity. One day she saw a flock of mandarin ducks, and these traditional symbols of monogamy led her to rue her own predicament. She wrote a poem complaining that although regular couples live together in simple harmony, she had to share her spouse with an enormous harem of beautiful competitors.[14]

> Spring breeze is light, water flowing,
> Hand in hand we seek fragrant blossoms across the small bridge.
> But how annoying the scene of the wild pond where my eye chances upon
> Innumerable mandarin ducks resting pair by pair!

In spite of relentless competition and anxiety, palace life was not always unpleasant. Harem women used their copious free time to practice musical instruments, read amusing books, embroider cloth, undertake religious devotions, and enjoy various amusements.[15] They also had ceremonial obligations. The most important rites honored the imperial ancestors. On the anniversaries of the death of each emperor and empress, the current empress dowager or empress would lead the palace ladies in conducting a grand memorial service.[16] These ritual duties broke the tedium of palace life and made harem women feel valued.

During the Song, the general level of education rose considerably, refining thought and behavior. High culture became a prominent aspect of palace life. Most noticeably, an increasing number of palace women wrote poetry. Not only did the empresses and minor consorts write in verse, but Daoist and Buddhist nuns, entertainers, and even servants attached to the palace also composed poems.[17] Their works touched on a range of themes.[18] Most works were conventional, celebrating the emperor and empress and expressing sanguine depictions of palace life. However, sometimes a consort used her writings to express discontent with her lot. Palace poets occasionally took on serious themes about matters of national importance, lamenting the army's defeats or expressing patriotic sentiments.

Ever since the advent of the imperial system, proximity to the throne had been a wellspring of power. During the Sui and Tang eras, several empresses and princesses overtly influenced affairs of state.[19] Most famously, Empress Wu Zetian (Wu Zhao, 624–705) usurped the throne and temporarily replaced the Tang with her own short-lived dynasty, reigning as the only female emperor in China's history. Wu's success in pulling down orthodox institutions and ruling in her own name traumatized the male elite. Over time, writers issued increasingly negative judgments of her reign, criticizing it as an unorthodox catastrophe.[20] Thereafter, emperors, officials, and thinkers concocted elaborate rules and ideologies intended to prevent another woman seizing power outright.

To prevent the rise of another Wu Zetian, eleven of the remaining Tang emperors did not even dare to bestow the title of empress on their consorts. They feared that an ambitious woman might exploit the position's prestige to destabilize the government. During the Five Dynasties era, however, rulers revived the custom of naming an empress, and the Song continued to observe this traditional practice. However, Song emperors took extreme care in selecting their empresses.[21] As before, the emperor's in-laws rose rapidly in status. To prevent consorts and their kinsmen from causing trouble, a potential empress's connections and personality underwent close scrutiny.[22]

Unlike the Tang dynasty, when emperors chose spouses with grand connections, many Song empresses came from relatively humble backgrounds. By selecting an empress from a modest family, the emperor diminished her prestige.[23] In the Tang era, 70.8 percent of empresses and consorts had been born into families of high officials, but during the Song only 26.8 percent came from such a grand background. Comparing the early Tang with the Southern Song, the numbers are even more striking. In the early part of the Tang, 91.7 percent of empresses and consorts came from the families of high officials. This declined to only 11.8 percent during the Southern Song. Only 16.7 percent of Tang empresses and consorts came from families that had not produced any officials, but during the Song, 51.2 percent came from a politically insignificant background.

Marriages of members of the imperial clan were also considered matters of state. The palace, not the immediate family of the prospective bride or groom, arranged these matches.[24] Kinswomen of the emperor married men from families with a distinguished record of government service, tying the imperial line to the officialdom. When a man married an imperial clanswoman, he was automatically recruited into the bureaucracy. If he already held office, he received a promotion. Emperors married their female relatives to officials and promoted these men within the civil service to gain useful allies who could shield them from potential rivals: generals, consort kin, and arrogant descendants of the medieval aristocracy.

In the violent era immediately prior to the Song, military prowess had been the key to supremacy. Generals and warlords dominated politics. Accordingly, when the Song began, emperors of the new dynasty assumed that generals would be very powerful. They sought to link some of them to the throne to ensure their loyalty in times of crisis. Emperor Taizu systematically married members of the imperial clan to spouses from military families, a strategy that his immediate successors continued. However, most emperors did not marry their kin to the most important generals, for fear of empowering them too much. They preferred to tie themselves to military families that had declined in status. These decayed in-laws would likely remain loyal to the ruler out of gratitude for having revived their families' fortunes.[25]

Due to the backlash against Wu Zetian, Song empresses and other palace ladies had far fewer powers than those of the early Tang.[26] Scholars justified increased restrictions by criticizing the empresses of past dynasties who involved themselves in politics and administration. They declared that historical precedent proved that empowering women invariably leads to disaster.[27] Officials protested strongly against any trace of ambition in the women around the emperor. Moreover, strict rules isolated palace ladies to a greater degree to prevent them from forming factions. And the symbolic position of these women declined as well. Deceased empresses had a lower place in the ancestral temple of the imperial clan than in earlier eras.[28] The movement to diminish the power and status of palace women extended beyond the empresses and high consorts to affect all women connected to the emperor.

Empresses had to navigate an increasingly hostile atmosphere. They responded by keeping a low profile and avoiding contentious issues. Some cloaked themselves in the mantle of high culture to appear admirable yet

benign. The forceful Empress Yang (1162–1232) softened her image by cul-
tivating the image of a refined lady dedicated to art and music. Other consorts
sought approbation by demonstrating virtue and sagacity. Song empresses
also patronized religious activities and presented themselves as paragons
of piety, a traditional means for consorts to attract approval.[29] Empress Liu
(969–1033) compared herself to the Queen Mother of the West (Xiwangmu),
a deity with an enthusiastic following, while Empress Wei (1080–1159)
devoted herself to the cult of the Four Sages, popular Daoist deities.

Empresses manipulated their clothing, lifestyle, and surroundings to construct a positive public image.[30] Empress Yang (1162–1233), for example,

Figure 2.1. Empress Gongsheng (Wikimedia Commons)

wrote a poem boasting about her frugality and simple lifestyle. She declared
that she disdained shallow ostentation and instead preferred to pursue bookish
pursuits amid an austere atmosphere.[31]

> Provisions for my Kunning Palace: just a single goat.
> Since assuming the proper seat, I manage literary affairs.
> Cherishing life and frugality, I pursue models of the ancient past;
> As exemplar for the palace ladies, I apply only light rouge.

This poem may have convinced readers who had never encountered Empress
Yang, but she was being extremely disingenuous. In fact, the empress resided
in a luxurious wing of the palace and led a life that was far from ascetic.[32]
Yang pretended to lead a spartan existence to avoid criticism. This strategy
was generally successful. While imperial historians often excoriated the
female regents of other dynasties, they tended to praise Song empress dowagers for their prudence and virtuous demeanor.[33] The carefully fabricated
public image of Song empresses has often misled subsequent generations into
assuming that they had removed themselves from the political arena.[34] Yet
sometimes they exerted significant authority, albeit in a far more subtle and
indirect manner than their audacious predecessors in the early Tang.

In spite of the various measures taken to limit female power, some Song
empresses nevertheless managed to influence state affairs.[35] A number of
emperors came to the throne as minors, so nine empresses dowager served
as regents. Given the traditional emphasis on filial piety as a supreme virtue,
young emperors felt morally obligated to defer not just to their mothers but
to surrogate maternal figures as well. This mind-set put an empress who
declared a regency in a position of authority over the titular ruler. Moreover,
because the Song imperial system lacked primogeniture, imperial consorts
sometimes tried to manipulate the imperial succession so that a younger son
of the previous ruler could ascend the throne. In antiquity, the right to rule
was inherited according to strict primogeniture, so younger sons who became
rulers seemed somewhat unorthodox. This hint of illegitimacy allowed an
empress dowager to take on more authority during his reign.

Empresses dowager had to contend with strident opposition from a bureaucratic apparatus far stronger and more confident than those of previous dynasties. The rise of the examination system had strengthened the bureaucracy, and
officials used their power to counter the pretentions of ambitious empresses.[36]
In particular, whenever a woman tried to interfere in the imperial succession, high ministers strongly resisted.[37] Not only did they consider female

involvement in government potentially dangerous, but it also diminished their own authority. Song Taizong's Empress Li (960–1004) plotted to depose the heir apparent and replace him with her own favored candidate, but the grand councilor thwarted her plan. Similarly, when Empress Dowager Liu (969–1033) tried to enthrone an emperor of her choosing, powerful officials steadfastly opposed her. To prevent these sorts of confrontations and ensure a smooth succession, a reigning emperor sometimes appointed an heir apparent.

Empress Liu (969–1033), the most powerful empress since Wu Zetian, had a major impact on the evolution of Song institutions.[38] Her successes cleared the way for subsequent consorts to exercise a degree of power during

Figure 2.2. Empress Liu (Wikimedia Commons)

the dynasty. Liu was the wife of Emperor Zhenzong. After Liu failed to bear children, she adopted a prince born to a lesser consort as her own son. When Zhenzong died in 1022, this prince ascended the throne as Emperor Renzong. The new monarch was still young and incapable of ruling on his own, so the Song government had to establish a regency for the first time. Empress Dowager Liu, the boy's adoptive mother, became regent.

Although the emperor reigned as the titular monarch, in fact Empress Dowager Liu acted as the real ruler of China for eleven years. Officials repeatedly warned her not to follow in the footsteps of the dreaded Wu Zetian, and Liu heeded their warnings. She kept a low profile and carried out her duties with prudence and moderation. Liu proved to be a talented ruler. Peace prevailed, and the administration ran smoothly. However, as Renzong approached adulthood, Empress Dowager Liu refused to relinquish her regency, as required by precedent. Her determination to cling to power and dominate an adult emperor tarnished her reputation. After Liu died, the emperor publicly condemned her.

In managing the government as a female regent, Empress Dowager Liu faced considerable obstacles. For the sake of propriety, she had to remain within the inner palace, so she rarely had face-to-face contact with important men, including high officials. To break out of her isolation, Liu cultivated unusually close links with the wives of high officials.[39] Because these women held honorific titles commensurate with their husbands' ranks, they could visit the palace. Liu frequently invited these ladies to social events, where she gave them messages to pass to their husbands. The empress dowager also employed servant women as go-betweens with the officialdom. Ironically, the low standing of these women gave them considerable freedom of movement, so the empress dowager could use female servants to deal with a wide range of useful people.

Empress Liu pioneered a new kind of regency. In the past, some female regents had earned resentment for their arrogant demeanor. Officials looked back on the reign of Empress Wu Zetian with horror, so Liu knew that any show of haughtiness would incite a furious backlash. With this in mind, she invented a novel style of female rule. Although Liu exercised supreme authority, she nevertheless defused potential opposition by acting with carefully calculated restraint. Moreover, whereas empresses dowager had traditionally promoted their blood relatives, Liu exercised power personally and did not favor her kinsmen. Because she came from a relatively low background, she probably did not regard her family as particularly useful. Instead, she used eunuchs to achieve her goals. By avoiding the emergence of a troublesome faction of consort kin, Liu limited potential opposition to her regency. Empresses dowager later in the dynasty, such as Empress Xiang

(1046–1101), imitated Liu's strategy and similarly defused opposition by declining to empower their kinsmen.[40]

Empress Liu fostered a novel ideology to legitimize her power.[41] Early medieval historians had used the term "two saints" (*er sheng*) to describe an emperor and his empress. This expression not only sacralized their conjugal relationship but also made the empress the moral equal of her spouse. Empress Liu took this idea even further by declaring that husband and wife constitute a single unit.[42] She then employed this rhetoric to legitimize herself as a holy ruler and an extension of her deceased husband. Liu commissioned various images of herself and her late husband, often in religious settings, to remind people of this link.[43]

Like Empress Liu, other ambitious Song consorts had to contend with implacable resistance from the officialdom as well. The experience of Empress Dowager Cao (1016–1079), wife of Emperor Renzong and adoptive mother of Emperor Yingzong, exemplifies the limitations of female power during the Song dynasty.[44] Yingzong suffered from physical and mental problems, rendering him incapable of carrying out his duties. Faced with a power vacuum, Empress Dowager Cao declared a regency. She wanted to dethrone the useless emperor and replace him with someone who could carry out the imperial role. However, the bureaucracy steadfastly opposed this scheme. Allowing the empress dowager to dethrone a sitting emperor would set a dangerous precedent. Moreover, a weak emperor allowed the officials around him to accrue more authority, so they probably liked having an incompetent monarch on the throne. When Emperor Yingzong's health eventually improved, the high ministers forced Cao to renounce her regency, and she found herself sidelined. This incident highlights the limitations empresses faced in even the most favorable circumstances. Empress Dowager Cao may have been able to serve as regent for an ineffectual emperor, but she lacked her own staff and depended on the male-dominated bureaucratic apparatus to get anything done. When the officials united in opposition, they could thwart her plans.

Antipathy toward ambitious empresses extended to other female members of the imperial household as well, so princesses also had their status lowered.[45] The Tang emperors had allowed their daughters great wealth and prestige.[46] However, this favoritism came at a cost. Tang princesses often dominated their husbands, ignored ritual propriety, and sometimes became involved in politics, earning them a reputation for being haughty troublemakers. Song emperors wanted to avoid these problems, so they limited the perquisites of princesses and reduced their ceremonial rank and income. The Tang government had a special office that handled the affairs of princesses, but the Song lacked this sort of bureau. Without advocates within the bureaucracy, princesses found themselves marginalized. Moreover, censors criticized any

princess who overstepped her proper role. The Song also subjected emperors'
daughters to stringent regulations. They had to behave moderately and maintain high standards of conduct. Song princesses reacted to these strictures by
becoming very cautious, and they had a reputation for meekness.

Emperors married off their daughters at age fifteen or sixteen. Although
princesses still received a generous dowry, their financial position was very
modest compared to their Tang predecessors.[47] They did not marry powerful
men but instead wed respectable minor gentry. Although marriage to a princess remained prestigious, Song emperors no longer allowed their sons-in-law
to assume high office. Moreover, whereas medieval emperors often married
off princesses to neighboring rulers to seal alliances, the Song court abandoned this awkward practice. Song princesses were also expected to follow
Confucian ethical injunctions. During the Tang, 23 percent of princesses married more than once. In contrast, only 5 percent of Song princesses remarried.[48]

The life of the Yanguo princess (1038–1070), daughter of Emperor Renzong, illustrates how the Song system barred the emperor's female offspring
from interfering in government matters.[49] Renzong showed Yanguo unusual
favor and granted her immense wealth, making her unusually audacious. She
dispensed her wealth to buy support and tried to participate in politics. When
high officials realized the extent of her ambitions, they pushed back forcefully. Originally Yanguo had ten officials staffing her residence, but government ministers remonstrated that such a large staff was inappropriate for a
princess and reduced the number of household managers to four. They also
criticized Yanguo for violating ritual norms. These attacks forced her to back
down. Thereafter she refrained from interfering with state affairs.

❦

The position of palace women under Liao, Jin, and Yuan also affected perceptions of female power in China. The Liao dynasty of the northeast established rules for palace organization earliest among these conquest dynasties.
These regulations emerged as a series of compromises between the native
customs of the nomadic Khitans and those of their Chinese subjects. The
resulting system linked inherited status, office, and marriage more tightly
than any other dynasty.[50]

The Khitan ruling class used marriage as a political strategy.[51] The Liao
rulers, surnamed Yelü, took their wives from a clan surnamed Xiao, and the
Xiao married their sons to the daughters of the Yelü, forming a reciprocal
marriage network. As the two clans intermarried generation after generation,
they developed a dense web of intertwined kinship ties. As an unintended
consequence of this mixing, women often ended up marrying their maternal

uncles or cousins.[52] This kinship system benefited both sides. Repeated inter-marriage with the ruling line raised the prestige of Xiao consort kin, while marrying with the most prominent clan reinforced the position of the ruling Yelü. Intermarriage also fostered a de facto political alliance between the imperial and consort clans. In return for supporting the rulers, members of the consort clan enjoyed immense privileges. The Xiao were extremely wealthy and served in key posts. This system also reduced the power of the emperor's agnates so that his blood kinsmen would not challenge him.[53]

Prominent Khitans also intermarried with the noble families of the Tanguts, Turks, Goguryeo, and other surrounding peoples to forge political alliances.[54] And Khitan nobles married with prominent ethnic Chinese families to build useful relationships in conquered areas. The ruling clan also married off prin-cesses for political gain.[55] Daughters of empresses wed men from the Xiao consort clan, but those born to minor imperial consorts could marry someone from a different clan. They often ended up being matched with high officials in the Liao government to help guarantee the loyalty of the bureaucracy.

Some Liao empresses exercised considerable authority.[56] Ambitious women sometimes managed to manipulate the dynasty's system and under-lying culture to achieve their personal goals. Liao empresses and consorts gained power in several ways. A talented woman could become a trusted adviser of the emperor and influence his decisions. Emperor Taizu's wife, Empress Chunqin (879–953), acted as one of his primary counselors.[57] This resourceful woman led troops and helped her husband assassinate rival chief-tains. When Taizu died in 927, she assumed control of the government and dominated her son Emperor Taizong. When he died, she tried to choose the next ruler as well. However, this time her opponents rose up in opposition. Chunqin lost the resulting civil war and suffered banishment.

The Liao adopted the Chinese custom of allowing an empress dowager to act as regent. When an emperor died, the dowager acted as regent until a new ruler was chosen. The empress dowager had considerable input in determin-ing which prince would become emperor, making her an important force at court. If the new emperor were still a minor, the empress dowager could declare a regency. When the husband of Empress Chengtian (953–1009) died, her son ascended the throne as Emperor Shengzong.[58] He was only twelve years old at the time, so Chengtian pronounced herself regent. Although Chengtian managed the government competently, she refused to relinquish her powers when the emperor came of age. With the aid of three supportive officials, she remained regent for twenty-seven years. Only in old age did she finally surrender control of the government and allow her son to rule.

Even adult emperors sometimes handed government matters over to their empresses when away from the capital. When Emperor Taizong went on a military campaign, he gave his wife, Empress Jing'an (d. 936), the authority to handle matters in his absence. Unlike the Chinese, Khitans considered empresses capable of leading troops. Khitan culture was highly militarized, and they considered the army the foundation of the nation. Men accepted a degree of female participation in military matters. Due to their nomadic background, elite Liao ladies rode and hunted, so Khitan men were accustomed to the sight of women on horseback in the company of armed men.[59] Several Liao empresses became important military leaders. Taizu sent Empress Chunqin out to lead a campaign against the Tanguts. She proved an able general and defeated them. And Empress Chengtian successfully defended Liao during a major war with Song.

Liao institutions developed out of tribal government, so the dynasty emphasized patrimonialism and kinship connections. Initially, the government was deeply intertwined with the ruler's family. This system allowed the ruler's wife to participate in important matters. Moreover, the Khitan marriage network worked in the favor of women who married into the imperial clan. Empresses dowager had impeccable pedigrees. Not only had they been married to an emperor, but they also came from the powerful Xiao clan, thus providing them with numerous allies in the upper ranks of government. When an empress dowager declared a regency, power temporarily shifted from the imperial clan (Yelü) to the consort clan (Xiao).[60] In the Song, the officialdom tried to keep the powers of the regent dowager in check. But in the Liao, many of the dowager's kinsmen served as officials, so they enthusiastically supported her regency. Raising her position empowered all of her kinsmen in tandem, so in contrast with the Song the officialdom strove to expand the empress dowager's authority.

Over time, the Khitans assimilated Chinese ethics, and female participation in politics gradually declined. But, while Chinese values tended to degrade the status of Liao empresses, they could use some of these values to their advantage. During the Liao dynasty, elite Khitan women studied the standard Chinese curriculum and were sometimes highly educated.[61] As in the Chinese heartland, the Khitans emphasized the importance of maternal instruction, so important families educated their daughters so that they could eventually teach their own children. Khitan empresses and ladies from wealthy families were extremely familiar with Chinese ethics, and they enthusiastically promoted Confucianism. Many epitaphs praise a Khitan woman for adhering to Confucian propriety. Empress Dowager Chengtian exemplified the Confucianized Liao empress. When she acted as regent for her son Emperor Shengzong, she made sure that he received a comprehensive Confucian education.[62] Chengtian modeled her own behavior after the Duke of Zhou and encouraged the Confucianization of the Liao bureaucracy. Although

Confucianism promoted gender hierarchy, this rich body of thought also included concepts such as filial piety and maternal authority that empresses could use to elevate themselves within the imperial family, thus potentially gaining political authority as well.

The Jurchens who established the Jin dynasty came from a similar nomadic background as the Khitans, yet in some notable respects the cultures and institutions of these two peoples differed. Jin rulers initially banned intermarriage with their Chinese subjects, as they feared assimilation.[63] However, this ban proved unworkable and was rescinded in 1191. The Jurchens were strictly exogamous. Because they married outside their immediate circle of kin, Jurchens were amenable to ethnic mixing. Many took Chinese spouses, and even the Jin emperors had ethnic Han and Khitan consorts. In general, there was considerable mingling between different peoples in this era, and even some emperors had mixed ancestry.[64]

The organization of the Jin palace changed over time, again due to steadily increasing Chinese influence.[65] Initially the Jin palace administration was very informal, and the ruler's concubines were not ranked. Over time, the Jurchens established a Chinese-style palace system and distinguished the rank of consorts through graded titles. Jurchen rulers had traditionally been polygynous, but after conquering China they only took one official wife, titled empress in the Chinese fashion. The Jin emperors chose their wives from elite families of the Jurchens and other nomadic peoples.

The Jin did not employ rigorous standards to select imperial concubines, and these women came from various backgrounds and ethnicities.[66] Initially Jurchen soldiers seized many Chinese women in war, similar to the traditional practice of bride capture. Some of these unfortunates ended up in the palace in lowly positions.[67] As before, the rulers took their major consorts from elite steppe families. Some Jin rulers practiced levirate and married their fathers' widows. They also selected beautiful women from the common people to enter the palace as minor concubines. Over time, the proportion of Han women in the Jin palace increased. Their status rose, and some became empresses and primary consorts. In 1138 the Jin instituted a more comprehensive system of female ranks.[68] Aside from palace ladies, the wives of nobles, princes, and high officials also received honorific titles commensurate with their husbands' offices. In rare cases, a woman could also earn a title as a reward for extraordinary personal accomplishments or service to the state, such as contributing to local defenses in time of war.

Like the Khitans, Jurchen women traditionally rode horses, hunted, and sometimes participated in war. After settling in China, however, Jurchen rulers expected their women to become more sedate and refined. Emperors emphasized the education of palace ladies.[69] Jurchen women had traditionally

been illiterate, and the ignorance of palace concubines at the beginning of
the dynasty caused problems. Unlettered women found it difficult to carry
out elaborate court rituals, and they could not manage complex palace
affairs. Moreover, as Jurchen rulers gained exposure to Chinese high culture,
they felt embarrassed by the tawdriness of their palace life. To remedy this
situation, they established a palace school to educate imperial consorts and
princesses in a standard Chinese curriculum. Palace women embraced these
educational opportunities, and the cultural tenor of the palace quickly rose.
The emperor's consorts mostly studied textbooks dedicated to female education and ethics. Ambitious students could delve into advanced subjects such
as astronomy, arithmetic, and the ancient classics.

Women of the Jurchen ruling clan traditionally had a voice in important
decisions. They helped settle internal quarrels and sometimes participated
in war. Yet, after the establishment of the Jin dynasty, palace women rarely
had significant political roles. As in the Song, Jin officials took measures to
limit the authority of empresses and other consorts. The Jin dynasty did not
have any female regents. When a woman influenced affairs of state, she did
so indirectly in a muted fashion. Empress Mingde, wife of Emperor Shizong,
gave her husband useful advice, and he regarded her as a trusted adviser.[70]
Nevertheless, to avoid criticism, she kept a low profile and did not take on an
overtly political role.

The conquest of China by the Mongols initiated a new form of government. Women had played important roles in the rise of the Mongol Empire.[71]
Prior to entering China, Mongol khans had married off daughters to powerful
men to build alliances, and Chinggis Khan (1162–1227) even took a Jurchen
princess as a minor wife to improve Mongol ties with Jin. Women married
to important husbands found themselves at the center of political life. Some
were shrewd and outspoken, and men listened to their opinions. They advised
their husbands and participated in assemblies (*quriltais*) where khans made
important decisions. The wives of khans received foreign ambassadors and
interceded on behalf of petitioners. After a husband's death, they might
become even more powerful, acting as regent and deciding key matters.
Women took responsibility for many tasks to free up their husbands to go on
distant campaigns. By empowering women within the family, men were able
to dedicate themselves to warfare and project Mongol power across Eurasia.

Female power peaked during periodic succession disputes.[72] Like other
steppe peoples, the Mongols lacked primogeniture. The selection of a new
ruler was often contested, and it could take years to bring together various
leaders, come to a consensus, and select a new khan. During these long inter-
regnums, a woman often served as regent. Most female regents simply maintained institutional stability, holding the government together until a new

Figure 2.3. Portrait of a Yuan dynasty lady (Metropolitan Museum of Art)

male ruler could take control. Occasionally they used this power vacuum to place a son on the throne, persecute opponents, or decide important policies.[73]

The wives of a few Mongol leaders stand out for having been particularly influential. Hoelun, the mother of Chinggis Khan, was extremely strong and capable.[74] Her competence made a deep impression on her son, and he considered women qualified to exercise leadership. When Chinggis began his ascent, he relied heavily on marriage politics.[75] He married and divorced his wives strategically to gain political advantage. Chinggis was polygynous and had up to four wives at a time, providing him with a pool of female talent. He gave the women close to him opportunities to rule. In fact, he relied heavily on his spouses and daughters-in-law to help administer his rapidly expanding empire. When Chinggis conquered new territory, he often assigned one of his wives to administer it. She established a royal court in the newly annexed region and oversaw administration. Chinggis married his daughters to the sons of other khans as a way to bind himself to important men. Their husbands received an honorific title and became warriors in the Mongol army, while his daughters remained behind to rule their husbands' domains.

Figure 2.4. Chabi (Wikimedia Commons)

The successors of Chinggis Khan took a very different view of female power. Instead of viewing kinswomen as a useful source of talent, they saw them as rivals and took steps to bar them from positions of authority. Also, as soon as Chinggis died, his daughters began to attack one another. Ambitious men soon acted to remove women from positions of authority. These measures quickly eroded female status and power. Although women had been instrumental in building and ruling the early Mongol Empire, after Chinggis they had little authority.

By the time the Mongols conquered China and established the Yuan dynasty, the position of women within their system had already declined. The Yuan rulers saw women largely as tokens in political marriages.[76] However, unlike the Khitans, the ruling line did not want to empower potential rivals by repeatedly intermarrying with a particular family or clan. Instead, Yuan rulers took multiple wives from different backgrounds, mostly from relatively powerless families.[77]

Koreans used this marriage strategy most successfully to link themselves to the Yuan regime.[78] The kings of Goguryeo were rightly terrified of their huge and bellicose neighbor. To maintain good relations with the Mongols, Korean kings regularly sent women to the Yuan court as tribute. Many Korean tribute women were highborn and educated, and some were skilled in music, dance, tea preparation, and cooking. Moreover, several kings of Korea married Mongol princesses. Intermarriage benefited both sides. Mongols used marriage ties to maintain their dominance over Goguryeo, and Koreans accepted their subservient status in return for a high degree of autonomy. The role of women in maintaining the relationship between the rulers of Yuan and Goguryeo highlights the low status of palace women at the time. They were not valued in their own right but were treated as items to be exchanged among powerful men.

Yuan consorts had different degrees of seniority. Only a son of the senior wife could potentially inherit the throne. In accordance with Chinese custom, the Yuan emperor gave just one of these women the title of empress. They controlled domains that consisted of both land and herds. In addition, empresses received tax income and engaged in commerce. Most Yuan empresses and consorts had little to do with politics. Chabi (1225–1281, called Empress Zhaorui Shunsheng in Chinese), the wife of Kublai Khan, was an exception. She was a niece of Chinggis Khan's senior wife, Börte, and her impressive pedigree seems to have given her unusually high standing at court.[79] Chabi acted as an adviser to her husband and interceded with him regarding key issues. She asked that captured imperial ladies of the defeated Song be treated well and opposed cruelty toward Chinese farmers.

Sorghaghtani Beki (d. 1252) was daughter-in-law of Chinggis Khan and mother of Kublai Khan. She received part of Hebei as her domain, which yielded a large income. Sorghaghtani encouraged the Mongols to adopt a more sophisticated and cosmopolitan style of rule, elevating the general level of administration. Dagi (also known as Targi, d. 1322) was the mother of Emperors Wuzong and Renzong. She managed their respective successions and decided the order in which they would reign. Budashiri (ca. 1307– ca. 1340), wife of Emperor Wenzong, also tried to manage the succession by exiling or executing opponents. Upon her husband's death, she served as empress dowager and dominated the state for seven years. However, she earned the antipathy of the young Emperor Ningzong, and he eventually sent her into exile.

Although most Yuan empresses had little influence, the sight of the ruler's women presenting themselves publicly in court and demanding a say in important matters disconcerted Chinese observers. In reaction, the rulers of subsequent dynasties took stringent measures to block the ambitions of palace women. At the beginning of the Ming dynasty, the founding Hongwu emperor placed strict constraints on his consorts to prevent them from following the example of Yuan ladies and block them from engaging in politics.[80] These measures set an influential precedent, and women rarely exercised much power for the remainder of imperial history.

Chapter 3

Wealth

The economy of the Song dynasty grew far more rapidly than before, generating unprecedented prosperity that transformed society in myriad ways. The law treated the household as the fundamental economic unit of society, so both family structure and the economy were transformed during this era, the changes in each affecting the other.[1] The intimate links between the domestic realm and the wider economy allowed many women to benefit from rising affluence.

Women could own and administer property, and a few gained control over a considerable amount of land or other wealth.[2] However, female property owners faced significant ideological hurdles. Households served as the foundation of production and consumption, so the government taxed households, not individuals. Chinese traditionally conceptualized the family not just as closely related kin who lived together, but more abstractly as a long line of descent that encompassed both ancestors and posterity. Succession through male heirs linked the diachronic family together, so elders considered it vital to keep assets within the patriline. Dowry implicitly threatened the family's continuation by removing collective wealth and depositing it with a different line of male descent. The ancients addressed this problem by prohibiting women from owning property. *Records of the Rites* (*Liji*) declared that a married woman should have no property of her own, on the assumption that everything should be mutually owned by the household and administered by senior men.[3]

Classical ideals did not always suit the circumstances of Song society. Many families lacked a competent man to manage collective assets, in which case a woman would have to step in and look after family wealth for the common good. Moreover, a bride entered her new home with a dowry that belonged to her personally. These realities ensured that women had the right to own and manage property, regardless of ideological objections.

At this time, economic changes fundamentally reshaped the household property system. From the eleventh century onward, it became common for people to own private property apart from family holdings. The shift toward individual ownership was never absolute, and society continued to regard property as ideally belonging to the family rather than its constituent members. Even so, as the economy developed, more property came into the hands of individuals, making it easier for women to control wealth.

Changing views toward ownership had a major impact on female property rights. Women acquired some of the new wealth generated by the vibrant commercial economy. Female property ownership elicited concern because it contravened both tradition and the classical rites. Women transferred dowry and inheritance from the family of their fathers to that of their husbands, so increasing dowries threatened the traditional inheritance system based on patrilineal descent. Conservative thinkers also feared that personal wealth would embolden women to challenge male prerogatives. These developments spawned moral panic in conservative circles, resulting in a backlash against women's property rights. The greatest Neo-Confucian thinkers of the day, including Sima Guang, Zhu Xi, and Su Shi, advocated reducing female ownership rights so as to uphold the integrity of patriarchal institutions.[4]

The new atmosphere of prosperity made people reconsider their views toward wealth. In the aristocratic society of the Tang dynasty, fortune was conventionally viewed as an accompaniment to status. Accordingly, Tang eulogies did not praise widows who endured financial hardship to remain chaste, as poverty implied debased social standing.[5] Attitudes toward money and work changed under the vibrant Song economy. It became far easier to acquire wealth, giving rise to nouveaux riches unrelated to the medieval aristocracy. As wealth detached from genealogy, poverty was no longer necessarily seen as a disgrace. In fact, a destitute widow who refused to remarry could garner praise for maintaining her integrity in the face of adversity. Epitaphs began to emphasize the poverty of chaste widows as a badge of martyrdom. A woman in straightened circumstances proved her fortitude by safeguarding her virtue and educating her sons.

Wealthy women were also held in high esteem. It was not unusual for a wife to own large amounts of property in her own name or for a widow to manage the estate of a deceased magnate. Real estate had become a highly liquid commodity, and gentry women actively bought and sold land and buildings.[6] They had the legal authority to enter into commercial contracts on their own behalf, and they used these instruments to acquire and dispose of property.[7]

Wives maintained links with their natal kin, and these relationships some-times had a financial dimension.[8] A bride received a portion of the fam-ily wealth as dowry. Thereafter, she and her blood kin might continue to exchange items of value on special occasions such as weddings and festivals. When a gentry woman bore a son, it was customary for her parents to pres-ent her (or her husband) with a piece of land as a gift for their grandson. If a married woman faced financial difficulties, her blood kin might step in and provide aid.

It seems that women frequently used their personal wealth to benefit their husbands and other family members. Most records of female property trans-actions describe a wife using her money to buy property for her husband. Women also helped pay for special family expenditures, such as a costly wedding or funeral and the educations of husbands and sons.

Song women demonstrated impressive generosity, and they often sup-ported charitable activities.[9] Ethical education stressed the importance of benevolence, and women of means often put this virtue into practice. Many women were devout Buddhists, and religious teachings also encouraged generosity. Epitaphs record many examples of female liberality. Women often gave alms to Buddhist clerics and funded the construction and repair of temples. Wealthy women funded infrastructure projects that benefited the entire community, such as bridges and irrigation projects. They also provided emergency food aid and relief funds to the victims of natural disasters. Some helped poor families pay for marriages and funerals, which could be ruin-ously expensive. Benevolent women also purchased medicine for the sick. Philanthropy was not necessarily a sacrifice, as it could bring benefits to the patron. A reputation for generosity could gain a woman acclaim, even as she remained cloistered. At a time when women were becoming increasingly secluded, charitable activities gave them an excuse to engage with the wider world, win public praise, and expand their range of contacts.

Of course, women were not entirely self-sacrificing. With rising amounts of currency in circulation and a wider range of available goods for sale, they also spent more on themselves. The rise of an increasingly refined market economy spurred consumption, and women were the prime customers for many luxury goods. They became more fashion conscious than before and spent large sums on clothing, jewelry, and cosmetics. They also purchased minor indulgences such as fresh flowers and scented items.[10] And women spent more on leisure activities, taking day trips to scenic suburban venues, visiting temples, and holding parties. Female spending on luxury goods was a significant factor in the rise of the commercial economy.

Figure 3.1. Women playing weiqi (Metropolitan Museum of Art)

For most women, their dowry constituted most of their personal wealth. Traditionally the groom's family presented a betrothal gift to the bride's side, and the bride's parents sent their daughter off with a dowry. Prior to the Song, betrothal gifts had generally been more valuable than dowry, but at this time dowry overtook bridewealth in value, transforming marriage finance. The ancient rites did not mention dowry and instead stressed the significance of the betrothal gift (*pincai*) from the groom's family to that of the bride.[11] The groom's parents presented this gift to formalize the engagement. The value of bridewealth fluctuated over time. In earlier periods, betrothal gifts were sometimes substantial and included land and moveable wealth. By the Song, however, betrothal gifts usually consisted mainly of small valuables and inexpensive items of symbolic significance. There were no clear guidelines, so the groom's family had considerable leeway in deciding what to give their new in-laws. Documents preserved at Dunhuang record the gifts presented by ordinary families. These included clothing, jewelry, cloth, cups, prepared foods, and meat. Urban residents often presented gold jewelry to their new in-laws.

As the value of dowry came to exceed that of the betrothal gift, the bride's side had to spend far more than the groom's family to finalize a marriage.[12] This situation ran contrary to previous practices. During the late tenth century, a woman's dowry was usually about half as valuable as the betrothal gift. These two sums started to converge during the Tang dynasty, and by the early twelfth century they were roughly equal in value. In the late twelfth century, dowries became about twice as expensive as bridewealth on average.[13] Traditionalists expressed concern about the rising value of dowries. The ancient rites had stressed bridewealth and ignored dowry, so classicists regarded the new customs as unorthodox.

Scholars have debated the reasons behind the switch in the relative values of dowry and the betrothal gift. There does not seem to have been a single cause. Several factors acted in tandem to alter the structure of marriage finance at this time. Most importantly, social change drove dowries higher. As the economy grew and mobility intensified, it became easier for a family to deploy wealth to raise their status.[14] Elite families offered large dowries to attract prestigious in-laws, thereby publicly demonstrating their social stature and gaining useful allies. This custom gradually trickled down to affect ordinary families as well, and even people of humble means began to dower their daughters more generously. In some regions, such as Fujian, extremely large dowries became the standard custom.

Increased social mobility made it difficult for gentry families to maintain their status over generations. To prevent the reemergence of hereditary aristocracy, the Song government provided literati with opportunities for advancement, and highly educated men from gentry families dominated the bureaucracy. However, opportunity also brought insecurity, as social position was no longer automatically inherited. To professionalize the bureaucracy and discourage heritable status, the government employed a rigorous examination system to select officials. The shift toward meritocracy made status more fluid. If a gentry family's sons and grandsons failed to pass the exams, they would steadily decline in wealth and standing. They had to use new strategies to preserve their position.[15]

These changing circumstances made affinal connections much more valuable than before. Educated and successful in-laws were a useful resource,

providing their marriage partners with cultural capital and educational exper-
tise. Moreover, behind the meritocratic facade, the Song civil service was in
fact extremely nepotistic. Minor officials were regularly denied promotion
if they lacked influential connections. To advance within the bureaucracy,
a man needed sponsors and connections. A son-in-law with a bright future
might provide the men of the bride's family with support to bolster their
careers. Given the increased utility of affines, families with daughters offered
large dowries to attract a son-in-law likely to succeed in the civil service.[16]

Families used dowry rather than bridewealth to gain these connections
because dowry was the more flexible of the two. Traditionally, the groom's
family recycled the betrothal gift and presented it to their daughter as part of
her dowry, making it less useful for attracting desirable in-laws. Moreover,
ritual and custom had little to say about dowries, so they could be readily
increased. As families offered large dowries to attract useful sons-in-law,
marriages often became blatantly financial in nature. This pragmatism fostered social mixing, and it became increasingly common for families of different economic levels to marry.

As dowries increased, it became possible for a poor scholar with good
prospects to quickly rise up the economic ladder by marrying the right
wife. Grooms began to seek a bride with a large dowry to facilitate their
own upward mobility. Some men were even willing to enter into matrilocal
unions for financial gain.[17] In these arrangements, a lower-status man married a woman from a more prosperous family that lacked sons. The wife's
family brought in an outsider to maintain the ancestral sacrifices and avoid
extinction. The husband took his wife's surname, lived with her family, and
became the heir to her parents' estate. Although people looked down on men
who joined their wives' families, some ambitious men were willing to endure
embarrassment to obtain economic advancement.

Although dowry generally increased in value during the Song dynasty, the
value varied considerably according to region, family assets, and individual
proclivities.[18] A dowry might include items such as household goods, clothing, gold and silver, jewelry, furniture, and real estate. The total value of this
package could be substantial. Epitaphs mention dowries sufficient to purchase
land and houses.[19] Most importantly, as during the Tang, a wealthy family
sometimes gave their daughter dowry land (*liantian*). In this agricultural society, people considered land the most reliable productive asset. The income
stream from a fertile piece of land could ensure a wife's economic security.[20]

Even the Song imperial clan embraced the new custom of expensive dowries and sent their women off with large sums paid for by the government.[21]
The amount of a clanswoman's dowry depended on her degree of relation
to the emperor. Princesses had the most generous dowries, about double the

value of a prince's betrothal gifts. Even more valuable than dowry, an imperial clanswoman's husband received privileges within the bureaucratic system, all but guaranteeing an honorable and profitable official career. Moreover, one son of each clanswoman automatically received an official post, guaranteeing the continued prosperity of her family for the next generation.

Economic development encouraged a pragmatic view of property ownership, so most people readily accepted the idea that women could own their own wealth. According to the law, a woman owned her dowry. To fully benefit, however, she not only had to own the dowry in name but also control it. Legal provisions safeguarding dowry became increasingly clear and specific through the course of the Song, protecting female property rights.[22] A couple did not own the dowry jointly, and it could not be merged with the property of a woman's husband. Nor did the dowry belong to a woman's natal family. It was owned solely by the wife.

Scholars have debated the degree of control that wives actually exercised over their dowry, and their management of land in particular. Some contend that the husband usually took control of his wife's dowry land, while others believe that spouses managed it jointly. It seems that in most cases a wife retained the right to freely dispose of her dowry, and if she remarried she could take it with her. Numerous legal cases and inscriptions confirm that judges actively protected a wife's right to own and manage her dowry wealth.[23] Brides preferred to receive dowry in the form of land. Transferring the title of real estate required official procedures, helping to protect dowry land from greedy husbands and in-laws.

Even though law and custom guaranteed a woman's ownership of her dowry, some Neo-Confucian thinkers nevertheless appealed to classical ritual to argue that it belonged to her husband. Largely due to the rising influence of Neo-Confucianism, Southern Song law diluted the property rights of women. Some jurists argued that because a couple constituted a single social unit, a husband had joint control of the dowry together with his wife. The government also began to discourage widows from taking dowry away from their husbands' families if they remarried. It also became more common for men to try to wrest away control of a woman's dowry. Husbands and their kinsmen tried to seize dowries outright. Various family members lodged lawsuits claiming a woman's dowry.[24] And siblings sometimes fought over the division of their mother's dowry after her death.

Social expectations also curtailed female financial autonomy. Family members often expected women to spend their dowries for the common good or to benefit others, and many wives used their personal wealth to support family endeavors. Even so, society did not require a woman to spend her dowry on others. Tang dynasty epitaphs rarely mention dowries, but during the Song it became common to praise a deceased woman who used her dowry to help her husband's family.[25] Because this sort of action was not required, a woman who spent her dowry in this manner attracted attention and commendation. Men wrote these epitaphs, so of course they praised women who used their assets to help their husbands.

Large dowries affected Song society in myriad ways. Dowry became one of the most important factors families considered when finalizing a match, altering the nature of elite marriage. The allure of money brought people from different backgrounds together, and various social groups intermarried more frequently. Also, women who received dowry land would have to marry a spouse from the same area. If she married a man who lived far away, it would be difficult for her to manage her landholding, so dowering women with land made it likely that they would marry locally. Dowry also facilitated widow remarriage. If a woman had a significant dowry that she could take with her if she remarried, she had a broader range of opportunities after her husband died.

Expensive dowries became a major financial burden for families with daughters. Parents sometimes had to put off a daughter's marriage longer than usual while they saved up an appropriate sum, and occasionally a woman never married at all for lack of a dowry. It was not uncommon for families to borrow money for a dowry, plunging them into debt. Sometimes they suffered impoverishment from the high cost of marrying off a daughter.

Large dowries also altered family dynamics.[26] A woman with money of her own felt more confident and enjoyed respect from her in-laws, so rising dowries empowered wives within the patriarchal family system. An unhappy wife with her own money would find it easier to leave a failed marriage and seek a better situation. Even so, the heavy emphasis on dowry could cause problems. Sima Guang fretted that if a dowry were too small, a woman's in-laws might abuse her, whereas a large dowry would make her arrogant.[27] He believed that individual property ownership, and female wealth in particular, threatened family harmony. To remedy this problem, Sima promoted the classical model of household wealth held in common and managed by a male elder. A financial marriage could also disrupt domestic life by bringing together spouses from different backgrounds. If wife and husband had dissimilar upbringing, their clashing behavior and values could raise tensions. The high cost of dowry also eroded moral standards. The death of a baby girl could potentially save the family a fortune, making female infanticide economically expedient. Critics complained that rising dowries encouraged infanticide, usually through drowning.[28]

The increasing value of dowries also altered the allocation of wealth within families. A large dowry constitutes what anthropologists call diverging devolution—the transmission of property to daughters, who removed family wealth from the male line of descent. As dowering daughters caused an exodus of wealth from families, they responded by trying to attract well-dowered brides for their sons. They needed an infusion of wealth from the dowries of wives to compensate for the money lost by dowering daughters.

Shifts in marriage finance spurred people to rethink female inheritance. Women received assets from blood kin either as dowry or inheritance.[29] One might assume that as the value of dowry increased, women's inheritance rights would decline. But surprisingly, in spite of the Confucian revival and rising dowries, the inheritance rights of daughters increased during the Song. Due to large dowries and liberal inheritance, women received more wealth from their natal families than ever before, moving unprecedented amounts of wealth away from the male line of descent and out toward affines.

The proportion of an estate that went to a daughter varied depending on whether or not she had a husband or brother. The basic provisions of Song inheritance law generally followed Tang precedents, but with some significant modifications.[30] During the Tang, a deceased man's sons divided up the estate equally. Authorities assumed that most of a man's assets would be passed down to his sons. An unmarried daughter received a share of the estate equal to half that inherited by her brothers. This amount would serve as her dowry when she wed.

If a couple had no surviving sons, the government declared the household "extinct" (*hujue*). Tang laws regarding extinct estates changed over time. In the early part of the dynasty, a married daughter could not inherit from her parents under any circumstances. If she lacked brothers, her father's kinsmen would divide up an extinct estate. However, a fiscal reform of 780 made women potentially liable to pay taxes, making the government amenable to female inheritance.[31] Previously, only men could be taxed, so inheritance laws kept property in male hands. Once the government started taxing women, it was no longer in the interests of the state to discourage female property ownership. From 836 onward, Tang authorities allowed married daughters to inherit property from an extinct household.

Many women lacked brothers, enabling them to inherit family wealth. It seems that during the Song, somewhere between 6 and 20 percent of families lacked a male heir, so extinct households were common.[32] Under Song law, a woman's right to inherit from her natal family depended on her marital status. A married woman with brothers did not ordinarily inherit from her parents.[33] Even in the case of an extinguished household, only unmarried daughters could receive a full share of the estate. A woman who had married and subsequently returned to her natal household received half of the estate. If married women were the only survivors of an extinguished household, they could inherit one-third of the total estate. Local officials oversaw the dispersal of large extinguished household estates so that the government could readily confiscate its share of property from extinguished households without unmarried daughters. They also tried to protect daughters from being cheated out of their rightful legacy and prevent husbands from seizing inherited wealth.[34]

In the Northern Song era, women enjoyed relatively liberal inheritance rights.[35] Daughters inherited a full share of their parents' estate, equal to their brothers. Even adoptive daughters and the daughters of concubines inherited a full share. And whereas under Tang law a deceased man's brothers could divide up an extinct household, during the Song a man's daughters inherited the extinct estate. Some scholars see these claims on natal family property not as true inheritance, but merely as a way to dower unmarried daughters.[36] However, the fact that unmarried daughters gained a full share of family property, equal to that received by their brothers, implies that this arrangement was indeed true inheritance.

During the Southern Song, female inheritance rights began to decline. A legal case from 1109, at the end of the Northern Song, shows a daughter and her brothers receiving equal portions of an estate. But after the state apparatus moved south, a daughter's share was worth only half that received by her brothers. The reasons for this regression are unclear. Perhaps it represents a deterioration in the general position of women. More likely, however, women's inheritance rights declined to compensate for dowry inflation.[37] As dowries increased in value, more resources were leaving the male line of descent and becoming the property of other families. From the standpoint of the natal family, intolerable amounts of wealth were being irrevocably lost. Decreasing the inheritance rights of unmarried women provided them with a decent dowry while stanching the flow of wealth from the male line.

Laws regarding matrilocal marriage also became increasingly explicit. These arrangements had always been considered unorthodox and even immoral, so legal regulation had previously been minimal. However, Song jurists took the realistic position that matrilocal households should have clear inheritance regulations.[38] In some cases, a son-in-law residing with his wife's family could inherit her parents' entire estate. However, if her parents had other children, or if the matrilocal marriage had failed and the son-in-law had moved out, his share would be reduced.

Wills became increasingly common at this time.[39] If a family had sons, the law clearly specified how the property should be divided, so a will was theoretically unnecessary. Nevertheless, writing a will allowed elders to allocate an estate according to their family's particular circumstances. The custom of writing wills further expanded female inheritance rights by enabling parents to direct a greater share of wealth to their daughters. A will governing the property of an extinct household usually bequeathed it to the family's daughters.

Song law regarding widows largely followed procedures set down in the Tang dynasty.[40] Only in exceptional cases would a widow inherit from her husband.[41] Usually she received nothing. As an outsider to the line of descent, a wife had no claim on the wealth of her husband's family. Even so, a widow would likely have a hand in managing her husband's estate, at least for a time. Song inscriptions frequently praise a woman for taking charge of family assets after her husband's death and managing them prudently.[42]

A widow's hold over her husband's estate depended on whether or not she had children. If she had sons, they would inherit the estate. In this case, if land was subsequently sold, even though the transaction likely required the widow's consent, the sale was conducted in the name of a son.[43] Although sons owned family property, the law forbade them from dividing it up while their mother was alive. Due to the dictates of filial piety, a widow's sons would likely defer to her wishes as they managed common property. They worked together under her supervision as long as she remained alive. In consequence, although a widow did not own her husband's estate, she might still control it. Even if she remarried, it seems that she might still have a say in the management of her deceased husband's estate, as her sons were still morally and legally obligated to obey her.[44]

If a couple lacked sons, the situation was more complicated. In this case, although the widow still did not own her deceased husband's estate, she assumed direct control over it. After her death, this property would pass to her husband's kinsmen. The couple's daughters might get a share as well. In taking over management of the estate, a widow had to assume all of her husband's responsibilities, such as caring for his parents. Because she did not own this property, she was not supposed to sell land or make major alterations. A widow who dispersed her husband's estate committed a serious crime and risked prosecution. Given the widow's tenuous hold over her husband's estate, if she lacked sons, her in-laws might try to seize it. These sorts of situations gave rise to acrimony and litigation.[45]

A man without sons would sometimes appoint a male heir before he died. However, many men died without a designated beneficiary. In this sort of situation, it was expected that his widow would appoint a male heir to inherit her husband's estate when she died.[46] Although the law did not require her to name the recipient, her in-laws would likely pressure her to clarify the line of inheritance. Although a widow could choose her husband's heir, she could not assign the estate to a man who was not related to him by blood. He had to be one of her husband's agnatic kinsmen. Because a widow had some leeway in the choice of heir, she would probably choose someone unlikely to claim the estate while she was still alive.

A woman who remarried and left her deceased husband's household could not take any of his estate with her. Moreover, her right to control this property ended when she remarried. A departing widow could only take her dowry. If she had sons, they would immediately assume control of their father's property upon her remarriage. But if the couple lacked children, her husband's kinsmen could divide up the estate.

When a woman died, her sons and daughters inherited her dowry.[47] It is not clear how the family allocated this wealth. Because classical ritual did not mention dowry, officials educated in Confucian dogma did not regard it as important, and the law did not thoroughly regulate dowry inheritance. Siblings probably had to reach a consensus on how to allocate their mother's property. In one case, after both husband and wife died, the man's parents were still alive. Three surviving sons took turns managing their mother's dowry land until their grandparents died.[48] This was clearly an ad hoc arrangement that the brothers negotiated to address their particular circumstances. Other families probably approached the problem with a similarly flexible mind-set.

Song law specifically denied a concubine any claim to her master's property. Even so, under certain circumstances she might benefit from his estate.[49] If a concubine did not have children and declared that she did not intend to marry, she could obtain control over a share of her deceased master's estate and use it for the rest of her life. If she married, she would forfeit any claim to this wealth. A concubine who had a son by her master could manage his share of the estate until he came of age. And if a man died wifeless and childless, his concubine might take over management of the entire estate in the manner of a widow and appoint an eventual heir. She could manage the property for the remainder of her life, and it would go to the designated heir upon her death. Also, a man could specify in his will that a concubine receive a share of his estate. The right of a concubine to control a deceased master's property and appoint an heir does not appear in Ming or Qing law codes, so the Song dynasty stands out as the high point for the property rights of concubines.

Not all female wealth came from inheritance and dowry. Some women worked outside the home to earn money. Economic development presented women with unprecedented opportunities. Even so, they generally regarded work as an unpleasant necessity. The women of wealthy families would only do symbolic labor, such as token embroidery or weaving. They avoided jobs outside the home that exposed them to public view. Literati regarded working women as objects of pity. They wrote of the sad life of elderly childless widows, women from poor families, or the wives of dissolute husbands who had to struggle to earn a living.[50]

Working women mostly performed domestic tasks. Wives were responsible for cooking, cleaning, laundry, and sundry household chores.[51] When a family lived in proximity to nature, women gathered wild foods in the forest.[52] They also made alcohol and sauces. Of all the work that women did at home, cloth making was considered the most important by far. Since antiquity, writers had lauded the manufacture of cloth as the most normative type of female labor.[53] Even though people of both sexes performed many different tasks during the day, it became commonplace to refer to female weaving and male plowing as representative gendered labor. Weaving was difficult and tedious. During the early Song, the state punished some female convicts by forcing them to work in textile workshops in the capital.[54] Because weaving was so unpleasant, people believed that this work displayed a woman's moral fortitude. Moreover, textile work upheld normative gender roles. As in other eras, Confucian moralists encouraged women to make cloth to express their inner virtue. Hundreds of Song poems about sericulture depict this sort of labor as a righteous activity.[55]

Although moralists lauded spinning and weaving as virtuous, women usually did this work to clothe their families and earn money.[56] For the average

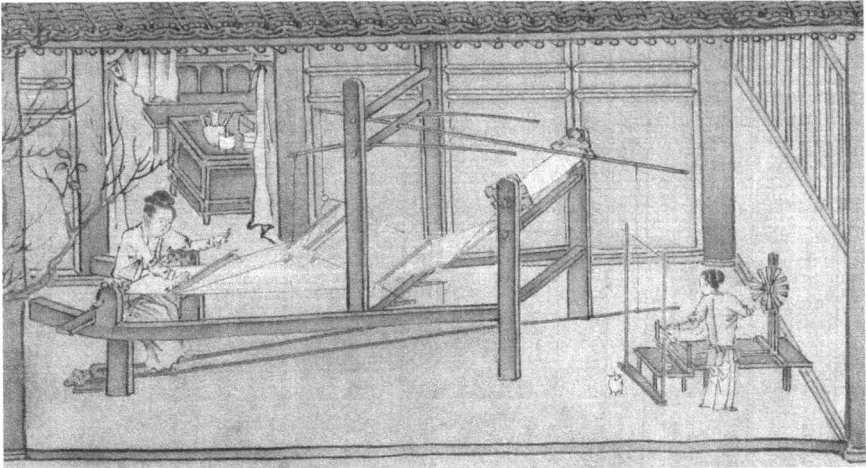

Figure 3.2. Working at the loom (Cleveland Museum)

farming family, making clothing was essential to their collective success. They saved a huge sum by making their own clothes rather than buying them. Any excess cloth could be sold for welcome income. Textile manufacture gave women a ready way to earn money, so destitute widows and other poor women turned to weaving as a survival strategy.

During this era, textile manufacture began to change. Inventors came up with improved machines for reeling, spinning, and weaving.[57] Some of these mechanical devices were extremely large and driven by waterwheels, so they could only be installed in workshops. Mechanization initiated the industrialization of Chinese textile production. Starting from the Song, cloth was increasingly made in factories staffed by men, thus depriving many women of the opportunity to earn money while working at home.

In spite of a growing economy, China remained a predominantly agricultural society, and most women lived and worked in farming households. Peasant women did many of the same tasks as their husbands.[58] While wealthy families hid their women from prying eyes, those from ordinary families had no choice but to work in the open. Economic necessity fostered more pragmatic and flexible attitudes toward gender relations, especially in the South. In Fujian, more women than men worked in the fields and markets.[59] Rural women in particular had little interest in stereotypes about gendered labor, and they did not feel ashamed to be seen working in the fields alongside their menfolk. In fact, rural people considered farm work a collaborative venture between husband and wife. Women prepared the fields for plowing, sowed seeds, transplanted seedlings, watered plants, hoed fields, harvested grain, tended the vegetable garden, and cared for livestock. After the harvest, they helped with the drying, pounding, and winnowing of grain. If the family grew cash crops, a woman might be involved in processing commodities such as tea or sugar. The wives of fishermen also helped their husbands with their work. In other words, peasant wives did whatever needed to be done. They even helped with difficult tasks such as digging and repairing irrigation works.

Overall, a woman's financial circumstances depended largely on her husband's profession. A merchant's wife often helped him run the family business.[60] These women had a special financial relationship with their husbands.[61] Itinerant merchants spent a great deal of time on the road, sometimes staying away from home for years at a time. By necessity, their wives had to be very independent and resourceful. Sometimes a wife managed one end of the business and coordinated sales with her husband in another place. In other cases, due to prolonged separation, husband and wife maintained separate estates.

The participation of women in military life, not usually a female realm of endeavor, illustrates how they sometimes helped fathers and husbands with their jobs. Numerous stories describe the exploits of martial women who fought on the battlefield and triumphed against male foes.[62] Although most of these tales were entertaining fantasies, some women did indeed live a military lifestyle and worked for the army.[63] Although women did not fight, they performed useful support work for the military. Even ordinary housework helped keep the camp clean and orderly.

The Song government wanted to raise morale and give the troops a greater sense of attachment to the land they defended, so they encouraged soldiers to marry and have children. The state even subsidized betrothal gifts to expedite the marriage of soldiers. Even so, soldiers had trouble attracting wives, as women rightly considered the military life hard and dangerous. Some soldiers captured enemy women and forced them into marriage. The government supported soldier marriages by allowing women to live with their husbands in military camps, even in distant border regions. Because these areas were remote and often unproductive, the state had to provide military rations for wives as well as their husbands. If a soldier died in battle, his wife received funds to finance her return home.

Women living in towns and cities had opportunities to work outside of agriculture, either on their own or as part of a modest family business.[64] Confucian concepts of female propriety limited their prospects. Women hesitated to work under the supervision of an unrelated man, and they did not consider it decent or safe to travel alone. Moreover, as most work was associated with one sex or the other, they were usually limited to stereotypically female activities. Female jobs varied by region.[65] Southern women were more pragmatic and performed a variety of jobs. In the north, where ritual restrictions tended to be stronger, they had few opportunities to work outside the home.

Due to the expanding economy, more women worked in commerce.[66] The scale of female-managed businesses was usually very small. Women had less capital than men, so they rarely did business that required a large investment or high risk. Also, custom excluded women from the most lucrative aspects of the economy. Women worked both as itinerant peddlers and as shopkeepers, selling a wide variety of items such as flowers, handicrafts, firewood, tea, cloth, and incense. Some worked in retail as their main job, while others did it as a sideline. Many female-run businesses sold food and beverages. Because women had experience cooking for their families, it was natural for them to use these skills to earn money. They fermented alcohol for sale and hawked street foods.

The business of male and female merchants differed in certain respects. Whereas men bought and sold luxuries or dealt in wholesale wares, women usually had less capital, so they sold inexpensive items. They also faced higher risks when doing business, as they were vulnerable to harassment and fraud. In most ways, though, women and men approached retail in a

similar manner. They helped to satisfy the growing demands of a society
with increasingly sophisticated patterns of consumption. And like their male
counterparts, women tried to avoid taxes and circumvent state monopolies,
sometimes acting as smugglers to earn higher profits.[67]

Most commonly, women worked in the service sector. Those without
capital or special skills might seek employment as a servant in a wealthy
household. Some women were bond servants sold by their families for a set
term of service. Others worked as managers or employees in teahouses, bars,
restaurants, and inns.[68] Women could also earn money as matchmakers, a profession that dated back to antiquity.[69] However, these women had a bad reputation and were popularly regarded as untrustworthy liars. Because women
traditionally served as family caregivers, they offered this service to others to
earn money. Some women sold medicines and worked in health care. Female
shamans conducted rituals to ward off the demons believed to cause illness
or complicate a delivery. Others trained as midwives or physicians, often
specializing in the treatment of gynecological problems.[70]

Since ancient times, it had been the custom for mothers from wealthy families to hand their babies over to servants to nurse and raise. They considered
child care a menial duty, so the household included resident wet nurses and
nannies.[71] Although wet nurses had the vital task of nurturing a family's progeny, they were usually lowly bond servants. The incongruity of their important responsibilities and low station could be awkward. Although wet nurses
came from the bottom rungs of society, they often developed close bonds
with the children in their care, and many people regarded their wet nurse as
their true mother. After reaching adulthood, a man would often continue to
shower affection on his former wet nurse. Some wet nurses received financial
support. They might be buried alongside the family they served. The famed
litterateur Su Shi even wrote a laudatory epitaph for his deceased nursemaid,
phrased in the manner of a filial son commemorating his virtuous mother.[72]

A small proportion of women also worked as prostitutes, performers, and
courtesans. The commercial economy commoditized goods and services,
including sex, so urban areas had numerous prostitutes of varying grades.[73]
Although the early medieval era had commercial prostitution, few men in that
impoverished society could afford to pay for sex. The sex and entertainment
industries became much larger during the Tang dynasty, and by the Song they
were highly developed. As before, the government strictly regulated prostitution to maintain order and uphold social hierarchy. Song laws on prostitution
largely followed the *Tang Code*, which distinguished prostitutes as a debased

group with limited rights. Officials regulated prostitutes within two separate systems that provided sexual services to civilians and soldiers.

Prostitution may have been legal and common, but society viewed it with increasing disdain. During the Tang dynasty, a high-ranking man could openly visit prostitutes and courtesans without harming his reputation. Although Tang law prohibited respectable men from marrying a courtesan, patronizing them brought no onus. By the Song, however, people derided a man who frequented the pleasure districts. Although music and dance were integral to refined literati culture, Confucian teachings disparaged sensuality. As prevailing ethics became increasingly austere, men looked down on commercialized performances and the women associated with them. An official could even be punished or dismissed if his superiors regarded his behavior as indecent. Song officials either avoided courtesans outright or dealt with them discreetly. Wealthy men kept talented concubines at home, which people considered more respectable than frequenting commercial establishments.[74]

Rising prosperity led to the emergence of large urban entertainment districts.[75] These areas offered far more than just sex. Men also went there to enjoy performances, food, wine, and a festive atmosphere. Establishments called tiled shops (*wasi*) offered refreshments and entertainment. Some venues were extremely lavish and specialized in a particular performance or service. Men visited pleasure quarters in search of companionship and to be entertained with music, poetry, and dance. As numerous venues competed for customers, the artistry of female performers increased.

The most highly trained women worked as courtesans (*changji*), who offered both entertainment and companionship to male patrons. These women were not only attractive but also highly skilled in music and dance. In addition, some courtesans flaunted their literary talent. The ability to compose poetry allowed these women to compare themselves to the educated wives of their literati patrons.[76] People appreciated courtesan song lyrics for their poetic value, and some became popular works of literature. These women developed extremely close relationships with favored clients, and men wrote poems depicting courtesans as friends, companions, and confidants.[77]

Although the officialdom increasingly avoided courtesans, wealthy merchants provided them with a new customer base.[78] Both courtesans and merchants lived in cities, making it easy for the two groups to interact. Although many people looked down on men from the world of commerce, courtesans treated them with respect, so merchants enjoyed their company. Lesser merchants were particularly enthusiastic patrons. As a man became more successful, he often adopted a more serious demeanor and abandoned his contacts with the world of entertainers.

While clients wrote poetry depicting courtesans as beautiful, talented, and vivacious, these women detested their profession. A poem by Yang Rui (fl. 1160) made it clear that behind the happy facade she rued her unfortunate circumstances.[79]

> It is not that I love the courtesan's life;
> It's the karma of a past life that has wronged me.
> Blossoms fall and blossoms open; each has its season.
> All depending on the god of spring.

Courtesans dreamed of marrying a good man and gaining a respectable place in society. But given the prohibition on intermarriage between respectable people and those of debased status, this ambition would be hard to realize. Because courtesans desired a conventional relationship with a man, they were famed for their fidelity.[80] When one of these women fell in love, she demonstrated intense loyalty. Nevertheless, due to prejudice and social barriers, she would likely end up frustrated, regardless of how well she treated her beloved.

Immediately after the Song, the status of courtesans fell considerably.[81] During the Yuan dynasty, men tended to value women more for beauty than talent, so there was less demand for skilled female companions. Yuan poems do not describe prostitutes as having any special ability or training. These women were merely selling sex. Of course, these unfortunate victims lamented their fate and hoped to eventually earn enough money to ransom themselves. A poem by a Yuan prostitute nicknamed Zhenzhen vents her anger at having ended up in such a terrible condition.[82]

> I was first a bright pearl held in someone's palm,
> But somehow fell into this Pingkang Ward.
> In front of others I feign all kinds of coquettish manners,
> But out of sight my tears flow by the thousands.
> At the end of spring in southern kingdoms, I pity being tossed adrift,
> Always at the beck of the eastern wind, planless, powerless.
> Increase, painful sorrow!
> Where are ten bushels of precious pearls
> To ransom *this* cloud girl?

In contrast to the Song, which prized refinement and erudition, the Yuan had a militaristic culture. The rough Mongol elite could not appreciate Chinese poetry or song lyrics, so performers had little reason to display literary accomplishments. As society coarsened, fewer men sought out skilled courtesans. Moreover, prostitutes had a very low status under Yuan law, and authorities did little to protect them from exploitation and abuse. Due to these hostile conditions, the courtesan world went into abeyance under the Yuan, only to be revived during the cultural effervescence of the late Ming dynasty.

Chapter 4

Religion

Over the centuries, Chinese institutions and secular thought became increasingly sophisticated, leading to the decline of religion as a social force. During the medieval dynasties, fervent piety was commonplace, and faith guided people's values and life goals. The rise of robust secular institutions, together with the Confucian revival, provided appealing alternatives. Yet, even in decline, religion still had an important presence in many people's lives. As before, the spiritual realm often appealed more to women than men. Numerous women devoted their lives to religious activities, and their faith informed their ideas and behavior.

In most respects, the faithful of both sexes had congruent religious beliefs and undertook similar devotions. However, women were more enthusiastic about certain observances. They were particularly prone to manipulate their diet to express piety, perhaps because of their traditional role as family cooks. Many women fasted or became vegetarian as devotional acts.[1] Some ate nothing at all for a set period of time, while others ate a reduced amount of food or limited themselves to simple fare. Buddhist women became vegetarian to express their compassion for all living things, while Daoists believed that abstaining from meat could help them attain longevity or even immortality. Many women temporarily limited themselves to a vegetarian diet while in mourning to express their grief and also to transfer accumulated merit to the deceased, which they believed would help their loved one achieve a better rebirth. Some even became lifelong vegetarians after the death of a parent. Chaste widows also occasionally vowed to abstain from eating meat for the remainder of their lives, distancing themselves from everyday family life and expressing moral transcendence.

The presence of a strict vegetarian wife or mother within a meat-eating household could be awkward. At the very least, women were expected to prepare the meat and alcohol used in ancestral sacrifices. And family members would probably demand that the family cook prepare them a conventional diet. Despite the awkwardness, however, meat eaters usually accepted a woman's vegetarianism without complaint, as they considered it a virtue.

Women usually undertook religious practice at home. Houses often had a dedicated spot for worship equipped with sacred images, texts, an incense burner, and other paraphernalia that enabled residents to perform ceremonies at their convenience. An extremely pious woman might seclude herself within the inner recesses of the home and devote herself to religious practice.[2] More commonly, women integrated sacred activities into their daily routine. Special events also offered opportunities for worship.[3] For example, during the Lantern Festival, women sacrificed to the Purple Maiden (Zi Gu) and playfully swiped vegetables from one another's gardens, a folk custom believed to bring good luck.

Some extremely ancient religious practices had continued up to the Song era. Shamans served their families and the community by invoking guardian spirits for tangible benefits.[4] Most frequently, female shamans undertook rites related to conception, pregnancy, and postpartum problems. They also addressed popular demand by performing ceremonies to cure disease. Although China had developed a large body of sophisticated medical thought, professional physicians and herbal medicine could be costly, and a shaman was an inexpensive alternative. Also, many people still believed that malevolent gods and ghosts caused illness, so they preferred shamanistic healing to conventional medicine. To seek a cure, the shaman and patient would usually worship the injurious deity together to mollify the angry spirit. Shamans might also employ curative dancing, rituals, and potions. While Daoist and Buddhist clerics also undertook healing rites, these practices were most strongly associated with shamanism. Beliefs varied considerably by region, however, and shamanism was popular only in certain places.

Although shamans invoked a range of deities, the Purple Maiden was one of the most common.[5] This goddess was originally an ordinary concubine who was cruelly persecuted and eventually killed by her master's jealous wife. People believed that a violent death can release supernatural forces and cause the deceased to become a ghost or spirit. In this case, the murdered concubine experienced an apotheosis and transformed into the Purple Maiden deity. Due to the lowly origins of this goddess, devotees worshipped her in the bathroom. The unorthodox characteristics of this strange deity attracted shamans to her cult.

The Purple Maiden was closely associated with spirit writing. During this ritual, someone would ask the goddess questions, and she would answer in writing. One or two people would hold a brush, and the faithful believed that the deity guided the movement of their hands and caused them to write out a reply on her behalf. At first worshippers only engaged in spirit writing on specific occasions, and they usually limited their queries to problems regarding sericulture. Over time, it became permissible to ask the goddess questions at any time, and the faithful inquired about a wide range of issues.

Women frequently learned shamanistic techniques from their families.[6] Some households specialized in these practices and passed down religious lore from one generation to the next, with the elders training younger family members in the esoteric wisdom of their ancestors. Women as well as men could learn these teachings. When a female shaman married out into another family, she might continue to practice her family's traditional rituals and hand down this knowledge to her children, spreading these beliefs. In other cases, individual women took an interest in shamanistic healing and sought out an informed teacher who could provide training. Most shamans worked part time, living a conventional life and practicing religious healing only occasionally. A small number were full-time professionals.

The reputation of shamans had been in decline for centuries. Literati dismissed them as petty charlatans who preyed on the credulous, and their popular image was little better. Many people considered shamans greedy and somewhat strange. In response to widespread prejudice, the Song government repeatedly issued injunctions against certain shamanistic practices.[7] This persecution had some impact. Many women's epitaphs mention that they had renounced shamanism, a point of pride for their families.

Skepticism toward shamanism among elite women was one aspect of a more general rejection of popular superstition by literati families. Epitaphs of elite women praised them for rejecting heterodox deities, religious taboos, and *fengshui*.[8] These skeptical women had clearly been influenced by their families. Men educated in the Confucian tradition tended to have a secular outlook, and they looked down on shamanism and other popular superstitions. Literati also felt duty bound to educate the common people and encourage them to use conventional medicine to treat their illnesses. They feared that people who sought shamanistic healing would forgo mainstream treatments and die unnecessarily. Also, superstitious people might believe that a sick family member had been cursed by a powerful deity and abandon the patient instead of seeking a cure. Moreover, certain shamans claimed to be able to harm people by issuing magical imprecations, and these claims threatened social order. For these reasons, educated men were often hostile toward shamans, and the women around them were likely to hold similar views.

In spite of enmity and periodic persecution, numerous shamans were active in every part of China, and many people sought their services.[9] The main reason shamanism endured was its supposed utility. The educated elite may have been skeptical, but many people sincerely believed that shamans could exercise extraordinary powers such as healing, rainmaking, prognostication, issuing imprecations, and communicating with supernatural beings. They sought the aid of shamans in times of need, particularly when faced with natural disasters, plagues, and droughts. Moreover, persecution ironically made shamans more independent and resilient. Previous governments had recognized shamans and regulated their activities to discourage abuses. This gave the state a degree of power over their actions. Persecution drove shamans underground, putting them beyond government control.

The Song and Yuan witnessed the rising popularity of a goddess called Mazu (Mother Ancestor) or Tianhou (Heavenly Consort), affecting how people regarded the holy feminine.[10] The goddess originated in Fujian, gradually gained devotees in other areas, and remains a mainstay of popular religion to this day, especially in Taiwan. Mazu was originally a goddess of the sea. According to legend, a Chinese envoy traveling to Korea by ship encountered a terrifying storm and thought he was doomed. A benevolent goddess then miraculously appeared and conducted him safely to land. The earliest worshippers were fishermen and sailors living in coastal areas, who worshipped her as the goddess of the sea. In the thirteenth century, the violent Mongol invasion disrupted agriculture in north China, so huge amounts of grain had to be shipped in by boat. Numerous southern sailors began frequenting northern ports, and they established temples to their favorite goddess so that they could worship her while in the north. Female deities had a high place in the native Mongol pantheon, so Yuan authorities supported the rise of Mazu worship. During the late imperial era, state authorities became concerned about the large number of strange and heterodox local deities. To remedy the problem, they decided to standardize popular religion. Local officials encouraged people under their authority to abandon minor regional deities and confine their devotions to a small number of sanctioned cults. During this standardization movement, the number of gods worshipped in China contracted considerably. Various manifestations of Mazu ended up as the key maternal deity in many areas, including some inland regions. She was the most important goddess in south China during the late imperial era.

The goddesses that people venerated varied according to region, background, and personal inclination. Maternal deities had very broad appeal. During the Song dynasty, the Sage Mother (Sheng Mu) surged in popularity, particularly in Shanxi.[11] This goddess underwent a complicated evolution. The Sage Mother developed out of a number of earlier goddesses, including Nü Wa, Xiwangmu (Queen Mother of the West), and Niangzi (also known as Lady Moji). Her cult also assimilated beliefs from the Pure Land school of Buddhism. By absorbing the attributes of so many religious figures, the

Sage Mother ended up with a wide range of powers and manifestations. In addition to her primary identity as a maternal goddess, people also beseeched her to control floods.

As before, there were many minor goddesses and female immortals associated with bodies of water. Many of these figures dated back to antiquity. The goddess of the Han River remained popular.[12] At this time, however, she was not just a focus of worship but also became a popular literary character, giving her a vivid identity. Poets enthusiastically praised the Han River goddess and imaginatively described her appearance and powers in far greater detail than before. Whereas previous descriptions had been somewhat vague, Song writers described her as extravagantly beautiful. By making this ancient deity into an alluring literary character, Song writers both secularized and vulgarized her image.

Daoism may have been less influential than before, but it remained attractive to female devotees. Inscriptional evidence suggests that there were about the same number of Daoist nuns in the Song as during the Tang dynasty, the high point of Daoism, so the religion still had an important place in female religious life.[13] As before, chaste widows saw life in a Daoist monastery as an alternative to remarriage. Even a few empresses were ordained after a husband's death.[14] During the Yuan dynasty, the Mongol elite patronized Daoism, giving the religion a further boost. Some nuns became socially prominent and enjoyed access to the palace.

Daoist beliefs changed over time. The pantheon gradually incorporated deities from other religious traditions, affecting creed and ritual. During the Song, the religion incorporated some new female deities. Daoist worshippers integrated the goddess Gaotang, traditionally associated with shamanism, into their pantheon.[15] Over the centuries, Gaotang had been progressively sexualized, but Daoists recreated her as a holy icon of female purity and morality.

Some women distinguished themselves as Daoist leaders and left their mark on the faith. The nun Cao Xiyun (1040–1115) stands out as perhaps the most important female thinker in the long history of Daoism.[16] It was not easy for Cao to become so prominent. She was born into a conservative family that discouraged female talent. Because Cao's parents forbade her from writing down her thoughts, she began to compose poetry, which she could memorize and recite orally. As a girl she would climb up to an isolated spot on the roof of her family's home to compose poems and commit them to memory. Cao spurned marriage and ran away from home to become a Daoist monastic.

Cao Xiyun gained a reputation for eccentricity and shocked people with her unpredictable behavior and disheveled appearance. Although Cao had initially embraced poetry out of desperation, she proved to be a talented writer of verse. She composed works of Daoist theory in poetic form, which made her writings stand out from prose texts. Expressing profound religious dogma in such a sophisticated and engaging manner won her many readers. Some of her ideas were highly original, and she stands out as a major Daoist thinker. Most importantly, Cao became the leading theorist of female internal alchemy (*neidan*), a complicated system of practices aimed at attaining wisdom and immortality. Cao's polished poetry and captivating ideas won the respect of the devout Emperor Huizong, who showered her with honors and constructed temples dedicated to spreading her teachings.

During the early Yuan dynasty, the Quanzhen school of Daoism became extremely popular. Many female clerics gravitated to this branch of their religion. Quanzhen Daoism emphasized asceticism and ethics, making it similar to Buddhism in some respects. Women involved in the Quanzhen sect practiced austerities and tried to extinguish worldly desires so that they could concentrate fully on spiritual pursuits. Yet, even as some branches of the religion put increasing stress on piety and ethics, the popular reputation of Daoist nuns declined. Yuan dynasty dramas depicted them as licentious and immoral.[17] The deteriorating image of Daoism eventually affected female attitudes toward the religion. In the late imperial era, women from good families hesitated to associate themselves with Daoism. They either practiced Buddhism or else turned to secular activities for fulfillment.

Although women engaged with many religious traditions, Buddhism was by far the most popular. The Buddhist establishment classified pious women into five categories.[18] The *upāsikā* (*youpoyi*) remained at home but took basic vows and engaged in regular worship. A more ambitious believer could become a postulant (*xingzhe*), a Chinese religious role that lacked an Indian equivalent. These women received religious education and training with the intention of eventually becoming a novice. Śrāmanerikā (*shamini*) were novice nuns who had taken ten core vows. Although they lived as monastics, they were still learning about the faith and had not yet been accepted as permanent clergy. An aspirant would then spend a two-year probationary period as a śikṣamānā (*shichamona*), after which she qualified to be ordained as a full nun or *bhikṣuṇī* (*biqiuni*).

Chinese Buddhism was constantly evolving, and during the Song and Yuan eras the faith changed in some notable respects. The identity of the bodhisattva Guanyin (Avalokiteśvara), one of the most popular figures of devotion, underwent a major transformation at this time.[19] When Chinese first encountered Guanyin, believers considered the bodhisattva to be male. During the Song, perceptions shifted, and henceforth Guanyin was usually seen as female. This extraordinary change in the gender of a key religious figure had a major impact on Buddhist dogma, amplifying the feminine dimensions of the faith.

Figure 4.1. Bodhisattva Guanyin as painted in the Chan (Zen) style, by Jueji Yongzheng (ca. 1300) (Cleveland Museum)

Guanyin's gender identity shifted gradually through a complicated process. Although Indian texts and images had conventionally portrayed Avalokiteśvara as male, worshippers initially did not associate this bodhisattva with any particular time or place. Chinese preferred their religious figures to have a concrete identity, so they positioned Guanyin within a detailed mythology. The apocryphal *Śuraṅgama Sutra* (*Da Fo ding shou leng yan jing*), written in China in the eighth century, described Guanyin as having thirty-two manifestations, six of which are female. This text made it acceptable to envision Guanyin as a woman. Around the year 1100, believers started to associate this bodhisattva with the legendary Princess Miaoshan, whom they admired for her compassion, chastity, filiality, and self-sacrifice. Miaoshan refused to marry, and lifelong virginity was a key aspect of her identity. Associating Guanyin with Miaoshan thus affiliated the bodhisattva with the rising cult of chastity. Not only did the feminization of Guanyin provide women with an important new focus of devotion, but the link between Guanyin and a pure virgin bolstered widow chastity by giving it religious sanction. Henceforth, devout widows could justify their decision to remain chaste by referring to the example set by Guanyin/Miaoshan.

The rise of the innovative Chan (Zen) school during the Song also altered the relation between women and Buddhism. Chan devotees reimagined Buddhist dogma and practice in radical ways, opening up new opportunities for women to participate in organized religious practice.[20] Mainstream Buddhists held mixed views toward women, and establishment figures often denigrated their intellectual and spiritual potential. The newly popular Chan sect put immense emphasis on the belief that each person is born with an implicit Buddha nature (*foxing*)—the ability to perfect oneself to the point of gaining enlightenment. According to traditional teachings, women as well as men have inborn Buddha nature. Largely due to the importance of this concept in Chan, over time the sect became increasingly open to female participation.

The men who wrote most Chan texts described women from their own gendered perspective. Initially, Chan writers followed mainstream Chinese Buddhist teachings and assumed that women have inborn limitations that impede their spiritual advancement. Early Chan texts tended to denigrate the achievements of nuns and other female believers, and women held a low position in the sect's formal hierarchy.

Those arguing in favor of women's spiritual capacity could refer to the influential *Lotus Sutra* (*Fahua jing*) to bolster their arguments. This scripture records a myth that describes how Dragon Girl (Longnü), daughter of the Nāga king, attained enlightenment, providing an example of a female character who reached the heights of spiritual attainment. Chinese writers also invented stories about women from humble families who became enlightened, stressing the idea that spiritual achievement is open to everyone, regardless of sex or status.

As depictions of female believers became increasingly positive, Chan leaders gradually accepted the idea that women have the potential to attain spiritual perfection. Over the course of the Song dynasty, Chan became increasingly open to female participation. Some women received transmission of the dharma within the Chan lineage, allowing them to play significant roles. Most prominently, the twelfth-century nun Miaodao gained recognition as a major teacher. She was the spiritual heir of the important master Dahui and helped revive the Linji branch of Chan.[21] As women gained prominence within Chan, the school attracted the enthusiastic support and patronage of devout laywomen.

As with pious men, relatively few women became clerics. Most remained in the mundane world. Buddhist laywomen were extremely numerous. About a quarter of Song epitaphs for women describe the deceased as a Buddhist believer.[22] Nor was the religion confined to China's heartland. Buddhism also attracted women living on the peripheries.[23] Many Liao dynasty women in the northeast were enthusiastic Buddhists, as attested to by hundreds of female names engraved on temple steles and the popularity of female names with religious associations. The Dunhuang caves in the far west contain images of Song-era women in Uighur garb making Buddhist offerings.

Women turned to Buddhism for various reasons, depending on individual background, proclivities, and circumstances.[24] Some were born into devout families and embraced the beliefs of those around them, while others turned to the religion out of personal interest. Sometimes the teachings of a monk or nun persuaded a woman to take up Buddhist practice. Many hoped that their devotions would bring them practical benefit, such as allowing them to give birth to a son, heal an illness, become wealthy, or perhaps eventually be reborn in paradise. Believers often turned to religion for solace when faced with difficulties, such as the death of a loved one or a severe illness of a family member. Widows used Buddhist teachings and institutions as a convenient framework for maintaining lifelong chastity.

Laywomen could practice their faith in many ways while remaining at home.[25] Most often, they read, chanted, and copied sutras, and they also burned incense to venerate religious images. Pious women did not have to undertake their devotions in isolation. Contacts with fellow believers could forge new relationships. Sometimes a household's women worshipped together as a group. They might encourage spouses and servants to participate in a home congregation. Women of different households also came together for collective worship. However, usually a woman would only enter the home of a man whom her husband knew and trusted, such as a friend or colleague.

Laywomen also visited temples to worship and study with Buddhist clerics. Those with sufficient means could engage in patronage, distribute alms, commission holy texts and images, and even pay to erect a shrine or temple. In addition, women participated in popular Buddhist festivals, which leavened their worship with a temporary atmosphere of celebration and fun. A believer could also demonstrate her piety by arranging to have a religious burial. Instead of being interred beside their spouses, some Buddhist laywomen preferred to be cremated and have their ashes interred in a pagoda, often near the remains of a famous monk.

People directed their Buddhist practice to address specific needs and desires, so inclinations and activities varied. Female worshipers approached the religion somewhat differently from their male counterparts. Over time the scope of female practice contracted. During the Tang dynasty, female Buddhists had studied a wide array of sutras with diverse content. By the Song, most of these works had declined in popularity, so women focused on the handful of sutras that remained popular. As the scope of women's attentions narrowed, their beliefs and worship practices became less varied than those of men. Out of the thousands of holy texts, women most frequently studied the *Diamond Sutra* (*Jingang jing*), the *Avataṃsaka Sutra* (*Huayan jing*), and the *Lotus Sutra* (*Fahua jing*). These three key scriptures informed their views of death and rebirth, ethics, and proper lifestyle, so their religious ideas tended to be more uniform than those of pious men.[26] Moreover, many women directed their devotions to the newly female bodhisattva Guanyin, making their version of Buddhism more overtly feminine.

The domestic world was largely a female domain, so women had a great deal of leeway in arranging the interior of the home. Pious laywomen could create an environment conducive to worship.[27] They often set up an altar and collected items used in worship, such as religious images and books, incense burners, candle holders, prayer mats, and meditation cushions. Although most women worshipped in public areas of the home, some preferred to undertake their devotions in a relatively private space, usually their bedroom. Chan stressed meditation, which required a quiet setting away from the hustle and bustle of daily life. The requirements of worship gave women an excuse to exercise more control over spaces in the home, increasing their authority over the domestic realm.

The most dedicated Buddhists could become nuns and devote themselves fully to spiritual pursuits. However, the reputation of nuns had declined since the religion's high point in the medieval era. Literati expressed increasingly negative opinions of Buddhist clergy, and their prejudice spread to society at large.[28] Neo-Confucian thinkers put great emphasis on female reclusion, and the relatively free movement of nuns troubled them. Conservatives considered nuns negative role models, tempting laywomen to break out of domestic reclusion. In addition, many literati accused nuns of having low morals. Literature often portrays nuns breaking their vows and committing crimes. Poetry even eroticized female clerics. Poets described young nuns as beautiful and stressed their capacity for love and sex. Sensationalistic writings fostered the popular belief that nuns were lowly troublemakers of dubious character. Nevertheless, some members of the elite continued to respect Buddhist nuns. Two Song princesses took the tonsure, and some wealthy families established temples to house their family's chaste women.[29]

The number of registered nuns fluctuated significantly over the course of the Song and Yuan. Overall, there were far fewer nuns than monks, with about seven monks for every female cleric.[30] Some women became nuns involuntarily. Former palace ladies, childless wives, and refugees may not have been particularly pious, but they sometimes ended up living in a temple for practical reasons. Some families forced a daughter to become a nun to avoid having to pay out an expensive dowry. Other women entered a convent to evade married life or else to obtain a higher standard of living. Sometimes a woman entered a monastery because a fortuneteller predicted that she was fated to become a nun. Many people believed strongly in fate, and they took these sorts of prognostications seriously.[31] Most commonly, though, it seems that nuns were genuinely devout.

Monastic discipline had declined, so authorities felt compelled to enact strict guidelines to regulate the clergy and enforce good conduct.[32] Chinese nuns had always been subject to more restrictions than monks, in line with the belief that women should be prohibited from male activities.[33] During the Song, nuns had to observe even more stringent official rules than before. As society put increasing emphasis on female reclusion, nuns had their movements curtailed. They could no longer travel freely to seek out the best religious teachers, so they had to make do with the education at their local monastery, regardless of quality. Because nuns had fewer opportunities to leave their temple and interact with the community, they became more removed from secular society. Nevertheless, many nuns had to support themselves financially, so they worked part of each day, making their lifestyle more like that of laywomen. Most often, nuns did embroidery, and some temples were famous for their needlework.

A nunnery was either public or private.[34] Public monasteries had links to the government and received imperial patronage. These institutions were prestigious and well funded. Private monasteries varied considerably. Some wealthy families founded temples to commemorate their ancestors, worship together, and provide a refuge for the family's chaste widows. Most private nunneries were funded by the community at large. Nunneries usually received the most enthusiastic support from wealthy local laywomen. Monastic rules required nuns to submit to the authority of monks, who were supposed to supervise them. However, the government also made efforts to separate male and female clerics to prevent relationships from developing. Keeping women under male control conflicted with separation of the sexes, and it is not clear how nuns dealt with these contradictory directives.

Women who wanted to join the formal clergy had to meet certain criteria.[35] Previously, nunneries would not accept novices younger than the age of ten. During the Southern Song, the state raised the age limit to fifteen. By that age a woman would be old enough to make a responsible decision about whether or not she wanted to join the clergy. Moreover, the state prohibited a woman from leaving home and becoming a nun if there was no one else in her family to care for elderly kin. A temple was responsible for confirming a prospective nun's identity and ensuring that she was not a criminal or otherwise disreputable. A registered nun had to receive a government-issued ordination certificate. The government wanted to limit the overall number of clerics to prevent too many people from leaving the productive economy. To obtain a certificate, a woman could either pass an examination or else purchase it. Sometimes the emperor dispensed these documents as largesse.

Although nuns faced more constraints than before, in most respects their way of life had not changed much over the centuries.[36] They dedicated hours each day to worship, studying and chanting sutras, and seeing to the quotidian matters of abbey life. As in every period, a small number of nuns gained notice for exceptional accomplishments.[37] These paragons observed monastic rules with unusual stringency, exhibited great erudition, or had notable success in transmitting the dharma. The monks who wrote Buddhist annals lauded the achievements of exceptional nuns. Religion was one of the few realms of endeavor in which a woman could exercise her talents and garner men's praise for attainments unconnected to family life.

Chapter 5

Learning

Most women spent their lives confined to the domestic sphere, a way of life that tended to foster complacency. Unworldliness conditioned them to accept conventional gender norms, so they usually expressed conservative values and cultivated a mild demeanor that those around them would find acceptable.[1] However, as the literacy rate rose, more women learned about matters beyond their immediate horizons. Reading gave women a way to break out of isolation in the home. Books exposed them to new ideas and values that sometimes contradicted what they had learned from their families. The rise of female literacy thus inspired new modes of gendered thought and provided women with fresh perspectives on the world.[2]

The rising importance of the examination system not only changed attitudes toward education among men but also promoted a more expansive view of female learning as well. The increasingly meritocratic administrative system relied on examinations to recruit talented officials. Ambitious men of the gentry spent years or even decades studying the classical canon so that they might pass a series of tests and obtain an official posting. The resulting obsession with study raised the culture of learning to an unprecedented level of intensity never seen before anywhere in the world.[3] During the Song dynasty, students had easy access to printed books, schools, and teachers. Widely available test preparation materials made it convenient for men to study privately at home, spreading the mania for education to even the most remote areas.[4] The obsession with learning led people to believe that almost everyone could benefit from some education. Primary education for ordinary people became common, and the government periodically aided promising male students from poor backgrounds.

The education system was primarily oriented toward teaching men. However, the rise of a comprehensive educational infrastructure, together with the increasingly popular ethic of lifelong learning, encouraged women to study as well. Passing examinations had become vital to success, so elite men sought to marry learned wives who could help them educate their sons.[5] As knowledgeable women became desirable marriage partners, it was no longer sufficient for a young woman to simply gain proficiency in domestic tasks. Daughters of the gentry also had to master a basic textual curriculum to prepare them for marriage. Influential men assumed that a woman from a good family should at least be literate and perhaps have some higher learning as well. Many epitaphs boast that a deceased woman had enjoyed reading, a point of pride for her children.[6] Nevertheless, female educational opportunities remained limited. Whereas a young man could attend a school or go to live with a famous teacher, women had to remain modestly cloistered, so they studied at home. The overall educational and cultural tenor of a woman's family determined what she studied and how much she could learn.

Some families became known for their high standards of learning and scholarship. Women who grew up in cultured households or married into them were expected to uphold the family's intellectual legacy. The Lü family of Donglai were one of the great literati families of the Song. Prominent for eight generations, many members of this family participated in politics and academic undertakings.[7] The Lü put great stress on maternal education. Mothers were their children's earliest teachers, so the family's men took care to choose wives with sufficient learning to fulfill their high educational aspirations. Nor were the Lü unique. Many other important literati of the Song came from similar backgrounds. For example, the Yuan family of Siming were also well known for choosing wives who could instruct their children.[8] Both the Lü and the Yuan relied heavily on women to help educate the next generation. This family tradition gave their sons a head start in preparing for the imperial examinations and provided their daughters with the necessary education to marry into equally cultured families.

As female education became more widespread and valued, Neo-Confucian thinkers expressed concern. They feared that education would empower women and alter the relations between the sexes in their favor. Learning might also make women bold, rude, and immodest. Conservative thinkers responded to these fears by debating the desirability of female education. Sima Guang (1019–1086) accepted the traditional argument that literacy allowed women to study ethics and ritual, making them better wives and mothers.[9] However, he did not believe that women needed to attain a very high level of learning. He also considered traditional female tasks such as weaving to be morally uplifting, so he believed that even women from wealthy families should master domestic skills in addition to textual learning.

Zhu Xi (1130–1200), the most influential Neo-Confucian thinker, also supported female education on pragmatic grounds. He accepted that an educated mother could teach her children and give them a valuable head start in life. He believed that great men were usually raised by educated mothers who had overseen their early instruction.[10] Zhu not only thought that a mother should teach her children their first lessons, but he also followed ancient authorities in assuming that she could educate the fetus in her womb. Ancient writers claimed that when a pregnant woman engaged in refined activities, such as reading or listening to beautiful music, her fetus would absorb these cultured influences. Zhu Xi accepted this belief, giving it renewed influence on contemporary opinion.

Like all Confucians, Zhu believed that the primary goal of education should be moral cultivation. In particular, he stressed filial piety as central to the education of both men and women. However, he thought that the sexes should apply this virtue in different ways. Zhu expected women to extend the scope of filiality beyond their blood kin to encompass in-laws as well. Although Zhu Xi promoted female education, he believed that women have limited intellectual capacity. Zhu assumed that they could not possibly understand the most difficult teachings, such as metaphysics. He thought that female education should focus on concrete matters that women would find readily comprehensible.

The palace had learned teachers and extensive libraries, so imperial consorts and princesses could become well educated. Some palace ladies took full advantage of these opportunities. They embraced literati values and became learned aesthetes. Empress Yang (1162–1232), consort of Emperor Ningzong, stands out for her refinement.[11] Yang is remembered as one of the most powerful women of the Song dynasty. Her weak-willed husband failed to carry out his duties, and the resulting power vacuum allowed his wife to influence important matters. Most importantly, Empress Yang helped put Ningzong's successor, Lizong, on the throne. In gratitude, the new emperor submitted to her authority. Yang's unusually high level of learning helped her navigate court intrigues and gain influence. Although she seems to have come from a fairly low background, Yang claimed to be the daughter of a cultured military official and played the role of an educated daughter of the elite. Empress Yang was an enthusiastic sponsor of the arts and distinguished herself as the most important female patron of the entire dynasty. She had excellent taste and promoted the brilliant artist Ma Yuan. In addition to appreciating the art of others, Yang was a respected calligrapher in her own right.

Empress Yang was not the only empress with good handwriting. A number of Song empresses and minor consorts were proficient calligraphers. However, connoisseurs have noticed that the calligraphy attributed to some of the dynasty's emperors and empresses looks suspiciously similar.[12] It seems that either empresses served as ghost writers for their spouses, or else the calligraphy attributed to both an emperor and his empress was in fact written by talented court scholars or eunuchs.

The influence of literati culture on women was not limited to the palace. Enthusiasm for education spread throughout society, affecting women from ordinary backgrounds.[13] Many people began to assume that an educated woman would be a good wife and mother, regardless of family circumstances. Literacy could give a woman a stronger grounding in ethics and allow her to better manage family matters. Even in an ordinary family, an educated mother could pass down her learning to her children.[14] Writers lauded the widow who managed to educate her sons, presenting her as a moral hero.

As in elite families, the education of women from common backgrounds stressed moral cultivation. Women sought broader cultural literacy as well. Whatever their goals, female students had ample learning material. A number of textbooks aimed at women had appeared in prior centuries. Many of these works remained popular, and the commercial printing industry made them widely available.[15] Song authors also wrote new books aimed at female students. Although most of these have been lost, it seems that these texts mostly focused on domestic ethics for daughters, wives, and mothers. Writers wanted to prepare women to carry out their expected family roles. At this time, Neo-Confucian thought began to have an impact on the content of textbooks.[16] Authors increasingly downplayed the relevance of female intelligence and talent and instead emphasized the importance of self-restraint. They enjoined women to obey their husbands, keep apart from men, safeguard their chastity, and hold themselves aloof from public life.

Women did not limit themselves to specialized textbooks. According to a comprehensive study of 206 female gentry characters in works of Song literature, authors describe 51 percent of these fictional women reading Buddhist sutras, 33 percent reading Confucian classics, and 31 percent reading history or literature. Only 10 percent are mentioned reading a textbook written specifically for women.[17] Fiction writers assumed that literate women had diverse interests and read a wide variety of works. However, female taste in reading matter had a notable distinction. It seems that women were more likely to read religious texts, much more so than men. Devout women frequently studied Buddhist sutras and other sacred texts, allowing them to learn from a sophisticated body of religious wisdom and engage with abstract ideas.

Women were also interested in art, calligraphy in particular.[18] Discerning aesthetes treasured the works of talented female calligraphers, some of which have been preserved down to the present day. A few women distinguished themselves in painting as well. Notably, Guan Daosheng (1262–1319) gained

Figure 5.1. Bamboo and stone, by Guan Daosheng (Wikimedia Commons)

attention for the unusual way that she painted bamboo.[19] Because bamboo conventionally symbolized masculine integrity, traditionally only men painted it. For a woman to paint bamboo seemed strange and even provocative. Not only did Guan defy this taboo, but she also depicted bamboo in a novel manner. Rather than employing a stereotypically feminine style of delicate lines and graceful forms, she painted with forceful brush strokes that viewers considered manly. Guan also integrated bamboo into a larger landscape rather than following convention and depicting it in isolation. Because of her daring innovations, many critics consider Guan Daosheng the greatest female painter in Chinese history.

During the Yuan dynasty, elite Han families strove to maintain high cultural standards, so they continued to educate their daughters.[20] Traditionally, nomadic women were illiterate. When the Mongols and their allies entered China, many did not believe that women ought to pursue an education. However, as the values of the Han elite influenced new arrivals, many accepted the value of female education. Over time, many Mongols and ethnic Semu (their allies from central and west Asia) adopted Han standards of family conduct. Some of them established ancestral temples, studied the Chinese classics, and composed family regulations. As part of the sinicization process, Mongols also came to value maternal instruction, giving their women a practical reason to study.

During the Yuan dynasty, girls continued to study at home, with their parents or other relatives usually serving as teachers. Sometimes a professional teacher would come in from the outside to teach a girl in her home, although this was fairly rare at the time. The Yuan curriculum for women adhered to the standard Song dynasty format. At first, young women usually studied specialized textbooks on female ethics. If they continued their education, they would then branch out to cover a broader range of subjects. Girls also routinely studied textile work and sometimes music.

A major goal of Chinese education was proficiency in literary composition. The gentry put high value on the ability to write acceptable poetry, so their daughters frequently received comprehensive training in this art. Some went on to distinguish themselves as skilled poets. Women could look back upon a long line of female role models for inspiration. In particular, Six Dynasties works had a major impact on their writing. That era had witnessed an awakening of female self-consciousness that continued to fascinate women in later eras. Song women showed a keen interest in early medieval poetry, and the open mind-set of those works stimulated their creativity and encouraged them to expose their own intimate feelings in verse.[21]

The number of known female authors from each era varies considerably.[22] According to one study, about 16.5 percent of surviving poetry by women was written during the Song. In contrast, Tang women produced 9.7 percent of the total, and less than 9 percent dates back to the entire pre-Tang era. The output of publicly circulated poetry by women clearly increased significantly at this time. Nevertheless, male critics still regarded women's poems with condescension. They dismissed women's writings as perhaps an amusing novelty, but nonetheless marginal when compared to the mainstream canon of male writers. Faced with such prejudice, few female poets gained attention. Women only wrote about one-tenth of 1 percent of works preserved in the massive compendium *Complete Song Poems (Quan Song shi)*.[23]

In part, the inconspicuousness of female writers reflects the relative paucity of works available to critics and editors. Poetry composition was one of the most important activities of cultured men. Literati produced reams of poetry, dwarfing women's output. Moreover, even when a woman wrote a good poem, male editors would likely exclude it from their collections. Although Neo-Confucians accepted the necessity of female education, they had an ambivalent attitude toward women's poetry, which they considered frivolous and sexually suggestive. Because women's poetry had a doubtful reputation, female poets usually did not dare to circulate their works publicly. Most had internalized restrictive gender norms and wanted to avoid embarrassment that might arise by attracting the attentions of strange men. Given these unfavorable circumstances, even though Song women undoubtedly wrote a considerable amount of poetry, the general public had few opportunities to see most of these works, and they were soon lost.

During the Yuan dynasty, female poets in the south far outnumbered those in the north.[24] Of the twenty-four women writers whose place of residence is known, twenty-one were southerners. The basic circumstances in these two regions diverged, affecting literary activity. The north declined economically and culturally under Jurchen rule and suffered terrible devastation during the Mongol invasion. Successive calamities brought down the literary infrastructure in the north, so there were far fewer writers than before, male or female. Moreover, during the Yuan, most of China's population resided in the south, which had become far more prosperous than the ravaged northern part of the country. The southern elite were not only more numerous and prosperous, but they had also accumulated considerable cultural capital, allowing their wives and daughters to gain skill at literary composition.

Few poems indicate communication among female poets or between creative women and their male peers.[25] Nevertheless, given the importance of poetry composition to literati identity, gentry women were expected to be able to write competent verse.[26] Women in literati households would surely

have shown their works to acquaintances and cultivated literary friend-
ships, as men did, even though outsiders would not have known about these
exchanges. Because female poets came of age among educated husbands
and brothers, their poems often imitated those of men. Women realized that
if they wrote in ways that men respected and found readily comprehensible,
male tastemakers would be more likely to take them seriously. This realiza-
tion resulted in a complex interplay between the influences of men's poetry
and women's unique styles and interests.

Li Qingzhao (1084–1155) was by far the most famous woman poet of the
Song, standing far above her female peers in renown.[27] Li acquired fame during her own lifetime and remains very highly regarded today. Many critics
consider her China's greatest female poet. In large part, Li owed her notoriety
to her brazen attitude. Whereas most talented women kept a low profile, Li
Qingzhao dared to circulate her poems widely. She also gained attention by
defying conventional expectations. She crafted highly original verses that
astounded male critics. Unlike most female writers, she did not always use
a delicate style, nor did she confine herself to polite and pretty themes. Li
often took on serious topics, such as history and politics, and treated them
forthrightly. Her brazen disregard for polite feminine norms shocked readers
and attracted wide attention.

In a characteristically clever poem, Li Qingzhao playfully teases herself
for her vanity.[28]

> A street vendor with a pole was selling flowers.
> I bought a branch, just ready to put forth spring.
> Their tear-stained rouge is lightly brushed,
> still bearing traces of morning dew from crimson clouds.
>
> Afraid he might say
> my face isn't as pretty as the flowers,
> I put some in my cloud-locks of hair,
> so he'd be forced to look at us together.

This poem centers on a hackneyed trope—comparing a beautiful woman to
flowers. But instead of naively associating the two in the usual manner, Li
pretends to be jealous of the flowers. In this way she subverts the clichéd
association of flowers and women and also hints that perhaps she might not
be as vain and shallow as she pretends. Her talent for reinvigorating even the
most worn-out theme won her an enthusiastic readership.

Li Qingzhao paid a high price for her boldness. Male critics may have praised
her poems, but they denigrated her as a person. They emphasized the fact that
after her husband died, she remarried rather than remaining chaste, implying

Figure 5.2. Qing dynasty painting of Li Qingzhao, by Cui Cuo (Wikimedia Commons)

that she had scant regard for propriety. They also portrayed her as fundamentally unhappy. These negative depictions suggest that even though outstanding talent is good in men, it causes women to become louche and dissatisfied.

These unjust reproaches exemplify how society punished female genius. Other women took note. Considering the mistreatment suffered by the era's most brilliant female writer, it is not surprising that few women dared to release their poetry to the general public. Most wrote in an uncontroversial manner and allowed only a small number of people to read their compositions. They usually confined themselves to innocuous themes such as religion. Men would not feel threatened by a female writer who portrayed herself as piously withdrawn from worldly concerns. A poem by Guan Daosheng conveys age-old Daoist sentiments, typical of women's religious poetry.[29]

96

The great positions in human life belong to princes and marquises,
But fleeting wealth, fleeting fame are not freedom.
How can they compare
With a single boat,
Appreciating the moon, chanting with the wind, and returning home to rest?

Female writers in the north were particularly interested in religious themes. About half of the surviving works by Jin dynasty women are about Daoism or Buddhism.[30]

Most often, women composed verses in the newly fashionable genre of song lyrics (*ci*) rather than writing older styles of poetry. Rhymed lyrics could be read or sung. Courtesans sang artistic lyrics for male audiences at private banquets and also in restaurants and teahouses. At the time, there were nine different ways to publicly perform song lyrics, so this was a highly sophisticated art. Because courtesans were trained professionals, they often sang very well, and their skilled performances accentuated the beauty of the lyrics. Men usually wrote the lyrics sung by women. Occasionally, however, a talented courtesan wrote her own lyrics.[31] Men and women tended to write different kinds of song lyrics.[32] While men employed difficult language and subtle allusions in imitation of formal Tang dynasty literati poetry, women wrote in a colloquial style that audiences found readily comprehensible. Sometimes women even structured their lyrics as conversational dialogues, integrating informal storytelling techniques with musical performance.

In addition to traditional forms of poetry, an unusual new form of written expression became common at this time. As the general level of education rose, men began to share their poetry with random passersby by writing on a wall in a public place. Travelers frequently wrote poems on the walls of inns to communicate with one another and share their thoughts about the journey. Sometimes an appreciative reader would record and publish one of these poems, making it widely available and preserving it for posterity.

Although most wall writers were men, women sometimes engaged in this literary activity as well. Most frequently, a woman traveling with her husband or father would write out a poem on a wall, bridge, or gate.[33] Women took to this type of writing because it allowed them to remain anonymous while sharing their poetry in public. Sometimes a passing man appreciated a woman's wall poem and copied it down, eventually publishing it or integrating it into his own writings. Various major collections of Song poetry contain thirty-four wall poems written by thirty-one women. Wall writers usually belonged to elite families. Twelve female wall poets are known to have been related to officials, three were gentry wives, and two belonged to the imperial clan.

The themes favored by female wall poets differed from those of their male counterparts. Men almost always used wall poems to remark on their current journey. Women sometimes also wrote about their trip, usually lamenting the difficulty and inconvenience of travel and complaining about having to follow a peripatetic man to distant places. Unlike men, however, women's wall writings were often deeply autobiographical. Women used the anonymity of this genre to reveal hidden emotions to passing male readers. Although some poets proudly declared their commitment to integrity and virtue, many works have a sad or anxious tone. Women often expressed feelings of insecurity, noting how they had to depend on the men around them. Sometimes a writer conveyed discontent with married life or hinted at love for someone other than her husband. In one moving poem, a woman states that she had been born into a good family that suffered impoverishment. Out of necessity, she had become a concubine and had to endure endless abuse from her master's jealous wife. While female poets usually confined themselves to benign topics, the informality of wall writing encouraged them to vent their passions and recall unpleasant memories. These poems gave male passersby startlingly candid insights into female psychology. As more women became literate and expressed themselves in writing, men discovered the breadth and complication of female emotions. They found these insights into the female mind both fascinating and deeply disturbing.

Chapter 6

Virtue

Song dynasty scholars explored many new and controversial ideas, making this a particularly fertile era in Chinese intellectual history. Not coincidentally, the Song was also a time of rapid social change. Thinkers struggled to apply traditional ideas to unfamiliar new situations, and they sometimes had to abandon or modify old beliefs to suit changed circumstances. As part of this intellectual ferment, female ethics became an important topic of discussion. For the academic establishment to pay so much attention to women's matters was itself novel. In antiquity, leading thinkers had rarely pondered women's proper place in society. They thought it sufficient to follow custom and tradition. However, conditions changed considerably over the centuries, and gender ethics became increasingly contested. The most creative thinkers of the Song era felt obligated to put forward definitive rules for women's conduct.

Song society encompassed many types of people living under a wide variety of local conditions. A woman's particular status and region affected her values, ideas, and behavior. Women in each place enjoyed varying degrees of autonomy. Southerners in Lingnan and Fujian often ignored the rites, while northerners tended to be far more conformist.[1] Individual circumstances were not always simplistically positive or negative. Gentry women may have had a high standard of living, but they also had to observe the most restrictive Confucian ethics and classical rites. In contrast, although women from merchant families had far lower social standing, they felt less bound to observe these restraints. Rather than trying to order their lives according to archaic ritual precepts, they tended to behave pragmatically.[2] For example, the widows of merchants had little compunction about remarriage.

Because women were responsible for raising children, they shaped the future generation and helped determine the long-term prospects of their families, so their ethical standards were always a matter of concern. Social changes at this time made female conduct increasingly important. As more men became wealthy, it became more common to bring concubines into the home, generating widespread domestic discontent. People also fretted that the rising commercial economy encouraged cynicism and selfishness. More women committed economic crimes, and magistrates increasingly dealt with female defendants accused of theft.[3] Many thieves were concubines or slaves who stole valuables from a member of their master's family. Women also defrauded outsiders, often using sex as a lure. Most frequently, a dishonest woman would seduce a man and then cheat him out of a sum of money.

The dynamic commercial economy treated people as commodities. Human trafficking became common as gangs kidnapped women and sold them into concubinage or some other form of servitude. During times of disorder, rape and abduction became widespread. The fall of the Yuan dynasty was preceded by more than two decades of terrible chaos, and many women suffered rape or committed suicide to avoid humiliation.[4] Female poets expressed their fear of sexual violence and exploitation in their works.[5] The rising threats against women's physical integrity sparked vigorous debates about sexual mores.

In the modern world, women often seek to maximize their personal freedom. However, in imperial China, it was not necessarily difficult to convince a woman to obey a restrictive code of ethics, as it was in her interest to cultivate a reputation for probity. Both sexes were extremely sensitive to threats to their public reputations. The enemies of the famed scholar Ouyang Xiu (1007–1072) accused him of having an affair with a niece who was living with his family.[6] Although these charges were likely without merit, he nevertheless found them extremely embarrassing. Even one of the most prominent literati of the era could be humiliated by rumors of sexual impropriety, and the reputation of the average woman was far more fragile. If a woman became the target of neighborhood gossip, her good name would be permanently ruined. The susceptibility of women to innuendo made them extremely sensitive to public opinion.[7] To have a decent life, a woman had to avoid public embarrassment. If her actions won the approval of others, so much the better. Some women even cared about their public image after they died, and they undertook difficult feats in order to guarantee their posthumous reputation.

This self-protective mind-set helps to explain why so many women willingly embraced stereotypical female virtues in spite of their restrictions. Women often made a show of filiality, chastity, wisdom, and prudence to gain repute. To be well regarded, they had to avoid appearing jealous, stingy, or dishonest. Parents even named their daughters after desirable female virtues such as submission.[8] The struggle to create a public facade of probity earned worthwhile benefits. If a woman gained repute for uprightness, her entire family could bask in her reflected glory. Virtuous women implicitly pressured the men around them to hold themselves to equally high standards. Song writers contrasted virtuous women with misbehaving men as a way of shaming their male readers into behaving better.[9]

Men of the gentry considered it important to marry a spouse of good character. An upright wife could be trusted to safeguard the family's ethical standards and pass down these values to the next generation. Epitaphs show that the gentry valued wise, virtuous, and talented women.[10] The Zhao family of Juye in Shandong, which produced generations of prominent literati, declared a bride's moral fiber to be far more significant than her family's genealogy or wealth.[11]

Song Confucians enthusiastically promoted austere versions of family rites, altering the dynamics of domestic life. The gentry wanted to reorganize the family according to orthodox Confucian dictates in order to raise the moral tenor of society, regulate rural areas, and maintain social order.[12] At this time it became common for families to write down rules of collective conduct and pass them down to their progeny. The genre of family instructions initially emerged in imitation of the *Admonitions for Women* (*Nüjie*) by the influential Eastern Han dynasty writer Ban Zhao (45–ca. 116), China's most famous female thinker. Although Ban directed her book at a female readership, the male elders of gentry families subsequently set down standards of family conduct to instruct their sons and grandsons. Families usually had oral rules, although they sometimes committed them to paper. These instruction texts addressed practical matters, often in a highly Confucian manner. The authors specified clear rules for handling issues such as property, residence, marriage, family membership, collective safety, and how the family should interact with local society. Most importantly, these texts described how family members ought to carry out their designated kinship roles, the management and distribution of family property, and the conduct of domestic rites.

A number of Song dynasty family instruction texts have been transmitted down to the present.[13] The authors usually applied general moral principles to the concrete details of family life, making them easy to understand and obey. When a family patriarch set down specific standards for conduct, he usually just repeated conventional ethical ideals. Some of these books do not mention women at all. When male elders described female duties, they most often demanded submission, separation of the sexes, and division of key tasks between men and women. Women were to properly manage the inner realm, treat elders with deference, and strive to be good wives and obedient daughters. Some books warned that women were likely to be jealous, selfish, foolish, and divisive, threatening family harmony. They enjoined men to prevent women from undermining the family's collective interests. Family instruction texts had a significant impact on gender concepts. Relatively few women studied the ancient classics or major ethical works in detail, so many families used their regulations as educational texts to inculcate Confucian ethics in their women.

One of these texts stands out from the rest, having been written by a woman for the benefit of her husband's clan. In 1159 a woman called Madame Mo released a book titled *Family Instructions of Dowager Mo* (*Mo taifuren jiaxun*).[14] She was the wife of a member of the Hu clan. Unusually, her husband's relatives admired her talent, education, and virtue so much that they chose her to lead the entire clan. Madame Mo issued regulations to impose order on clan members and regulate their dealings with one another. Her book shows the influence of Neo-Confucian ideas fashionable at the time, demonstrating how a conservative education could convince a woman to embrace values that were seemingly opposed to female interests.

⚬══✦══⚬

Confucianism was never a unitary school of thought. In every era, leading thinkers debated key issues, ranging from moral conduct to textual interpretation. During the Song dynasty, the Neo-Confucian movement challenged previous interpretations and put forward innovative views. These thinkers sought to strip away centuries of mysticism and commentaries and try to recapture the intended meanings of canonical ancient texts. They also put forth a metaphysical system intended to serve as the foundation of a rational and objective body of ethics.

Many historians have assumed that conservative Neo-Confucian values caused the overall status of women to decline during the Song. However, this assertion has come under scrutiny. Even if female autonomy regressed in some respects, attributing these changes to new ideas about metaphysics probably overestimates the effects of elite philosophy on society at large. The Song may have been the golden age of Neo-Confucian thought, but these ideas initially had very limited impact. Neo-Confucians were merely a vocal minority within a much larger intellectual community whose members tended to have far more moderate and conventional views. Over time, however, Neo-Confucian views gained considerable authority, eventually becoming official state orthodoxy during the Yuan and Ming dynasties. The conservative views of Song Neo-Confucians toward gender had significant influence on late imperial society.[15]

Neo-Confucians rejected mysticism and apocryphal teachings and reappraised the ancient classics in search of wisdom. For example, they frequently employed quotations from the *Classic of Poetry* (*Shijing*) to justify their views on gender topics. In addition to classical scholarship, however, they also underpinned their ideas with novel metaphysical concepts. These ideas initially grew out of their classical studies. Although Song Confucians revered all of the classics, they were particularly fascinated with the *Classic of Changes (Yijing)*. This divinatory text is replete with vague statements and ambiguous images that could easily be construed to prove whatever a thinker wanted to promote, and Neo-Confucians found this malleable text extremely useful for justifying their novel assertions. They appealed to the authority of the *Changes* to reconstruct the foundations of Confucian ethics, including ideas about gender norms.[16]

Tethering family ethics to an elaborate system of metaphysics provided new ways to justify moral priorities. Instead of relying on received traditions or ethical treatises, Neo-Confucians appealed to the *Changes* to validate a conservative vision of gender relations based on rigorous separation of the sexes, gendered division of labor, and female reclusion and passivity. Ban Zhao had decreed that women should submit to men, and the Neo-Confucian thinker Zhu Xi employed the system of the *Classic of Changes* to bolster this assertion.[17] Metaphysical hierarchies became the templates for ideal marriage relations, with dominant husbands and submissive wives. Neo-Confucians could also appeal to the *Changes* to condemn female jealousy as a violation of the natural order of the cosmos.

Although none of these ideas were new, legitimizing them via the metaphysical scheme of the *Changes* lent them far greater authority than before. Neo-Confucians used metaphysics to justify a hard line on gender relations. They presented women's ethics not simply as traditional teachings, but as objective necessities integrated into the fundamental fabric of the universe. Violating gender norms was not only immoral but courted disaster by destabilizing cosmic forces. Moreover, whereas the rites had traditionally only applied to the elite, linking gender to metaphysics and cosmology made it equally applicable to ordinary people. Neo-Confucians sought to purge heterodox popular customs regarding family and kinship and replace them with far more restrictive standards.[18]

Sima Guang was an early Neo-Confucian whose ideas served as the foundation of the Neo-Confucian reassessment of gender relations.[19] He had extremely conservatives views. While serving as an official, he steadfastly opposed reform. In his writings, he expressed alarm at the erosion of traditional gender norms. To keep families stable and society in harmonious equilibrium, he thought it imperative to restrain women and force them to observe basic standards of good conduct.

In particular, Sima fretted that economic prosperity had commodified marriage and sexuality. Like other Neo-Confucians, he disliked lavish dowries, which made marriage seem like a cynical commercial transaction instead of a solemn union grounded in the ancient rites.[20] He also feared that large dowries had shifted too much wealth to women, tilting the balance of power in their favor. A wife's dowry had become so important to a family's overall financial standing that men were disturbingly dependent on female wealth. Moreover, women with property could become independent of men, detaching themselves from the patriarchal kinship system. To counter these developments, Sima Guang sought to use stringent ethics and ritual rules to strengthen the gender hierarchy. Like other Confucians, Sima believed that only by organizing society as a series of interlocking hierarchies could stability and propriety be guaranteed.

Sima Guang wrote at length about women's proper place in the family. He took most of his ideas about gender from the classics and earlier writings on the subject. Since antiquity, moral theorists had expected men and women to adhere to similar virtues, even though each sex expressed them differently. Sima also accepted this corpus of time-tested virtues but presented them in innovative ways that addressed contemporary issues. He also applied newly fashionable metaphysical theories to justify gender hierarchy. In addition, he put great emphasis on female participation in domestic rites, largely because these rituals presented women as subsidiary to men. Stressing the rites thus further strengthened hierarchy within the home.

Most importantly, Sima Guang emphasized the importance of rigorously separating men and women. In his view, the onus of keeping the sexes apart should fall most heavily on women. He expected them to remain in the inner quarters of the home from age ten onward to shield themselves from the humiliating male gaze. Although the rhetoric of reclusion had increasing impact after the Song, typical behavior had already started to change at this time. Women were becoming increasingly demure and avoided going outside. When they had to leave the home, they often wore veils and traveled in closed sedan chairs to hide from prying eyes.

Otherwise, Sima Guang promoted conventional female virtues described in women's educational texts. He demanded that women be gentle and submissive, refrain from expressing jealousy, and embrace useful qualities such as cleanliness, frugality, and industriousness. Significantly, even though he considered lifelong fidelity highly praiseworthy, he did not believe that widows had to refrain from remarrying. Sima understood the difficulties that unmarried women faced. His moderate approach to this issue shows that he maintained a degree of empathy. He sometimes saw beyond the constraints of ideology and recognized the severe challenges women faced.

Zhu Xi issued the most influential Neo-Confucian pronouncements regarding women. Even though Zhu did not write any works dealing specifically with female ethics, he mentioned gender matters while addressing other topics.[21] These piecemeal ideas eventually had immense impact. After the Song, subsequent governments canonized his teachings as state orthodoxy. Students preparing for civil service examinations had to learn his classical commentaries by heart. These writings included pronouncements on gender roles, so the late imperial elite were deeply familiar with Zhu's views on the matter.

Zhu Xi's ideas about women did not diverge dramatically from those of earlier thinkers. He was extremely familiar with Sima Guang's writings and often used these ideas as the basis for his own pronouncements regarding gender. However, Zhu put increased emphasis on the importance of female virtue. He considered women's adherence to high ethical standards a hallmark of civilization. Zhu criticized the Tang dynasty in this regard. He complained that because the ruling house had barbarian roots, they did not follow the orthodox rites for women.[22] He believed that this laxity had led to some of the problems that plagued the dynasty.

Zhu Xi was not a fanatic. His opinions on gender matters were often pragmatic and flexible. Nor can he be dismissed as an unalloyed misogynist. Zhu considered women capable of ethical cultivation and thought that both sexes should strive to realize similar virtues. However, he believed that because men and women have different social roles, they manifest virtue in different ways.[23] Most importantly, whereas men dealt with the wider world beyond the home, domestic roles structured women's lives. As a woman assumed new identities within the family, developing from daughter to wife to mother, she took on a series of moral duties.

Although Zhu Xi recognized women's capacity for self-cultivation and moral achievement, he believed that they have more limited capabilities than men. He used metaphysics to argue that women's innate nature limited their potential achievements.[24] Zhu considered the yin/yang dichotomy to be a cosmic template for female and male. Theorists regarded yin as inferior to yang in many respects, so Zhu reasoned that yin women are fundamentally weaker and less capable than yang men. He considered it reasonable for women to be passive and reclusive and to obey their vigorous yang counterparts.

Zhu Xi adhered to the conventional Confucian position regarding female education.[25] He considered education not just the attainment of knowledge but more fundamentally a lifelong process of moral improvement. By studying ethical texts and applying these teachings to her own life, a female student could realize her moral potential. Self-cultivation had practical benefits. A woman who became a better person through education could fully support her husband, instruct her children, correctly perform the domestic rites, and maintain a high ethical tone within the home. Given this pragmatic defense of women's education, it seems that Zhu Xi did not see it as inherently good.

He considered female education expedient, as it allowed women to carry out their family duties better.

Even though Zhu encouraged female education and praised specific women for their literary accomplishments, intelligence, and high character, he nevertheless believed that women should be confined to the domestic realm. He certainly did not want education to empower women or prepare them for public life. To the contrary, Zhu believed that women should be strictly prohibited from participating in government affairs lest catastrophe befall the state. To that end, even highly placed women should meekly obey the men around them. While these obligations might seem unfair to women, Zhu believed that men had even more onerous responsibilities. Because women had to remain within the home, the family's success or failure depended mostly on its men. Although women had to restrain their impulses and seclude themselves within the inner quarters of the home, men were under far more intense pressure to work hard and allow the family to flourish. From Zhu's perspective, men faced much higher expectations and undertook heavier burdens than women.

Zhu Xi's view toward specific female virtues largely followed classical ritual and the ideas of Ban Zhao.[26] In fact, he championed Ban's writings, and her high standing in the traditional canon of Chinese thought comes largely from his approbation. However, social conditions had changed substantially since antiquity, so Zhu could not simply repeat what had been written centuries earlier. He had to interpret earlier ideas to make them relevant to his own time. Most significantly, Zhu put enormous stress on the need to confine women within the home. While various thinkers had promoted reclusion for centuries, Zhu's imprimatur lent this idea unprecedented urgency. The growing strictness of female reclusion in the late imperial era can largely be attributed to Zhu Xi's promotion of this practice.

Zhu also wrestled with the question of widow chastity. Previous Confucian thinkers had often felt torn on this issue. While the emphasis on a wife's lifelong fidelity to her spouse had increased over time, the Confucian ethical scheme also demanded benevolence, making these thinkers amenable to widow remarriage. Zhu understood the difficulties that widows faced and realized that poor women had no choice but to remarry when their husbands died. In one instance, he even chided a student who criticized a poor widow for remarrying. Nevertheless, he found the thought of a woman marrying more than one man during her lifetime discomfiting.[27] More than previous authorities, he stressed the desirability of widow chastity and expressed stronger disapproval of remarriage. Zhu Xi's assertive position on this issue eventually had a major impact on Chinese ethics. The influence of these views helps to account for the intensification of chastity rhetoric in the late imperial era.

Cheng Yi (1033–1107) put forward a far more radical vision of female virtue.[28] As with other Confucians, Cheng saw the revival of ancient standards of conduct as the way to elevate the moral tone of contemporary society. This goal inspired him to take an extremely conservative position on many issues of the day. Intense pride in his distinguished family background also helps account for his hard line on moral questions. Cheng regarded his family's reputation for integrity as their most precious legacy. His mother had also been unusually strict. She held herself to exceptionally rigorous ethical benchmarks and demanded that those around her do the same. Her obsession with ethical purity had a major impact on the behavior of their entire family. Cheng concluded that because women wield so much influence over other family members, they must be held to the highest standards. Although Cheng's hard-line views seem to have emerged in reaction to the particular circumstances of his own family, he ultimately demanded that others take a similarly rigid stand.

In most respects, Cheng Yi followed conventional Neo-Confucian thinking on female ethics. He emphasized the importance of women's obedience and fidelity and promoted widow chastity. Cheng accepted Neo-Confucian metaphysical teachings, grounded in the *Classic of Changes*, as the template for organizing interactions between the sexes. He summed up this position with assertions such as "The order of greater and lesser between men and women is the great regularity of Heaven and Earth."[29] Appealing to cosmic metaphysics as a model for gender relations allowed him to modify traditional expectations and introduce more stringent demands regarding female integrity.

Through this chain of reasoning, Cheng not only praised and encouraged chastity but sacralized it. He believed that widow chastity conforms to the metaphysical structure of the universe. For a woman to remarry violates the cosmological framework underpinning our world. Cheng gained infamy for his declaration that if a poor widow refused to remarry and subsequently starved to death for the sake of virtue, this was an extremely small matter. This shocking assertion followed from his belief that a virtuous person should be willing to sacrifice his or her life to uphold propriety. Although Cheng Yi's ideas in this regard were more extreme than those of his contemporaries, his thinking was not unprecedented. Many previous authorities had also demanded female fidelity, and they sometimes used forceful language.[30] Nor was death for the sake of virtue a heterodox belief. The classical Confucian canon contained similar teachings. The ancient sage Mencius wrote, "Life is something I desire; righteousness is also something I desire. If I cannot have both, I will forsake life and select righteousness."[31] Cheng Yi seems to have been following Mencius in demanding that a widow be willing to sacrifice her life for the sake of conjugal fidelity and sexual integrity.

Cheng Yi's strongly worded opposition to widow remarriage should be understood within the intellectual context of the time. Like Sima Guang and Zhu Xi, Cheng Yi believed that widowers as well as widows should ideally shun remarriage.[32] Cheng may not have demanded that men commit suicide to demonstrate loyalty to their wives, but he saw conjugal fidelity as a reciprocal obligation. Although future generations tended to ignore this aspect of the Neo-Confucian moral program, in fact these thinkers made substantial demands of men as well as women.[33] And even though Cheng Yi used dramatic language, he did not expect his readers to follow these pronouncements to the letter. Even members of his own family, who were unusually conservative, did not observe these harsh dictates. Two women from the Cheng family are known to have remarried. Cheng Yi seems to have assumed that families would take a woman's particular circumstances into account when deciding whether or not she ought to remain chaste or wed again. He employed extreme language for rhetorical effect as a way to shock the reader into appreciating the importance of fidelity.

Cheng Yi's pronouncements on female virtue did not represent mainstream opinion within the Neo-Confucian movement, much less Song society as a whole. Cheng exemplified the sternest social element of the time. These reactionaries ardently opposed political reform and sought to bind society within a rigid moral straitjacket. Cheng's extreme beliefs were far from typical even among the literati, and they differed considerably from the far more pragmatic mainstream mind-set.

Moreover, the importance of female behavior within Cheng Yi's overall ethical program should not be exaggerated. He wrote little about women, and gender relations were not a major component of his overall vision. Although he held extreme views regarding widow chastity, he saw this as a minor feature of a much larger ethical project. Nor did these ideas have much impact beyond a narrow academic niche. In sum, historians have tended to exaggerate the importance of Cheng Yi. Neo-Confucian thinkers may have considered widow chastity exceptionally virtuous, but they still accepted remarriage as a routine matter.

⚬══✖══⚬

Although debates about widow chastity now attract the attention of historians, in fact discussions about the nature of human desires or appetites (*qing*) were much more central to Song intellectual discourse. The passions had long been an important topic of discussion.[34] Critics believed that the emotions expressed in ancient poetry have considerable value as a medium that reveals humanity's moral essence. Normally a person's inner values are hidden from others. Emotional reactions toward particular events put these principles on public display, making intrinsic character traits visible to observers. Song thinkers associated the emotions with elements in their new metaphysical systems, lending them even greater depth and significance.

As people considered women more emotional than men, views toward the passions affected perceptions of female character. Confucian thinkers had conflicted ideas about the desires underpinning our emotions.[35] Due to the rising prominence of metaphysics, thinkers such as Zhu Xi considered desire a natural tendency instilled in humanity by Heaven. Nevertheless, even if *qing* is natural, particular desires might not conform to moral principles. Obeying the passions might lead a person to act badly. Zhu Xi accepted the optimistic Mencian position on human nature, seeing it as fundamentally good, so he believed that human passions are basically moral and tend to inspire people to behave well. However, other thinkers were less sanguine.

Mencian confidence in human nature raised a quandary in Confucian ethical theory. If human nature is fundamentally good, why do so many people behave badly? This conundrum led many Confucian thinkers to reject the naive Mencian view. Some took a contrary position and pinpointed emotion as the major inspiration for evil acts, associating *qing* with the negative side of human nature. This interpretation was informed by classical metaphysics, which held that each person has both yin and yang elements. Whereas benevolence arises from yang, desire and other emotions emerge out of yin, which had long been associated with the feminine. According to this explanation, *qing* is basically a negative quality, so people should be taught to control their emotions. Extirpating strong passions allows good impulses to prevail.

Neo-Confucian thinkers saw untrammeled desires as the main cause of women's malfeasance. But given the difficulty of controlling the emotions, they realized that it is much easier to rein in women by restricting their movements. Ever since antiquity, various writers had demanded that men and women remain physically separate, with women confined to the "inner" (*nei*) realm while allowing men to move freely in "outer" (*wai*) places. Inner and outer were abstract concepts and not necessarily specific places. However, inner was usually identified with the private recesses of the home. The effectiveness of injunctions dividing the sexes fluctuated over time, and actual behavior was often fairly lax. Nevertheless, in general, Song women became much more reclusive than before, establishing a new benchmark for female conduct that endured until the end of the imperial era.[36] Ethical writings put increased emphasis on confining women to the inner quarters of the home, and literature explored the disasters that might occur when people violated these injunctions. Scholars further bolstered gender separation by declaring it a reflection of the metaphysical system of the *Classic of Changes*. A variety of texts, ranging from family regulations to funerary inscriptions, praise this virtue as a moral imperative.

The rising emphasis on separating women and men affected daily life. At the apex of society, palace rules carefully segregated residents by sex.[37] Imperial consorts and daughters did not attend regular palace banquets, as numerous men were present. Instead they held separate celebrations in the inner halls of the palace, with titled ladies from the outside as their guests. Women at the bottom of society also remained largely separate from men. Authorities kept male and female criminal suspects apart, housing them in different cells.[38] A detainee could hire a prostitute as her servant. For both high and low, division of society by gender was part of quotidian life.

This keen emphasis on segregating men and women resulted in part from moral panic. Due to rising prosperity, people enjoyed unprecedented mobility and moved around much more than before. However, increasing openness brought risks as well as opportunities. Women were particularly vulnerable.[39] Song records contain numerous accounts of women who were robbed while traveling. These incidents occurred in every region of the country, affecting women traveling on land and by boat. Robbers came from a wide range of backgrounds and included Chinese and foreign soldiers, monks, riverboat captains, and roving gangs of thugs. Wealthy women were particularly at risk, and many robbery victims belonged to the gentry. Not only did these women carry valuables, but they were most likely to travel long distances. Gentry women sometimes followed husbands or fathers to an official posting in a distant province or accompanied a husband journeying to study or take an examination. During times of chaos, some women traveled in search of refuge, often going to distant places, making them easy prey for criminals. Female victims of robbery frequently died during attacks. Some were killed by bandits, while others committed suicide to avoid rape.

The emphasis on female reclusion was a reaction to the threats that women faced in a fluid, mobile, and dynamic society. Many people demanded that women hide themselves in the inner parts of the house for their own safety. They imagined the female quarters of the home as a remote haven protected from the prying eyes of strange men. Ouyang Xiu described the ideal women's abode as safely isolated.[40]

> The inner courtyard deep, so deep, how deep is it?
> Willows pile up mist;
> Blinds and curtains are of endless layers.

The house was a spatial mechanism that controlled people's movements.[41] Restricting women to a small space in the depths of the house made it easier for men to dominate them. Unable to go outside, women found themselves removed from the wider world of public affairs. They had no choice but to confine themselves to family matters and rely on men to deal with outsiders.

Although female seclusion became more intense at this time, these restrictions could never be absolute. Sometimes a woman had to deal with men outside the home, such as when they met with government officials or handled legal cases.[42] It was also customary for women to occasionally venture out of the inner quarters for pleasant outings.[43] They visited gardens to enjoy seasonal blooms, traveled to picturesque spots, and even went out in the evenings to admire nighttime scenery. Women visited ancestral shrines, Buddhist temples, belvederes, and beautiful buildings, as well as sites of interest such as irrigation works and city walls. They also participated in public festivities during major holidays, viewing lanterns and enjoying music and dances. Overall, in spite of markedly hardening rhetoric, it seems that separation of the sexes remained extremely uneven. Younger women tended to be the most securely cloistered, as they attracted the most attention from men. As a woman aged, she gained more freedom. Elderly women could interact with men without the risk of embarrassment or humiliation.[44]

Female reclusion and separation of the sexes was primarily intended to maintain women's sexual integrity and guarantee their fidelity to one man. People had varying attitudes toward this constellation of related virtues. The severity of these strictures varied by personal inclination, social class, and region. Some people elevated chastity into the supreme expression of a woman's character, while others maintained flexible views of female sexuality and conjugal fidelity. Not only does Song literature describe prostitution and extramarital sex, but there are also many accounts of strong-willed wives who exercised authority within the home.[45] And, in both north and south, cultural factors worked against stringent reclusion. Southerners had little regard for unrealistic ritual restrictions, while northerners received influence from nomadic peoples who lacked strict gender segregation.[46] Strident rhetoric about chastity often conflicted with actual behavior, which could be far more temperate.

Even as Confucian thinkers tried to bring marriage and family into conformity with classical standards, actual practices remained diverse. Ethnic Chinese living under the Liao and Jin dynasties inevitably absorbed some of the values of the conquering elite.[47] The Han subjects of Liao sometimes entered into levirate marriages, marrying a kinsman's widow to keep her in the family. There were also sororate marriages. When a woman died, her sister might wed her brother-in-law to replace the dead wife. Even in Song, where the law prohibited these foreign marriage customs, epitaphs nevertheless describe people engaging in levirate and even sororate.[48] Although the inspiration for sororate may have come from steppe culture, Chinese could justify the replacement of one sister with another as a practical arrangement. The gentry often limited themselves to closed marriage circles, presenting many widowers with a limited number of potential spouses. If a widower married his wife's sister, he could uphold his family's traditional circle of marriage partners. Moreover, she would likely be a good mother for her sister's children. Given these advantages, even though moralists looked askance at these pragmatic arrangements, sororate marriage was not uncommon, particularly among the gentry.

Song law permitted women to remarry.[49] Widows could not legally wed while still in mourning, but in 1090 the government shortened this period to one hundred days to expedite remarriage. Ordinary people were not hostile to second marriages. Even if a mother remarried, her children continued to treat her with filial devotion, showing that her marriage to someone other than their father did not break the bond between mother and child. Song fiction mentions numerous female characters who married two or three times.[50] Even women from prominent families are known to have remarried, and their behavior did not provoke scandal.[51] The thriving commercial economy seems to have fostered a very pragmatic attitude toward many issues, including remarriage. Even among the gentry, financial factors rather than idealistic moral teachings often determined whether a woman would divorce or remarry.[52] This pragmatic spirit favored remarriage. Poor widows sought a new husband out of economic necessity, while men coveted the dowries of wealthy women and tried to entice them to wed anew. Other considerations also factored into a widow's choices, such as her age, whether or not she had a son, and her relationships with her natal kin and in-laws.

From a woman's perspective, remarriage was possible, expedient, and acceptable. Nevertheless, a second marriage seemed morally dubious. For centuries, mainstream Confucian ethics had derided widow remarriage as a violation of conjugal fidelity. Song Neo-Confucians intensified this critique. Given the rising condemnation of remarriage, although it remained common, a second marriage tainted a woman somewhat in the eyes of others. Widows remarried more often than not, but they would likely feel embarrassed to enter the home of a new spouse.[53]

Episodes of chaos also affected attitudes toward chastity. Successive invasions by Khitans, Jurchens, and Mongols sent waves of humanity southward in search of safe haven. The resulting upheaval exposed women to enormous risks, and many suffered rape. Moreover, many men died during these invasions, leading to sudden surges in the number of widows. Due to these calamitous circumstances, widowhood, remarriage, and women's physical integrity all became topics of great concern.[54] As before, men wanted a virgin bride, so a woman who had been violated would find it hard to marry well. Restricting women to the inner quarters helped to safeguard the virginity of young women so that they could eventually make the best possible match. Even the rise of footbinding seems to have been related to notions of sexual purity. Although footbinding began as an aesthetic and erotic practice, this mutilation also curtailed women's movements and kept them from wandering far from home, helping to preserve the virginity of unmarried women and the chastity of wives.

The rising cost of dowry likely made elite families put a much higher premium on their daughters' virginity. As dowries became more expensive, it was important to get a good return.[55] Elite families were willing to furnish a lavish dowry in order to attract a son-in-law with a good future. However, as long as a woman remained unmarried, she was highly vulnerable. Families feared that a lothario might impregnate their daughter to force her into marriage. This turn of events could bring a huge windfall to a low-born man. He could forge an alliance with prestigious in-laws, obtain a large dowry, and elevate his social standing. Yet, from the standpoint of the bride's family, this would be a disaster. If their daughter became pregnant and had to marry down, her dowry was completely wasted. As the cost of dowries rose, families fretted about keeping their daughters virginal until the wedding. Anxiety about premarital virginity expanded to cover all aspects of female sexuality, developing into a fixation with female chastity in general.

Society looked on all forms of extramarital sex with increasing disapproval.[56] Tang dynasty literature had sometimes described sexual liaisons in a matter-of-fact tone. In contrast, Song writers condemned the adulterous wife for shaming her husband and ruining his reputation. Authors described illicit sexual encounters differently depending on the social station of the people involved. They were particularly derogatory about trysts between people at the bottom of society, portraying these encounters as lurid debauchery. Female participants in extramarital intercourse suffered the most opprobrium, as they had shamed their male kin. Religious figures warned that those guilty of illicit sexual acts would surely suffer karmic retribution. A man might even resort to violence to clear his good name. Yuan drama depicts heroic male characters killing lascivious women, and audiences apparently considered this sort of retribution appropriate and even righteous.[57] As cuckoldry brought increasing humiliation, many husbands took stronger measures to ensure that their wives remained faithful, strictly confining them within the inner quarters of the home.

Song rape law reflected hardening views toward female physical purity.[58] Laws governing sexual violence became more detailed than before. Song jurists treated rape as adultery by force, so they appended rape law to the statute on adultery. When a married woman reported a rape, authorities immediately suspected her of having committing adultery. It was up to her to prove that the act had not been consensual, which she could usually only substantiate if a struggle had left visible traces on her body. If a married woman reported rape but was then declared guilty of adultery, she could be sentenced to two years of penal servitude. Because victims faced an unrealistic burden of proof, it seems that they rarely came forward to report rape. Considering that a married rape victim would likely be condemned for adultery, it made sense for wives to seclude themselves within the home for their own protection. Punitive rape laws made it dangerous for women to encounter unfamiliar men, and they reacted by retreating into the safety of the home.

Although circumstances increasingly pushed women toward reclusion and chastity, people still considered the unmarried woman's life hard and uncertain. When Li Qingzhao reached old age, she wrote a poem that describes widowhood not as moral heroism but as a sad and humiliating state. In addition to lamenting the decay wrought by old age, she goes on to rue the loneliness of widowhood and looks back with nostalgia on her happy youth.[59]

> But now I am a bag of bones,
> My hair disheveled and turning gray—
> I'm afraid to be seen when going out at night.
> Far better I should from
> Behind a lowered blind
> Just listen to other people's laughter.

The death of a spouse instantly plunged a woman's life into crisis. Men were almost always older than their spouses, so they often predeceased their wives by many years. Widowhood could last a long time. Among a group of Jin dynasty epitaphs for women, the average age at death was 59.34.[60] If a woman's husband died when she was young, she might have decades ahead of her. Given the potential length of widowhood, the decision of whether or not to remarry could not be taken lightly.

Widows found themselves torn between remarriage and lifelong chastity. Either option posed difficulties. A widow without property would find herself destitute.[61] Literature depicted the stereotypical widow as a lonely and pathetic figure living on the margins of society. Even so, remarriage also presented challenges. A woman entering a second marriage had a lower status in her husband's family than a virgin bride.[62] She would usually have to leave her sons behind with her in-laws when she departed.[63] Fear of losing her children could convince a devoted mother to forgo remarriage. Also, when a widow left her deceased husband's family, her in-laws sometimes filed lawsuits to seek the return of all his property.[64] In-laws and even adult children sometimes tried to claim her dowry.

In spite of the drawbacks to chaste widowhood, this status offered certain benefits.[65] Both government functionaries and prominent thinkers promoted the cult of chastity, lending it greater prestige than before. This sacrifice would make a woman's family proud, as it raised their collective reputation. For the lower gentry, a chaste widow in the family demonstrated that they embraced the values of the upper elite.[66] The individual could also gain commendation, even if she were poor. During the Tang, the writers of eulogies usually connected female virtue with high social status, as they considered good character heritable. Because of this assumption, they did not praise poor widows. In contrast, Song thinkers put far more emphasis on merit earned through individual effort. Posthumous Song encomia celebrated poor widows as martyrs who managed to hold themselves to the highest moral standards in spite of material deprivation. If a poor widow also educated her sons, she deserved even stronger praise.

Widowhood was not just a way for a woman to bolster her reputation. She could also help those around her deal with practical matters. A chaste widow could stabilize a family by caring for the elderly and preventing bloodlines from becoming tangled. Also, a widow enjoyed certain tangible rights.[67] Most importantly, she could manage her husband's estate. In theory, a widow was supposed to obey her son, but this injunction was rarely practical, as her child was likely still a minor.[68] In reality, a widow usually ended up controlling her dead husband's estate. Widows of wealthy men thus had a rare opportunity to gain respect not just for their conduct but also for affluence. A childless widow could decide which of her husband's kinsmen would inherit the estate when she died. Widows could also freely arrange the marriages of their children without the interference of a husband.[69]

During the Song, widow chastity was reinterpreted as an expression of filial piety, altering its cultural implications and imbuing the practice with additional moral sanctity. This shift grew out of the gradual expansion of the scope of filial piety. In antiquity, this virtue had initially only applied to fathers and sons.[70] Over time, the rubric of filial piety expanded to cover mothers and daughters as well. By the early medieval era, Confucian authors lauded women who exhibited exemplary devotion toward their husband's parents.[71] When a Song widow declined remarriage and remained in her deceased husband's home to serve his parents, people interpreted her behavior as a moving sacrifice for the sake of filial piety.[72]

For widows, there were many advantages to remaining in a deceased husband's home, managing his estate, and caring for his parents. Even so, widows who did not remarry usually returned to their own families. People assumed that a chaste widow would want to live out the remainder of her life among blood kin.[73] When she left her in-laws, she took her dowry with her. Even though some people argued that a departing widow should leave part of her dowry behind with her in-laws, widows do not seem to have heeded these calls. The desire to keep dowry wealth in the family helps explain why a widow's in-laws were sometimes eager for her to remain with them. Extending filial piety to cover the relationship between a woman and her husband's parents provided a convenient justification for encouraging widows to act in the interests of their in-laws.

Figure 6.1. The Classic of Filial Piety, *by Li Gonglin (ca. 1085)* (Metropolitan Museum of Art)

The state also actively promoted widow chastity, making it increasingly prestigious. The emperor's relatives embraced the state promotion of chastity. Although Song emperors permitted women of the imperial clan to divorce and remarry, they also sometimes provided stipends to widows with limited means to allow them to remain chaste.[74] The imperial clan seems to have dealt with these matters in an ad hoc manner.

The bureaucracy issued commendations, called *jingbiao*, to recognize exemplary moral achievements of both women and men. A woman could receive official kudos for chastity, filial piety, loyalty to the state, and even for making a significant contribution to the community, such as paying for infrastructure repairs or helping to defend an area under attack. Ever since the Han dynasty, the state had periodically issued these sorts of awards. The Song expanded the commendation system to unprecedented proportions.[75] Central and regional governments each issued commendations, acting independently of one another and employing different administrative frameworks. There were several types of commendation. An exemplary woman could receive an honorific title, and her family might be permitted to construct a memorial gateway, shrine, stele, or tomb tablet in her honor. She might also receive tangible awards, such as material goods and exemption from tax and corvée duties. Although many families sought recognition for their widows, commendations remained relatively infrequent compared to later eras. The Qing dynasty government handed out so many accolades that elite families did not even bother to apply, as the awards had lost their exclusivity.[76] In the Song, however, state commendations for chaste widows still held great prestige for both the recipient and those around her.

Official concepts of female virtue were primarily a form of elite male discourse.[77] Powerful men promoted particular types of female virtue, such as fidelity, to serve their own interests. They also used women's integrity as a tool of politics. During the Song era, China was surrounded by powerful and aggressive peoples: Khitans, Jurchens, Tanguts, and eventually Mongols. After the Jurchen invasion, the government retreated to the south, far from the traditional heartland of orthodox culture. Authorities ruling over a rump state felt weak and humiliated.[78] To regain a measure of respect, they took a harder line on moral issues, including chaste widowhood.

Distress over the loss of north China made loyalty an imperative political virtue.[79] The Southern Song court wanted to attract men of talent southward and reward them for remaining steadfast in spite of the dynasty's travails. For this reason, loyalty became a key theme in biographical and historical writing. The emphasis on this value influenced attitudes toward female virtue. Writers lavished praise on the faithfulness of widows, implicitly contrasting their loyalty with inconstant men who refused to follow the emperor southward. To further highlight the importance of loyalty, writers concentrated on dramatic stories of widows who maintained their chastity in spite of terrible privations or who committed suicide to safeguard their honor. As chastity rhetoric took on an overt political dimension, it became increasingly extreme.

The state apparatus did not want people to perceive the official promotion of chastity as cynical expediency. Historical discourse had long been a major vehicle for expressing ideology, so Song officials justified their political values by projecting them into the past. They adjusted theories of dynastic decline to justify state sponsorship of the cult of chaste widowhood. Tang and Song historiography put great stress on the belief that female immorality can provoke dynastic collapse.[80] This theoretical shift justified hard-line female ethics. Restricting the behavior of women limited the chances that they would endanger the dynasty by interfering with important matters or behaving wrongly.

As chastity rhetoric intensified, the ways that women expressed this virtue became more extreme. During the Tang, self-mutilation had become an increasingly respected way for people to express their commitment to a moral ideal, such as filial piety. These measures continued into the Song.[81] Sima Guang praised widows who mutilated themselves to escape forced remarriage.[82] Other accounts list numerous women who cut off their flesh to concoct a medicine used to treat an elder, usually a parent.[83] There are more records of filial cannibalism from the Song than from the entire time before the dynasty. The Yuan government even issued two edicts prohibiting self-mutilation in the name of filial piety in a futile attempt to stem this burgeoning practice.

Women occasionally committed suicide to dramatically express their decision to remain permanently chaste. Of course, not every female suicide was undertaken to express righteousness. Most women killed themselves due to passion, mental illness, or to escape unbearable circumstances. Because people who died a violent death were believed to become angry ghosts, vengeful women occasionally killed themselves with the hope of gaining supernatural powers and exacting retribution on those who had wronged them. Relatively few suicides were committed for the sake of chastity.

Because female suicide had various motivations, when a woman killed herself, the family and community had to explain her self-destruction. This was an important point, as the motives of a suicidal woman determined the nature of her funeral.[84] If she had killed herself in a fit of pique, her family would feel embarrassed and reduce their obsequies. Instead of being interred in the family cemetery, she might be buried where she died or in an isolated spot. The survivors might even feel afraid of the deceased, as popular belief held that someone who committed suicide out of extreme passion might become a malevolent ghost. To appease this restless spirit, they might conduct special religious ceremonies during the funeral to propitiate her, discouraging her from returning to earth as a ghost.

In contrast, if the suicide's family declared that she had killed herself for the sake of a virtue such as chastity, she would receive an unusually elaborate funeral. The family genealogy would document her suicide so that future generations could brag about her sacrifice. They might even report this exemplary death to the authorities in the hope that official chroniclers would record her martyrdom in local historical records. Some suicidal women received posthumous honors through the state commendation system. Because the treatment of suicide differed substantially according to the perceived motivation of the deceased, it was in the interests of the victim's family to declare that she had killed herself for the right reason. Even if her in-laws had bullied a woman until she took her own life, it would be convenient for them to claim that she committed suicide for the sake of virtue, turning potential disgrace into honor. For this reason, the true motives behind many female suicides allegedly undertaken in the name of virtue remain suspect.

Chapter 7

Image

During the momentous transition from Tang to Song, popular views toward women and the ways that women presented themselves to the world both changed significantly. This shift in female persona had varied causes. Women responded to social changes by behaving differently, so people perceived them in novel ways. In addition, men promoted new views of gender. Since men produced almost all visual and literary representations of women, they could shape female imagery to serve their own priorities. The male domination of women's representation is readily apparent in painting. Artists created female subjects for the male gaze, situating them in places, costumes, and poses deliberately chosen to appeal to the sensibilities of male viewers. Artists painting women did not do so in response to their subjects' concerns. Instead they employed an explicitly male mode of gendered visual discourse. Stereotypical representations of women sometimes worked against female interests by reinforcing the patriarchal underpinnings of society and politics.[1]

The increasingly negative portrayal of Wu Zetian, the consort who overthrew the Tang dynasty and declared herself emperor, illustrates how male interests shaped standard ideals of womanhood.[2] Empress Wu brashly defied traditional male privilege, and recollections of her reign traumatized elite men for centuries thereafter. Song and Yuan literati wrote about Wu with increasing venom, depicting her as illegitimate and immoral. In reaction to this critique, high-placed Song women took great pains to avoid behaving in ways that recalled this reviled historical figure. Although women around the emperor might still exert some power, usually indirectly via male intermediaries, they nevertheless cultivated a public image of disinterested humility. Most confined their activism to unthreatening realms such as religion and the arts.

Amid this reassessment of womanhood, a diversity of new female images emerged. Popular fiction presented readers with various female types. Three kinds of female characters were most common.[3] First, readers enjoyed stories about imperial consorts. Instead of presenting high-placed ladies as moral exemplars in the manner of the standard histories, fiction writers were much more interested in gossip and scandal. They titillated readers with glimpses of hidden palace life, usually of dubious accuracy. The second group of female characters consisted of supernatural beings, including immortals, ghosts, and demons. Finally, fiction depicted ordinary women as well. Because readers were familiar with everyday female life, these descriptions were usually fairly realistic. Popular fiction often focused on unexceptional women from low backgrounds, such as vendors in the marketplace, providing historians with valuable glimpses of quotidian life.

Writers were also extremely interested in courtesans. However, Song tales differed noticeably from Tang descriptions of courtesan life. Whereas Tang fiction tended to depict courtesans as beautiful and romantic figures inhabiting an opulent realm of pleasure, some Song writers took a more realistic perspective and described these women's hardships in detail. They turned the courtesan from a romantic fantasy into an object of pity.

Song love stories also differed from Tang prototypes, revealing changes in ideal relations between the sexes.[4] During the Tang, the female romantic ideal was often a supernatural being, such as an immortal or ghost. In contrast, Song love stories focused on mortal women. Authors often depicted them in a positive manner as brave and decisive. Whereas circumstances frequently frustrated Tang romance, Song love stories often had a happy ending. A typical tale concluded with the loving couple united and those around them accepting their relationship. But even though Song romantic literature took on a more positive tone, love stories had become less numerous than before. The Confucian educational curriculum made readers highly sensitive to the inherent conflict between emotion and the rites, so they felt increasingly uneasy about couples who sought relationships based on romance in defiance of the tradition of arranged marriage. Even though love stories became more positive, they made readers feel increasingly uneasy, causing such stories to decline in popularity.

Although male writers sometimes promoted free love, women had a more realistic view of their situation. Life was not always as rosy as it seemed in popular fiction, and not every woman had a lover to keep her company. Zhu Shuzhen (ca. 1063–1106) wrote a poem describing her unbearable loneliness and isolation.[5]

> I walk alone, sit alone
> Chant poems and raise my glass alone
> Even go to bed alone.
> I stand still, my spirit grieving,
> No way to defend myself against the troubling spring chill.

Who notices these feelings of mine?
Tears have washed away the powder and rouge till not even half is left.
Sorrow and sickness have each had their turn.
I've trimmed the lamp's cold wick to the quick, but dreams won't come.

Women could use poetry to reflect on their lives. When they contrasted their actual circumstances with cheerful literary clichés, introspection could give rise to disappointment. Zhu's poem reinterpreted the timeworn trope of the miserable solitary woman. As before, people considered intense desire for a loved one a largely feminine trait.[6] Although Six Dynasties boudoir poetry had also featured unhappy women, those characters were pining for an absent man. In contrast, this woman is not lonely because her male lover is absent. There is no male loved one. Her sense of desolation comes from the feeling that she is alone in the world with no hope for happiness in the future.

As with visual art, the ways that male poets approached female subjects shaped ideas about womanhood. Visual representations of women often followed written descriptions, particularly stock images from poetry, so as literature changed, artistic depictions of women shifted in tandem. The ideal female characters described in the ancient *Classic of Poetry* (*Shijing*) provided the basic template for normative representations of women.[7] These poems not only stressed the ideal woman's appearance but also emphasized her virtue. Ancient poets believed that although lofty character is invisible, it nonetheless constitutes an important aspect of a woman's overall beauty. However, Song poets treated women in a variety of ways, presenting artists with a range of possibilities. The Confucian revival intensified the stress on female propriety. Some artists did not even dare to depict the female body, as they feared that painting a beautiful woman would seem inherently licentious. Instead they employed a symbol, such as a flowering tree, to evoke the feminine in a tastefully indirect manner.

The profusion of new poetic and philosophical works gave rise to conflicting ideas about the ideal woman. While some creators dealt with female issues primly, not all were so high-minded. Some looked back to more engaging depictions from the past. Sensual poetry in the sixth-century collection *New Songs from a Jade Terrace* (*Yutai xinyong*) described women as gorgeous yet lovelorn.[8] Although these beauties wear extravagant garments and live in luxurious surroundings, they feel bored, frustrated, and generally miserable. The rise of *ci* lyric poetry during the Song translated the content of sensual boudoir poetry into an au courant literary mode, renewing its influence and disseminating these decadent images of female life to a contemporary audience.[9]

Because early medieval poetry so often described women as enclosed within a luxurious boudoir, many readers assumed that the model woman

Figure 7.1. An ideal beauty of antiquity (Metropolitan Museum of Art)

ought to reside in opulent surroundings. They considered the luxury of a woman's environment an important component of her overall beauty. Tang dynasty painters used bright colors to evoke a sense of brilliant feminine luxury and depicted women as graceful, sumptuous, and imposing. However, they rarely framed female figures within a concrete background. These dazzling women seemed to exist in black space. Empty surroundings implicitly emphasized the woman herself, focusing the viewer's attention on every nuance of her body, clothing, hairstyle, bearing, and movement. Female figures in Tang art took on an air of superhuman perfection. Artists did not intend to depict real women. Instead they used their art to express a highly aestheticized vision of ideal femininity.

The abrupt destruction of the aristocracy and their attendant culture at the end of the Tang cleared the way for new and very different female images to emerge. Northern Song critics began to use a specific term for paintings of beautiful women, calling them *shinü*.[10] Yet, even as this genre became clearly defined, it went into decline. While Tang viewers had appreciated paintings of beautiful noblewomen, Song connoisseurs began to consider this subject matter vulgar.[11] Some classical texts associated beauty with licentiousness, so literati were loath to ascribe this quality to women of good birth. Instead of appreciating a woman from a high background for her beauty, they considered it proper to laud her character or talent, as in didactic images of virtuous women associated with moral biography.

As Song literati redefined the proper representation of women, artists moved beyond shallow depictions of physical beauty to imbue female subjects with greater depth. Song painters depicted the ideal woman standing amid a detailed background. Placing a female figure within a particular context made her seem more realistic. This technique also made a spatial context part of a woman's identity. Luxurious or ordinary surroundings allowed the viewer to assess the female figure's position in society. Significantly, as in literature, Song artists often depicted women of lower status, a novel subject that suited contemporary popular taste.[12] Painters such as Wang Juzheng (active in the late eleventh century) and Li Song (1190–1230) represented ordinary women in poses and situations chosen to highlight their realism. Sometimes these commoners seem very attractive, in spite of their humble standing. These painters extended the scope of beauty beyond the privileged elite to encompass ordinary women as well.

Most radically, the ideal female subject no longer had to be attractive. People realized that plain women could also be interesting and worthy of attention. For example, during the Song, it became extremely common for women to wrestle in public, and even residents of the palace sometimes watched these competitions.[13] Women usually competed with one another,

*Figure 7.2. Painting of a poor woman, by
Wang Juzheng* (Wikimedia Commons)

but sometimes they wrestled with men. This form of popular entertainment became widespread, and even stage dramas included scenes of female wrest-ing. The rising interest in female wrestlers was part of a larger reassessment of womanhood in general. Overall, the focus of female images shifted away from superficial beauty and invited the audience to ponder more meaning-ful aspects of female life. Painters depicted ordinary women who managed to thrive in spite of their humble station. They did not expect the viewer to despise these women for their low status. To the contrary, artists expected that the sight of unexceptional women engaged in mundane activities would arouse interest and empathy in viewers.

⊙══✦══⊙

Since antiquity, the classical rites had demanded that men and women be clearly distinguished and kept apart. Ideally, gender was to determine an indi-vidual's work, appearance, behavior, and physical location. This assumption permeated every aspect of society. To cite just one example, many unem-ployed scholars became physicians during the Song and Yuan dynasties, and they injected moral concepts from the classics into medical theory.[14] Physicians assumed that women's bodies differ fundamentally from those of men and assigned distinctive treatments for each sex.[15]

Difference was not necessarily parity. People considered the female body essentially unclean due to menstruation and childbirth. The apocryphal *Blood Bowl Sutra* (*Xue pen jing*), which expresses twelfth-century beliefs, taught that a woman could go to hell simply as punishment for her unavoidable physical pollution.[16] According to this revision of Buddhist thought, the uncleanness of the female body made being a woman inherently sinful.

Because people considered each sex distinct, they assumed that a woman should contrive an appearance that conformed to standard gender norms. However, for many women it was not enough to simply look generically female. They manipulated their bodies and accoutrements to project a carefully crafted individualistic persona as well. Fashions in clothing and hairstyles steadily changed over time, so the beautiful Song woman looked very different from her Tang precursors.

The Confucian revival came to fruition during the Song, exerting a significant influence on how women presented themselves in public.[17] Aristocratic flamboyance and nomadic culture both had a profound influence on Tang dynasty fashions, and women's clothing departed notably from earlier prototypes. In contrast, Song Confucians revered antiquity and attempted to revive certain old ideas and customs. They encouraged women to reject exaggerated Tang fashions and revive the sorts of unassuming clothing allegedly worn by the ancients. Palace ladies looked to the apocryphal *Rites of Zhou* (*Zhouli*), which allegedly described the institutions of that ancient dynasty, for guidance on how to dress for ceremonial events. They wore items of clothing carefully graded for each kind of occasion, in line with classic ritual.[18]

Confucians also encouraged people to adopt a sober mind-set, so in some respects the cultural atmosphere became more austere. In response to these ideas, fashions became far more sedate than before. Low-key colors became popular, and clothing had demure lines. Tang ladies had favored suggestive garments that emphasized the curves of the wearer's body, and low-cut fronts sometimes revealed décolletage. By the Song, women regarded such sensual clothing as vulgar and even obscene. They favored garments designed to hide the shape of the body, not accentuate it. Women also rejected the early eighth-century vogue for voluptuous physiques. As in antiquity, the ideal Song woman was slender. Even hairstyles became far simpler than before.[19]

Because Song women rejected Tang extravagance for classical modesty, even highborn ladies wore relatively simple clothing, downplaying the link between luxurious fashions and high status.[20] They deliberately took a contrary approach. Everyone knew that a wealthy woman could afford to dress extravagantly, so if she chose to present herself to the world wearing simple garments, those around her interpreted her humble appearance as an expression of sober virtue. Elite women sought praise for seriousness instead of vain luxury. However, simplicity did not mean austerity. The Southern Song tomb of Huang Sheng (1226–1243), imperial clanswoman and wife of a local magistrate, contained 201 pieces of clothing. Of these, 56 percent were made from silk fabric.[21] Although less flamboyant than Tang fashions, a wealthy Song woman still had an extensive wardrobe of finely crafted garments.

Simpler clothing did not have to be unattractive. Garment technology and production methods advanced during this era, making well-tailored attire readily available.[22] Previously, family-owned shops and individual tailors had produced garments in small quantities. During the Song era, although most people still wore one-off clothing, more sophisticated alternatives had begun to emerge. The scale of manufacture expanded, and distribution became more efficient. Techniques for spinning, weaving, and dyeing all advanced. Whereas garment production had traditionally been a female preserve, male craftsmen entered the booming industry. Expert tailors cut and sewed garments. Their participation elevated the status of textile work and increased workforce specialization and manufacturing quality. Large manufacturers also produced better fabrics. Traditionally, women working at home had woven silk thread into thick tabby cloth, but professional workshops used superior looms capable of producing lightweight silk gauze. Due to these changes, the garment industry became more professional than ever before, and quality rose. Not only was the average garment higher quality than before, but cloth also became less expensive, so women from modest social backgrounds could dress better.

Changing taste affected other aspects of female appearance as well. Although clothing became simpler, cosmetics became more artificial. Some women applied extremely affected makeup. Portraits of Song empresses portray them with stark white faces highlighted by theatrical red cheeks.[23] Women valued pale skin because it implied that they demurely sheltered within the inner quarters of the home and did not work outside, signifying both virtue and high status. Liao cosmetics were even more stylized.[24] Khitan women used the fruit of the Mongolian snake gourd (*Trichosanthes kirilowii*) to concoct a yellow paste that they rubbed on their faces in winter. This thick coating protected their skin from the harsh cold air. They periodically added fresh coats of makeup, building up an increasingly thick layer of yellow paste on their faces until they finally washed it all off with the arrival of spring. People thought these women's yellow faces made them resemble gilt Buddhist statues, so they called this paste Buddhist makeup (*fozhuang*).

The most dramatic alteration that Chinese women made to their appearance entailed a painful mutilation. It became more common than before to break the bones in women's feet and wrap them tightly in cloth bandages to reduce their size.[25] Although there seem to have been cases of footbinding during the Tang dynasty, poets did not yet mention it. This custom became visible during the subsequent Five Dynasties era. Both literature and the visual arts confirm that during the Song, footbinding became more common than before. By the end of the dynasty, some gentry families bound their daughters' feet as a matter of course. However, the extent of footbinding at this time should not be exaggerated. It remained an elite practice over a limited range. Only during the Ming dynasty did footbinding spread down to ordinary families across the nation.

The rise of footbinding fundamentally altered female life. Mutilating the feet made it difficult for women to walk. They became confined to the home out of physical necessity, making it far more difficult for them to participate in the wider world. Moreover, the excruciating pain that resulted from walking on compressed broken feet became an accepted part of female life. Constant pain made it difficult for women to concentrate, and victims lived a passive existence out of necessity.

Two factors facilitated the upsurge of footbinding at the time, one material and the other ideological. During the Tang era, houses had minimal furniture, and people sat on floor mats. Even when chairs and tables came into fashion in the tenth century, some conservatives considered it vulgar for a woman to expose herself by sitting on a chair rather than assuming a reserved pose on the floor. As long as women sat on the floor, footbinding could not become common, as it would be extremely difficult to stand up on tender mutilated feet. The introduction of tables and chairs into the home made bound feet feasible.[26]

Footbinding may have become practicable at this time, but why did people start to consider it desirable? Initially it seems that some women bound their feet to make them seem more attractive and even erotic. Women covered their tiny feet with beautifully embroidered cloth shoes, and poets lauded these "lotuses" as the pinnacle of beauty. When footbinding became the norm, men mocked women's natural feet as crude and ugly. The rise of Neo-Confucianism also gave bound feet an additional moral dimension. Although some of these thinkers considered footbinding inhumane, it happened to accord with their program for restricting women to the domestic sphere. A woman with bound feet had her movement severely curtailed, so she could not possibly be independent. She had no choice but to depend on men for her basic needs. By necessitating female reclusion and dependence, footbinding made the virtue of modest reclusion into a physical necessity. As the prestige of the Neo-Confucian school grew, more people appreciated the implicit link between footbinding and female virtue, justifying this cruel erotic practice as an expression of ethical probity.

Chapter 8

The Conquest Dynasties

Throughout China's history, powerful foreign tribes and kingdoms periodically rose up along the northern and western frontiers. Usually the Chinese state could successfully defend against intermittent incursions, but when the government fell into decay, foreign peoples had an opportunity to invade and conquer. During the Tang and Song eras, China faced several powerful neighbors. To the west, the Xi Xia kingdom combined central Asian culture with Chinese administrative techniques to construct a sophisticated state. Khitan nomads in the northeast established Liao, modeled on China's native dynasties. Then the Jurchens charged down from the steppes and conquered north China, establishing the Jin dynasty to rival the rump Southern Song dynasty in the south. Finally, the Mongols invaded China. Having honed their military skills in combat with a wide array of opponents across Eurasia, the Mongols readily defeated both Jin and Song and unified China under the Yuan dynasty.

The impact of the various conquest dynasties on gender relations is one of the most controversial topics in Chinese history. For most of the twentieth century, historians regarded China's native ethics as fundamentally restrictive and contrasted them with the allegedly relaxed customs of neighboring steppe peoples. They assumed that because Tang dynasty culture absorbed so much foreign influence, women had a high degree of autonomy.[1] In contrast, Neo-Confucianism and nativist orthodoxy supposedly made society far more conformist during the Song era, restricting female movement and expression.

This interpretation depicts China's native culture as fundamentally conservative on gender issues. When foreign influences weakened restrictive Confucian values, people of both sexes supposedly had more room to pursue their desires. Historians have applied this assumption to an even larger

131

issue as well. During the Ming and Qing dynasties, in some respects women had fewer rights and opportunities than before. Female inheritance rights declined, the cult of chastity intensified, and more widows committed suicide.[2] It became the norm for women to bind their feet, seclude themselves within the home, and adhere to highly restrictive rites and ethics. Generations of scholars attributed the conservative turn in gender ideals to the rising influence of Neo-Confucianism. They believed that when Confucian orthodoxy prevailed, female status declined.

The Korean scholar Seol Baehwan has issued an eloquent defense of this viewpoint. He argues that steppe values were amenable to female interests, so the status of women rose under the Yuan dynasty.[3] Seol holds that women throughout the Mongol Empire enjoyed higher status and more freedoms than their counterparts under Sinocentric dynasties. Moreover, he points out that Mongol women exerted significant authority within the family, elevating their overall social standing. Seol also emphasizes the military and political importance of elite Mongol women, particularly during the early phase of the empire. They rode well, accompanied their husbands on military campaigns, and provided invaluable logistical support, contributing to Mongol victories.[4] Chinggis Khan empowered his female kin and used them to rule both allies and conquered regions. Some Chinese scholars have adopted a similar view, arguing that because Mongol culture lacked the restrictions of Neo-Confucianism and the classical rites, Chinese women enjoyed more autonomy under the Yuan dynasty.[5]

In recent decades, revisionist historians have questioned the assumption that steppe customs favored women. To the contrary, they argue that many aspects of pastoral culture opposed female interests. Instead of attributing the decline in female status to Song Neo-Confucianism, they point to the impact of the autocratic Jin and Yuan dynasty systems.[6] According to this reinterpretation, changes in the legal and financial systems under the conquest dynasties curtailed female autonomy and put women firmly under the control of male kin.[7] The historian Tan Xiaolin sums up this view by proclaiming that during the Yuan dynasty, women were completely objectified and commoditized, and the government viewed them as little more than reproductive tools.[8] Others point to the intensification of chastity rhetoric under the conquest dynasties, seeing this as a harbinger of the conservative gender ideals that defined social relations in the late imperial era.[9]

The status of women from the Song dynasty onward remains a subject of debate. Historians have set out opposing models to explain when and why Chinese gender relations became more stringent. Some see the turning point as the Song, while others attribute it to the conquest dynasties of Liao, Jin, and Yuan. To understand the history of women after the Tang, it is vital to pinpoint when gender attitudes began to significantly harden and why this transformative shift occurred.

○━━◆━━○

Historians and anthropologists have taken note of the powers exercised by women in various societies on the Asian steppe. Given this backdrop, some authorities have suggested that nomadic influence generally raised the status of Chinese women. In fact, given the intricate interaction between native and steppe customs, it is clear that these practices had a complex influence on Chinese society. Many steppe customs were inappropriate for a sedentary society, diminishing their impact. When invaders from the steppe settled down, they rapidly assimilated Chinese habits and values. Moreover, Mongols, Jurchens, and Khitans had distinct kinship and political traditions, so the incursions of each steppe people influenced China differently.

Most fundamentally, the economic dimensions of gender relations differed in nomadic and sedentary societies. While both sides had gendered division of labor, allotting key tasks to one sex or the other, the productive capacity of Chinese women was generally lower than that of female nomads. From the Song dynasty onward, Chinese women were increasingly restricted to the home, confining them to domestic tasks and textile production. In contrast, because conditions on the steppe were so harsh, all members of a pastoral society, including women, had to work very hard just to survive. Khitan and Jurchen women undertook many kinds of work and helped provide food for their families. They oversaw domestic tasks, prepared meals, cared for children and the elderly, and also hunted, fished, and herded livestock.[10]

Mongol women also worked very hard.[11] In addition to domestic chores, they milked animals, made butter and cheese, processed meat, tanned hides, and made felt and leather goods. Because women contributed significantly to provisioning their families, they were far more economically productive than most Chinese women. They also loaded, unloaded, and drove the carts filled with the family's tents and possessions whenever they moved to a new area. Even though Mongol women usually only fought in emergencies, they received military training, and many were highly skilled at riding and archery. When the men went away to fight, women usually remained at the home camp and took on male tasks in addition to their own duties. The flexibility of gendered work roles allowed the Mongols to fully mobilize their men as soldiers in time of war.

Although Mongol aristocrats dowered their daughters with livestock and a trousseau, ordinary women did not receive any dowry. A wife's wealth usually came from her husband's family. A bride received a portion of the husband's livestock to manage, often when she bore a son. Although wives did not receive regular income from their husbands, they might be given a share of the spoils of war. Upon a woman's death, her sons inherited their mother's share of the family property. Because of the gender inequality of property ownership, in spite of the relatively high productivity of Mongol women, men controlled most wealth and property.[12] Inheritance was matrilineal, passing from man to man down the maternal line of descent, so men were the heirs to family wealth.

In some respects, married nomadic women had more freedom than their Chinese counterparts.[13] Some steppe marriages were matrilocal. When a man resided with his wife's family, she had a higher standing within the marriage. Women's divorce and remarriage rights were comparable to those of men. For example, many Liao princesses divorced, usually because they did not get along with their husbands. However, nomads considered the marriage bond extremely important and looked down on infidelity. The Mongols severely punished both sexes for adultery.

Significantly, peoples of the steppe did not value widow chastity.[14] Mongols also placed little value on a bride's virginity. Moreover, a widow often married a kinsman of her deceased husband, in contravention of the increasingly important Chinese ideal of lifelong fidelity. The motivation for levirate was largely financial. Having paid out a costly betrothal gift, pastoral peoples assumed that a woman belonged with her husband's family for life. They did not see this custom as merely pragmatic. Nomads justified it through religion, claiming that because a widow would be reunited with her first husband after death, she should not allow herself to be defiled by a man who was not her husband's kinsman.

Although those unfamiliar with levirate might consider this custom odd, a widow probably saw remarriage with a husband's relative as a good option. She could not subsist by herself amid the harsh environment of the steppe. A woman had to live with a family to survive, so it made sense for her to stay with her deceased husband's kin. Marrying an in-law kept the family together and allowed her children to grow up among supportive paternal relatives. Yet, in spite of these advantages, the wives of khans and nobles often declined remarriage. Wealthy Mongol women had the financial resources to survive on their own. The fact that wealthy widows refused levirate marriage suggests that most women saw it as an expedient measure.

The kinship customs of conquering nomadic peoples affected the values and behavior of their Chinese subjects to varying degrees. Epitaphs document considerable Khitan influence on the marriages of Han living under the Liao dynasty.[15] At that time, traditional Chinese incest taboos broke down. Relatives and people of different generations married without shame. Moreover,

Han women often remarried, and some ethnic Chinese families even practiced levirate. When a woman died, a younger sister who had not yet married might take her place as the widower's wife. Because nomadic customs and values differed so much from Chinese norms, influence from these cultures also affected women's quotidian behavior. Yuan dynasty comedies depicted some female characters as passionate, heroic, and just.[16] Their bold actions defied restrictive Confucian stereotypes. Instead of reclusion and obedience, these female characters sought respect for authenticity and self-assurance.

Pastoral women traditionally exercised some political power, and they sometimes participated in government under the conquest dynasties. Khitan empresses, backed by their powerful kinsmen, often took part in politics. The Liao elite educated their women, and some used this learning to write about policy matters.[17] Privileged women remonstrated with the emperor over particular issues and expressed their concern for the nation. Khitan men often accepted this advice, showing that they considered it permissible for a woman to participate in politics. Of all the conquest dynasties, the Mongols had the most influence over Chinese society.[18] Yuan empresses and consorts did not modestly hide themselves behind screens, as was the Chinese custom. Instead they appeared openly at court and dealt with officials directly. A few Yuan women played significant political roles, and the dynasty had female regencies.[19]

In light of the prerogatives that pastoral women enjoyed, it might seem reasonable to assume that steppe influence had a liberating influence on Chinese gender mores. In fact, the evidence points to the opposite conclusion. Scholars who regard pastoral influence as emancipating usually identify the Song dynasty as the turning point when women's overall circumstances began to decline. They stress the rise of Neo-Confucianism, which allegedly supplanted pastoral values and intensified traditional gender restrictions. However, the influence of Neo-Confucianism on the lives of Song women should not be exaggerated. Elite thinkers writing commentaries on classical texts did not have much immediate impact on popular ideas and practices.[20] Moreover, Neo-Confucianism was just one school of several during the Song, and not the most prominent. Even within the Neo-Confucianism camp, hard-liners such as Cheng Yi were marginal figures.

Ultimately, Neo-Confucianism had a critical long-term impact on Chinese society, but the effects were delayed. The official embrace of Neo-Confucianism began in the Yuan dynasty. After conquering China, the Mongols realized the utility of using Confucian values to rule their subjects. Chinese advisers convinced Mongol leaders to legitimize their unpopular regime by basing policies on strict interpretations of traditional ethics, so the Yuan promoted the most stringent form of Confucianism as a way to claim moral legitimacy.[21]

This project significantly altered the mechanics of Chinese law and administration. By embracing Neo-Confucian ideology, Yuan official practices diverged from milder precedents and placed unprecedented restrictions on women. The government amended laws regarding property and inheritance to reduce female autonomy. And whereas women could previously bring lawsuits to court on their own behalf, a woman had to find a man to represent her before a magistrate.[22] The influence of Neo-Confucian gender concepts endured after the fall of Yuan. During the Ming dynasty, officials continued to employ Neo-Confucian values as the basis of law and administration, introducing these stringent principles into everyday life.

Overall, the level of freedom in China for both men and women decreased under the conquest dynasties. This decline had begun even before the Yuan. Jurchen invaders enslaved many people, including war captives, criminals and their families, and debtors.[23] Slaves performed critical tasks and were integral to the economy. Although slavery had previously been legal, under the Tang slaves were neither numerous nor economically important. The devolution of the northern Chinese economy into a slave system under Jin administration highlights the decline in individual freedom under autocratic alien occupation.

Under the brutal Jin dynasty system, women lost basic rights.[24] Although most Jin dynasty law has been lost, surviving fragments include provisions regarding marriage and property. In many respects, Jin law adhered to precedents from earlier Chinese dynasties. The state forbade marriage between people of extremely different social status or the same surname, distinguished wife from concubine, and forbade polyandry. Other provisions, however, reflected the alien priorities of Jurchen culture. Whereas the Song code harshly punished the murder of a spouse, Jin law allowed a man to kill his wife with impunity. It also became more difficult for women to escape an intolerable marriage. Whereas Song officials could invoke "righteous separation" (*yijue*) to dissolve an abusive marriage, it seems that Jin authorities did not consider domestic violence problematic. In addition, the financial status of women declined markedly. Because Jin law discouraged the division of family property, it became less convenient for women to remarry. And it seems that a divorcee or widow who left her husband's family could not take her dowry with her.

The Yuan dynasty legal system was similarly unsympathetic to women's concerns. Mongol custom had a strong influence on Yuan jurisprudence, affecting the legal status of Chinese women.[25] While Chinese had traditionally been limited to one wife, Mongol men sometimes had four or five spouses. Generally speaking, polygyny degrades the status of women in the home. A man with several wives tends to regard them as his social inferiors. Mongol men took this disdain to an extreme by treating wives as property. A Mongol who killed a man in battle could claim his wife as booty. Husbands could abandon their wives for any reason. Although killing a wife was not entirely legal, a murderous husband merely had to pay a fine equal to that for killing a slave.

Unfortunately, Yuan dynasty law is difficult to reconstruct, as the Mongol emperors never promulgated a systematic code. The Yuan derived some basic principles of justice from earlier Mongol law. Around the year 1218, Chinggis Khan enacted a comprehensive law code called the *Great Yassa*.[26] However, he kept these provisions secret, and they were only known to officials. The surviving fragments of the *Great Yassa* show that it codified traditional Mongol customs and values as law. The *Yassa* mandated marital fidelity, and an adulterer could be put to death. Children born to a concubine were considered legitimate offspring. And after a man's death, his son could decide what to do with his father's wives. He could either marry them (although of course not his own mother) or else wed them to someone else.

Circumstances in China differed considerably from those on the steppe, rendering many Mongol laws superfluous, objectionable, or insufficient. Moreover, China already had a long and sophisticated legacy of jurisprudence. Yuan officials used either Mongol or Chinese law, depending on the particular situation. Enforcement was ad hoc, and the populace was often unaware of what laws they should obey. Because the Yuan state lacked a comprehensive or systematic code of law, magistrates looked to a patchwork of edicts and precedents to render their verdicts. The results of this haphazard process were often unpredictable.

Yuan marriage law departed from Chinese norms. Provisions shifted over the course of the dynasty.[27] Initially Mongol authorities maintained the Jin code, which resembled Song law in most respects. However, within a few years judges began to force their Han subjects to follow certain Mongol kinship practices. Over time, more Han officials entered government service, and they reasserted Chinese values. In an effort to preserve their culture under an oppressive alien regime, Han officials embraced the most conservative version of Chinese ethics. They codified Neo-Confucian principles, mostly drawn from the writings of Zhu Xi, as law. Although the Ming elite looked back on the Yuan with distaste, they nevertheless followed many of these precedents and maintained Neo-Confucian ideology as a lodestone of law and administration. From the Yuan dynasty onward, women had fewer rights than before.

In some respects, the incorporation of Neo-Confucian gender ideals into the law simply codified common kinship rules.[28] As with clan custom, a woman lacked an independent legal or social identity and instead shared that of her husband. However, Neo-Confucian influence further increased the authority of senior males over family members. A daughter was legally obligated to obey her parents, who could force her to marry whomever they chose. Also, crimes were to have a heavier punishment if committed by a junior family member upon a senior rather than vice versa.

In other respects, the legal status of women under the Yuan dynasty deteriorated dramatically, departing significantly from traditional law and custom.[29] In previous eras, if a husband abandoned his wife and disappeared, she could remarry after a set period of time. During the Yuan, a husband's unexplained disappearance meant that a woman could never remarry. Even more drastically, a husband could legally kill a "guilty" wife if he believed that she had committed a serious transgression.

The financial position of women retreated as well. Because Mongols did not usually dower their daughters, they considered this custom unimportant. Yuan authorities decreased women's control over their dowries. Although ethnic Han brides still received a dowry, their husbands controlled this wealth and could dispose of it as they wished. Moreover, Mongols could not accept the idea that a woman could remove property from her husband's family. Unless a husband expelled his wife without citing a legitimate cause, she could not take her dowry with her if she left his home. A widow could not even leave with her dowry after her husband's death. In other words, if a woman divorced or remarried, she lost her dowry. This crucial change in the property law made it much more difficult for women to remarry and helps account for the visible increase in chaste widows from the Yuan dynasty onward. Even so, a widow's in-laws might try to force her to remarry so that they could seize her dowry outright.[30] Under the altered dowry system, widows and their in-laws had different interests, and they sometimes found themselves at odds.

In contrast with Southern Song law, which expanded women's inheritance rights to an unprecedented degree, the Yuan legal system severely curtailed inheritance by daughters. As before, a woman could not inherit from her husband, although she might manage the estate until a son came of age. A childless widow could control the estate for the rest of her life, as long as she did not remarry. However, the law reduced a daughter's right to inherit from her parents. A woman could only inherit a portion of her parents' estate if she had no brothers and her natal household had thus become "extinct" (*hujue*). In this situation, daughters could inherit one-third of the estate, and the government confiscated the remainder.

Yuan officials also reconceptualized marriage finance. Among steppe peoples, men inherited family property. However, a man had to pay out a costly bride price to acquire a wife, transferring a significant amount of wealth to her family.[31] Because nomads owned little property, grooms frequently worked for a bride's family for a period of time in lieu of bride price.[32] Men considered bride service highly burdensome and saw it as a test of their spirit. Given this backdrop, it is not surprising that Yuan officials emphasized the importance of the betrothal gift. Yuan marriage documents spelled out the value and contents of the betrothal gift in detail.[33]

During the Yuan dynasty, people increasingly regarded marriage as a financial transaction. Due to the importance accorded bridewealth, Yuan authorities allowed a woman to end her marriage through payment.[34] While a husband could divorce his wife without paying a financial penalty, her family had to return the betrothal gift to buy her freedom. Yuan case law includes instances of husbands or in-laws selling a woman to obtain betrothal gifts, akin to selling a wife.[35] Moreover, as a wife belonged to a man and his family, a woman who committed adultery was severely punished. One adulteress received forty-seven strokes of a cane, after which she was sold into slavery.[36] Men sometimes rented out their wives, a practice called *dianqi*. The woman lived with another man temporarily until she bore him a child, after which she would return to her husband.[37] This custom was common in the south, particularly in parts of Zhejiang. Also, because women had tangible financial value, kidnappers abducted women to sell as wives.[38] Overall, it is clear that Mongols saw the wife as a husband's property, as he had purchased her by paying a bride price. From the Mongol perspective, when a woman married, she became chattel. Although ethnic Han attitudes were not so extreme, Yuan law and administration affected how ordinary people thought about marriage, which helps account for the diminished position of Chinese women from the Yuan dynasty onward.

The Yuan dynasty saw a marked intensification of the cult of chastity, and it became more common for widows to resist remarriage. Given traditional attitudes toward marriage and widowhood among steppe peoples, it might seem unexpected for chastity rhetoric to harden during a conquest dynasty. In some respects, nomadic marriage customs were less restrictive than those practiced by Chinese. Pastoralists often allowed their children to choose their own spouses, tolerated elopement, and even practiced ritualized wife theft, with the groom pretending to steal his bride from her family.[39] Most importantly, whereas Chinese considered widow chastity virtuous, pastoral peoples practiced levirate. They expected a widow to marry a husband's kinsman so that she could stay in the family. Prior to the Yuan, Khitans and Jurchens both saw levirate as a standard custom. Among the Khitans, it might even have been mandatory.⁴⁰

When pastoral peoples entered China as conquerors, they had to resolve the blatant contradictions between their traditional marriage practices and extremely different Chinese customs and values. They found it very difficult to harmonize dissimilar and sometimes contradictory bodies of family ethics. Due to the high number of incongruities, policies regarding marriage and kinship changed over time. Initially the Jin government declared that ethnic Han could not practice levirate, as this was not their traditional custom. When a Han widow finished mourning her husband, she had to return to her natal family, who would arrange for her remarriage. Subsequently, however, the Jin changed the law and allowed Chinese to engage in levirate marriage, as some Han wanted to imitate the customs of the pastoral ruling elite.⁴¹

Official Yuan attitudes toward levirate also shifted over time.⁴² Some Chinese adopted this custom voluntarily, and officials occasionally forced a Han widow into a levirate union against her will. In reaction, some widows publicly declared themselves chaste to avoid being forced into an unwanted levirate marriage. Emperor Wuzong declared that a chaste widow had to remain with her in-laws in conformity with Mongol tradition, while Emperor Renzong allowed Chinese women to return to their natal home. A great deal of surviving Yuan case law involves levirate marriages, as this alien practice frequently provoked lawsuits.⁴³ Generally speaking, it seems that Mongol administrators applied rules regarding levirate unevenly. Poor widows were most likely to be compelled to marry a deceased husband's kinsman. A widow might even willingly accept this arrangement, as it could have financial and practical advantages. However, wealthy women usually managed to resist being pressured into levirate unions.

During the conquest dynasties, judicial authorities struggled to balance conflicting views of ideal widowhood. The solutions they devised affected the official treatment of chastity and remarriage for the remainder of imperial history. This clash of values first became evident under the Liao dynasty. Khitan domestic life differed significantly from Chinese norms. Traditionally, the Khitan family was extremely hierarchal. Parents had absolute authority over their children, and husbands stood above their wives. Elite men took multiple wives. Some even married several sisters at the same time.⁴⁴ Whereas Chinese had practiced sororal polygyny in antiquity, they had long ago abandoned the practice and subsequently condemned it as blatant incest.⁴⁵ Emperors, princes, and other high-ranking men could even kill their wives and concubines with impunity. When Emperor Daozong of Liao ordered Empress Xuanyi (empress 1055–1075) to commit suicide after she had been falsely accused of adultery, he was exercising an established prerogative.⁴⁶

The Khitans even occasionally practiced human sacrifice. When a ruler or noble died, his family might kill his wife and concubines and place their bodies in his grave to accompany him to the afterlife.[47]

The Khitans put great stress on a woman's sexual integrity. They believed that a sexually abused woman not only suffered humiliation personally but also cast shame on her entire family. For this reason, prior to the establishment of the Jin dynasty, the Khitans deliberately violated and degraded Jurchen women, even those of good family, to humiliate their Jurchen vassals and emphasize their dominance.[48] Nevertheless, Khitan women enjoyed liberal divorce rights. Some divorced and remarried several times.[49] Liao princesses in particular frequently divorced, as these proud women found it difficult to get along with their spouses. Khitans also practiced levirate marriage, so a son married the wives of his deceased father (other than his own mother).[50]

In addition to their traditional practices, Khitans adopted customs from Han Chinese culture and religion. Liao dynasty Khitan family ethics thus combined native traditions with values from Confucianism and Buddhism. The Khitans also enthusiastically embraced education grounded in Confucianism and the classics. Young Khitans were immersed in this body of learning at an impressionable age, molding their value system along Chinese lines. The Khitan ruling elite did not limit education to sons but schooled daughters as well, influencing their ideas and behavior.[51]

These ethical systems had a major impact. Confucian teachings eventually led the Khitans to forsake levirate. They imported other Confucian ideas as well, such as strictly gendered domestic roles and filial piety. Most dramatically, the Liao rulers abandoned human sacrifice. Confucians abhorred this cruel practice, leading Liao emperors to renounce the custom. Elite Khitan women began living their lives according to Confucian precepts.[52] Epitaphs for the Liao elite routinely acclaimed deceased women as paragons of Confucian virtue. While most of these texts commemorate men, they often mention mothers and wives as well. While these tributes were not intended as objective portrayals of women's actual behavior, epitaphs nevertheless reveal general moral priorities. These inscriptions often describe women by using language and values lifted directly from Chinese moral biography, such as Liu Xiang's influential Han dynasty collection of narratives about exemplary women. Epitaphs routinely describe deceased women as filial daughters, devoted mothers, and obedient wives.[53] The Liao government also tried to enforce certain Confucian ethical priorities, and rulers prohibited titled ladies from remarrying.[54]

After the Jurchens conquered north China and established the Jin dynasty, they experienced a cultural trajectory akin to that of the Khitans.[55] Like the Khitans of Liao, the family life of the Jurchens who established the Jin dynasty also differed from Chinese norms.[56] Traditional Jurchen customs were very harsh toward women in some respects. For example, some people believed that if a man sacrificed both a woman and a white horse, he could gain magical powers.[57]

Jurchen women did not traditionally receive dowries. Instead, men presented the bride's family with a generous bride price. Having paid out a considerable sum, the husband's family wanted to keep his widow with them after he died, so a kinsman of the deceased would marry the widow in a levirate union.[58] This custom seems to have depressed female status. Levirate sometimes required a woman to marry a deceased husband's kinsman of the same generation as her son, reducing her to a kinship position below her husband.[59] Overall, the Jurchens had a relatively relaxed view toward the marital bond. Female adultery was not taken very seriously, and divorce and remarriage were not uncommon.

At the beginning of the Jin regime, the Jurchens continued to observe their native kinship traditions. They did not yet see divorce and remarriage as moral failures, and they had no concern for the sexual integrity of captive women. During the fall of north China, the Jurchens captured numerous Han women to serve in the palace, where they were treated like slaves. Over time, however, the Jurchens soon realized the advantages of using native Chinese customs to rule their resentful subjects. The Jin dynasty rulers Taizu and Taizong even sought to sinicize Jurchen society in the belief that Chinese culture suited their new sedentary lifestyle.[60] To this end, they encouraged the Jurchens to educate themselves in the Chinese manner. They established schools at each administrative level as well as a special academy for officials. When Jurchens received a classical education, they became familiar with Chinese ethics and adopted some of these values. And as the Jurchen nobility intermarried with prominent Han, they embraced Chinese family practices such as concubinage.

Confucianism is an extremely ambiguous term that covers a large body of ideas disseminated by various thinkers over many centuries. This school of thought included a range of ethical priorities that sometimes conflicted. Some Confucian ideas could potentially empower women, such as filial obedience to one's mother.[61] In general, however, Confucian gender concepts limited female autonomy. When Jurchen rulers adopted Confucian values, they disempowered palace ladies, encouraged widow chastity, and even lauded female martyrdom. The language on many Jin dynasty epitaphs followed that used in comparable Song inscriptions, stressing a deceased woman's adherence to Confucian probity. As Jurchens intermarried with ethnic Han, they absorbed Chinese concepts of conjugal propriety. Jurchen women embraced chastity ideals, and some widows refused to remarry. Epitaphs praise Jurchen widows who chose to remain chaste. Jurchens gradually abandoned other native marriage practices that conflicted with Chinese norms, such as sororal polygyny, and adopted Chinese customs, including concubinage. Over time, Jurchen family life increasingly resembled that of Han Chinese.

Although the Mongols had far less interest in Chinese culture than the Khitans and Jurchens, after settling in China they nevertheless became increasingly amenable to Confucian ethics. Initially the Mongols did not promote lifelong marital fidelity. Many continued to practice levirate, and they probably found the behavior of Chinese widows difficult to comprehend. However, the chaos unleashed by the Mongol conquest and the slapdash Yuan administrative system threatened women's security. Soldiers terrorized civilians and bandits roved the land, making the preservation of chastity a major challenge. Some women committed suicide to avoid humiliation. Historians recorded a few of these cases to convey the threats faced by women of the time, depicting them as martyrs to chastity.

The Yuan dynasty saw a major shift in orthodox thought. Although the most important thinkers of the Neo-Confucianism school lived during the Song, the Chinese had relegated them to the intellectual margins. Ironically, it was the Mongols who made Neo-Confucianism a state ideology. After traumatizing the Chinese with an invasion of merciless savagery, a small number of Mongol occupiers had to govern a vast population of embittered and contemptuous subjects. To stake a claim to moral legitimacy and prove themselves civilized, from the mid-Yuan onward the dynasty's officials embraced extremely conservative interpretations of classical ethics. In doing so, they made Neo-Confucianism state orthodoxy for the first time.[62]

As part of the Confucianization of Yuan administration, Mongol authorities embraced Chinese filial ethics and actively promoted them among their own people.[63] Yuan law included measures to enforce filial piety, such as prohibiting children from dividing up the family estate while either parent was still alive, barring people from marrying during obligatory mourning for a parent, and even preventing people from feasting or enjoying music during that time frame. Yuan court scholars annotated the *Classic of Filial Piety* (*Xiaojing*) and issued a collection of narratives about filial exemplars. Filiality became an increasingly prominent theme in popular culture as well. Six surviving Yuan dramas highlight the issue.

Significantly, whereas filial devotion had originally been a male concern, at this time it became increasingly identified with women. The scripts of popular stage plays put greatest emphasis on the deference owed to mothers. Conditions of the time account for this shifting emphasis. In the aftermath of the violent invasion of China, many men had perished, so there were far more widows than before. These women often headed up broken families, and their sons had to obey them. The sudden increase in the number of widows made obedience to mothers a significant moral issue.

The degree of sinicization of Mongol and Semu women varied considerably. While many showed little interest in Chinese customs, others became highly assimilated and strove to live up to Confucian ideals.[64] Commemorative epitaphs for Mongol women often praised them for observing Confucian virtues and the rites. The section on didactic female biographies in the *Yuan History* (*Yuanshi*), the standard history of the era, honors six non-Han women as martyrs to chastity. Confucianization also affected official policies toward women. The Yuan reestablished the *jingbiao* commendation system to honor chaste widows and other righteous women, offering them prestigious awards and financial support.[65]

Popular culture absorbed these stringent views about female virtue and promoted them among ordinary people, spreading the reach of Confucianized female ethics to all levels of society. Yuan dynasty dramas depict a wide range of female types.[66] Some are virtuous wives who genuinely love their husbands and behave in an exemplary manner. Other female characters titillated audiences with their louche behavior, seeking out sexual encounters and adulterous romance. They could sometimes be vicious as well. This gallery of wicked women implicitly warned audiences of what happens when people foolishly ignore Confucian ethics.

Yuan jurists sought to impose stringent moral standards on society at large. In doing so, they deployed the power of the state to bolster Confucian patriarchy. As part of this project, Yuan authorities altered the connection between bridewealth and dowry. During the Song dynasty, families had come to see dowry and betrothal gifts as a reciprocal exchange. Yuan officials followed Mongol custom and instead stressed the betrothal gift as the foundation of marriage finance, reducing the importance of dowry. Although the classic rites required the presentation of a betrothal gift to legitimize a marriage, in ancient times this was usually a symbolic offering. In contrast, Yuan authorities assumed that the groom should pay out a considerable sum as bridewealth. Chinese law assimilated the Mongol concept that a wife had been effectively purchased through bride price, effectively commoditizing women and lowering their status to chattel. The Yuan treated women as property in other ways as well.[67] When the Mongols invaded China, they immediately enslaved many women. A woman could also be enslaved if her father or husband could not pay the fine incurred for a crime. During this era, female slaves became a common sight in wealthy homes.

With women increasingly looked upon as property, when a family paid out a betrothal gift to obtain a bride, many people assumed that they had acquired permanent authority over her.[68] Yuan officials deliberately made it much more difficult for a widow to leave the home of her in-laws. Unlike the Song, if a widow remarried, her deceased husband's family could confiscate her dowry. This change made it very costly for widows to enter a new union. In consequence, women became much more thoroughly integrated into the families of their husbands. These developments shifted the circumstances of Chinese widows to accord with Mongol tradition. Conditions in China differed from those on the steppe, so these values had uneven applicability. According to Mongol custom, when a father died, his son could decide what do to with his father's wives.[69] In Yuan China, however, the dead man's parents often had the most authority over his widow. Whereas previously a widow's parents usually had the greatest influence over her decision to remarry or remain chaste, from the Yuan dynasty onward the widow's in-laws prevailed.

With increasing numbers of widows forced to remain with their in-laws, they tried to turn necessity into virtue. Over time, a woman's relationship with her parents-in-law intensified. People gradually extended the rubric of filial piety to make a woman's bond with her in-laws as important as that with her parents, if not more so. Given this mind-set, when a widow's parents-in-law forced her to remain with them, she could valorize her predicament as an expression of exemplary virtue. As the details of marriage finance changed, the psychology of chastity took a new turn.

Yuan administration strengthened the authority of husbands over wives in other ways as well.[70] The government curtailed female divorce rights, making it virtually impossible for a woman to escape an unhappy marriage. Yuan officials also prohibited the wives of soldiers away on distant campaigns from marrying someone else, even if a husband had disappeared and was presumed dead. They also prohibited the wives and concubines of government officials from remarrying so as to guarantee that they would not desert a man away on a distant posting. The government accepted the idea that a man had the right to use violence to discipline his wife, and it seems that domestic abuse became much more common at this time. Surviving records detail various types of violence ranging from curses to beating, branding, and mutilation. Most dramatically, Yuan authorities allowed a man to kill an adulterous wife and her lover on the spot with impunity.[71] Although the rights of women declined appreciably during the Yuan, there was one bright spot. The thorough incorporation of a woman into her husband's family bolstered her power over her children.[72] A man was prohibited from arranging his own marriage as long as either of his parents remained alive, a rule that shows the power of widows over their offspring.

The Ming state extirpated some Mongol customs from the law, prohibiting levirate for example. Even so, Yuan legal practices had a long-term impact. The Ming maintained Yuan regulations that diminished female property rights. Most importantly, late imperial law continued to prohibit a widow from taking her dowry with her into a new marriage.[73] The Mongols had traditionally used levirate to keep wealth from leaving the male line. When they settled in China, levirate became highly controversial, so they used the Chinese custom of widow chastity to achieve the same result. Making it difficult for a widow to leave the family of her deceased spouse would help keep her dowry with the husband's line.[74] This change in property rights constituted a major shift in women's financial standing and helps account for the rapid rise in widow chastity from the Yuan era onward. As under the Yuan, a Ming widow who left the household of her deceased husband forfeited her dowry to her in-laws. Ming law also preserved Mongol tolerance for the use of violence against women. In line with Yuan precedent, a man could murder an adulterous wife or concubine on the spot with impunity.[75]

In sum, Yuan law and administration had a long-lasting impact on Chinese gender relations. From this time onward, remarriage became far more costly for widows. Most still remarried in spite of the difficulties, but an increasing number remained chaste, often living out their lives in the household of their deceased husband. For some, neither remarriage nor chastity seemed like a good option. An increasing number of widows martyred themselves through suicide, ostensibly in dedication to the virtue of conjugal fidelity.

Didactic female biographies helped shape views of ideal female behavior in China and neighboring countries. Yuan dynasty literati embraced this literary genre, making depictions of female role models much more common. These texts reflect the changing behavior of widows.[76] Significantly, the content of these narratives shifted to focus on extreme and even violent behavior. Although Liu Xiang's original Han dynasty collection of female biographies generally celebrated peaceful qualities such as righteousness, wisdom, and talent, this genre took a violent turn. Female martyrdoms occurred in several ways. Many took place during wartime, when women committed suicide to avoid being raped by bandits or renegade soldiers. Widows occasionally killed themselves to avoid being forced to remarry against their will. A woman occasionally killed herself soon after her husband's death to accompany him to the grave, under the assumption that a widow's life was meaningless. Some of these widows may have committed suicide because they saw no good options for their postmarital life.

The encyclopedic *Complete Collection of Illustrations and Writings from Early to Current Times* (*Gujin tushu jicheng*), completed in 1725, includes 282 accounts of female chastity martyrs from the 312 years of the Song and 854 similar narratives for the 98 years of the Yuan.[77] These figures give the impression of a sudden spike in female suicide in the Yuan era. Also, of the 187 biographies of exemplary women in the *Yuan History*, the standard account of the era, the authors recognize 161 for their chastity, of which 81.4 percent died an unnatural death.[78] Earlier dynastic histories had mostly lauded widows who quietly lived out their lives without remarrying, but the *Yuan History* has few pacific narratives of widowhood, focusing instead on martyrdom as the new standard for chastity.

The shift in chastity rhetoric toward violence and self-destruction is partly attributable to Mongol influence.[79] Traditionally, when a high-status Mongol died, his subordinates would commit suicide or undergo human sacrifice to follow him to the grave. This practice attested to the status of the deceased and allowed his followers to dramatically demonstrate their fealty. Minor wives of polygynous Mongol men sometimes committed suicide upon the death of a husband as well. More frequently, a Mongol widow would mutilate herself to show her grief. During the Yuan, the Chinese cult of chastity absorbed the Mongol spirit of self-sacrifice and integrated this culture of violence into the prevailing Confucian moral framework. Ideas about female ethics underwent a major transformation, becoming far more demanding than before. This change in how chastity was manifested marks a major disjunction in the development of Chinese ethics, affecting women's lives for the remainder of imperial history.

Conclusion

The Tang–Song Transition and Women's History

The standard model of Chinese history identifies the Tang–Song transition as a fundamental turning point. The economy, society, politics, and culture all underwent major changes at this time. Through this process, a conservative medieval state transformed into a far more dynamic, prosperous, and refined society, initiating a new phase in the history of China. Although historians stress the overall importance of the Tang–Song transition, they debate its relevance to gender relations. The roles of women and men did not necessarily change in tandem with other aspects of society, so historians need to ask whether or not this period also marks a key disjunction in women's history.

Until recently, most scholars assumed that gender relations tracked other historical trends, so the changes constituting the Tang–Song transition must have fundamentally transformed women's lives. However, the matter is not so simple. There were many types of women, and they interacted with the people around them in various ways. Even within the same household, a wife, daughter, concubine, and servant residing in proximity would have led very different lives. Moreover, imperial China was extremely large and incomprehensibly complex. It is difficult to make simplistic judgments and sum up an entire era as better or worse for women. The numerous components of Chinese society did not necessarily change in unison, and broad shifts did not affect each constituent feature in the same way.

In light of these interpretive difficulties, historians increasingly question the relevance of the Tang–Song transition to women's history. The previous consensus assumed that the emergence of Neo-Confucianism soon altered relations between the sexes. In fact, although Neo-Confucianism unquestionably had a major impact on late imperial society during the Ming and Qing dynasties, its short-term effect on Song society is questionable. During the Song dynasty, Neo-Confucianism was as yet new and marginal. Most thinkers of the time took a far more moderate, pragmatic, and flexible approach to female ethics. Because the impact of Neo-Confucianism was so gradual, its emergence did not constitute a sudden rupture with past values and behavior.

During the Song era, women's basic place in the family did not alter dramatically. As during the Tang, people put great stress on filial piety, and the standing of mothers within the family remained comparable. Families still valued daughters largely because they could be married off to useful affines. However, as the Song government became increasingly bureaucratic, people sought a different kind of son-in-law. Rather than seeking out a man with the most prestigious genealogy, as during the Tang, elite families often put more stress on talent. They wanted a son-in-law who would likely pass the increasingly important civil service examinations and succeed within the highly competitive bureaucratic system.

Changes in family finance altered the domestic kinship structure. Song law gave women greater inheritance rights than ever before. Although a wife still could not inherit the property of a deceased spouse, she had liberal rights to manage his estate if she lacked sons or if her son was still a minor. And even as the average dowry increased in value, women retained control over this wealth. They could decide how to spend it, and they took it with them if they left a husband's home due to widowhood or divorce. Most significantly, daughters could inherit a significant portion of the parental estate, giving them a far greater claim on family wealth than before. In respect to women's financial position, there was clearly no regression from the Tang. To the contrary, Song women had more financial autonomy and a greater claim on family wealth than ever before.

The influence of women on government institutions developed in a different direction. The early Tang dynasty was a high point of female power. Several princesses and consorts led influential factions that exerted great influence over policy. Most dramatically, Empress Wu Zetian temporarily overthrew the Tang, usurped the throne, and ruled on her own behalf as a female emperor, a unique event in China's long history. Although Empress Wu was generally competent, her unorthodox reign nevertheless shocked powerful men. Song officials reacted by restructuring imperial institutions to limit the authority of highly placed women and prevent another episode of blatant female dominion. In general, this plan succeeded. Although subsequent empresses and empresses dowager sometimes exerted a degree of influence, they always felt abashed to be seen overtly wielding authority. Potentially powerful women shielded themselves from criticism by assuming an air of disinterested virtue or devoting their attentions to uncontroversial cultural and religious projects. In sum, when compared with the Tang, the Song saw a clear diminution of female political power.

When comparing the overall circumstances of female life during the Tang and Song periods, although there were many differences, both negative and positive, the transition between these two epochs does not stand out as a major turning point in women's history. While the Tang–Song transition affected particular aspects of women's lives, it did not involve a notable decline in female status.

Recently a number of scholars have forcefully argued that instead of the Song, the conquest dynasties of Liao, Jin, and Yuan should be seen as the key era of transition in Chinese women's history. As more research on these complicated eras comes to fruition, a picture of changing gender relations has begun to emerge. At first glance, it seems odd to attribute declining female status to the influence of nomads, as these cultures lacked the restrictive Confucian ethics and classical rites that had traditionally circumscribed Chinese women's autonomy. To the contrary, Mongol, Khitan, and Jurchen women often exercised considerably authority within the home and even participated in public affairs. Most visibly, the wives and daughters of Chinggis Khan played a significant role in the expansion of the Mongol Empire, managing the households and wealth of absent warrior husbands, administering conquered and allied territories, and participating in succession conflicts.

The position of Chinggisid women had deteriorated considerably before the Mongols established the Yuan dynasty. And once nomadic peoples settled in China, they tended to embrace restrictive Chinese gender values. Moreover, pastoral law and custom, those of the Mongols in particular, traditionally gave women fewer rights than their Chinese counterparts, and the legal and administrative systems of the conquest dynasties embodied these principles. In addition, under the Yuan, the Mongols also sought to win respect from a mistrustful populace by embracing the most conservative strains of Confucian thought, ironically positioning themselves as the defenders of traditional Chinese ethics.

Changes to the law most clearly reflect a major shift in the treatment of women. Yuan legal practice integrated both repressive Mongol gender values and also restrictive Neo-Confucian ethical concepts, treating women significantly worse than the legal regimens under the Tang and Song. The Mongols put such great emphasis on bride price that they treated a wife as chattel that had been purchased from her family, degrading women in the eyes of both the officialdom and society as a whole. A wife who left her husband's family forfeited her dowry to them, making it costly for widows to remarry. The law also prohibited the wives of absent soldiers and government officials from wedding someone else. Domestic abuse was basically decriminalized. A man could even kill an adulterous wife with impunity. It also became much more common for women to be enslaved and for husbands to temporarily rent out

Figure C.1. Yuan dynasty painting of palace ladies (Cleveland Museum)

a wife to another man. Ming and Qing dynasty law retained some of these oppressive precedents, making the Yuan a clear turning point in female legal status.

Women tried to make the best of a deteriorating situation by portraying the restraints they had to observe as voluntary choices made in the name of virtue. Male authors cooperated with this project, as they preferred to think of the women around them as paragons of virtue rather than victims of oppression. People put unprecedented emphasis on the filial bond linking a woman with her parents-in-law, promoting it to the same level of importance as the duty owed to parents. When a widow remained with her in-laws after her husband's death, she did not admit that she did not want to lose her dowry. More likely, she would explain her behavior as motivated by filial piety, wifely fidelity, and maternal duty. These expressions of virtue were not necessarily insincere. Women often internalized their survival strategies and embraced them as genuine personal values, altering the standard mentality of womanhood in the process.

After carefully examining the available evidence, it is clear that the conquest dynasties, and the Yuan in particular, stand out as the time when women's general status went into decline. The Yuan dynasty may have been relatively brief, but it was perhaps the most consequential era of Chinese women's history. Henceforth women faced far more restrictions than before. They had no choice but to adapt their behavior and psychology to cope with their new circumstances, seeking creative ways to thrive within the confines that society had thrust upon them.

Glossary

bi	婢
Bohai	渤海
Cao (empress)	曹
Cao Xiyun	曹希蘊
Chai Jingyi	柴靜儀
Chan	禪
Chang'an	長安
changji	娼妓
Cheng Yi	程頤
Chengtian	承天
Chunqin	淳欽
ci	詞
Da Fo ding shou leng yan jing	大佛頂首楞嚴經
Dahui	大慧
dianqi	典妻
Donglai	東萊
er sheng	二聖
Fahua jing	法華經
fengshui	風水
foxing	佛性
fozhuang	佛妝
Fujian	福建
Gansu	甘肅
Goguryeo	高句麗, 고구려
Guan Daosheng	管道昇
Guanyin	觀音
Gujin tushu jicheng	古今圖書集成

155

Han (river)	漢
Hangzhou	杭州
Hongwu	洪武
Hu (clan)	胡
Hu Shi	胡適
Huang Sheng	黃昇
Huayan jing	華嚴經
Huizong	徽宗
hujue	戶絕
jian	賤
jili	笄禮
Jing'an	靖安
Jingang jing	金剛經
jingbiao	旌表
Juye	巨野
Kaifeng	開封
Li (empress)	李
Li Qingzhao	李清照
Li Song	李嵩
Liang Hongyu	梁紅玉
liantian	奩田
Liji	禮記
Lin Yutang	林語堂
Linji	臨濟
Liu (empress)	劉
Longnü	龍女
Lü	呂
Luoyang	洛陽
Ma (Semu family)	馬
Ma Yuan	馬原
Mazu	媽祖
Miaodao	妙道
Miaoshan	妙善
Mingde	明德
Mo (madam)	莫
Mo taifuren jiaxun	莫太夫人家訓
Moji	摩笄
Naitō Konan	内藤湖南
nei	内
neidan	内丹
Niangzi	娘子

Ningzong	寧宗
nühu	女戶
nüshi	女使
nüxia	女俠
nüzhu	女主
Ouyang Xiu	歐陽修
pincai	聘財
Pucheng	浦城
qie	妾
qing	情
Qingming	清明
Quan Song shi	全宋詩
Quanzhen	全真
Renzong	仁宗
rubi	乳婢
Semu	色目
shamini	沙彌尼
Shangyuan	上元
Sheng Mu	聖母
shichamona	式叉摩那
Shijing	詩經
shinü	仕女
Shizong	世宗
Sima Guang	司馬光
Siming	四明
sui	歲
Taiping guangji	太平廣記
Taizong	太宗
Taizu	太祖
Tianhou	天后
wai	外
Wang Juzheng	王居正
Wang Qinghui	王清惠
Wanggu	汪古
wasi	瓦肆
Wei (empress)	韋
Wenzong	文宗
Wu	吳
Wuzong	武宗
Wu Zetian	武則天
Wu Zhao	吳嬰，吳曌

Xi	奚
Xia	夏
Xiaojing	孝經
Xi Xia	西夏
Xiang (empress)	向
xingzhe	行者
Xiao	蕭
Xuanyi (empress)	宣懿
Yan Rui	嚴蕊
Yang (empress)	楊
Yang Miaozhen	楊妙真
Yanguo (princess)	兗國
Yelü	耶律
Yi Jian zhi	夷堅志
Yijing	易經
yijue	義絕
youpoyi	優婆夷
Yuan	袁
Yuanshi	元史
Yutai xinyong	玉臺新詠
Zhang Yuniang	張玉娘
Zhao (of Juye)	晁
Zhaorui Shunsheng	昭睿順聖
Zheng Yunduan	鄭允端
Zhenzong	真宗
Zhongshu	中書
Zhu Shuzhen	朱淑真
Zhu Yuanzhang	朱元璋
Zi Gu	紫姑

Notes

INTRODUCTION

1. Some feminist theorists promote a concept called performativity, arguing that although social context bounds a person's life, she can nevertheless still exert agency to affect this context and decide how to interact with it. Yang, "A Pictorial Autobiography," 269–270.

2. Tackett, "Great Clansmen."

3. Miyakawa, "An Outline of the Naito Hypothesis"; Fogel, *Politics and Sinology*.

4. Yi, "Social Status," 132–133, provides tables that show the chapters dedicated to the biographies of empresses, consorts, princesses, consort kin, and virtuous women in the standard histories, including those for the Song and Yuan dynasties. Ni et al., *Zuijia nüxing miaoxie cidian*, defines a large number of Chinese terms traditionally used to describe women.

5. Chang and Saussy, *Women Writers of Traditional China*, 113.

6. For example, between 1207 and 1236, the registered population of Cizhou decreased 85 percent, the registered population of Jinan decreased 82 percent, and the population of Yan'an decreased 89 percent. Many communities experienced similar depopulation. Liu, "Jindai hukou yanjiu," 95.

7. Von Glahn, *The Economic History of China*, 216–219.

8. Qi, *Songdai jingjishi*, 44–57.

9. Von Glahn, *The Economic History of China*, 208–209, 216–219, 225, 242, 245.

10. Tackett, *Destruction of the Medieval Chinese Aristocracy*.

11. Zhang, *Hunyin yu shehui*, 125–126, 139–140.

12. Bossler, *Powerful Relations*, 12.

13. Duan, *Tangdai funü diwei yanjiu*, 124–125.

14. Birge, "Chu Hsi and Women's Education," 325.

15. Bailey, "Chinese Women Go Global," 244.

16. Isay, "To Regain Self-Affirmation," 111.

17. Bernhardt, "A Ming-Qing Transition."

18. Biran, "Periods of Non-Han Rule," 129, 133.

19. Rossabi, "Notes on Mongol Influences on the Ming Dynasty," 200.

20. Biran, "Introduction: Nomadic Culture," 2.

21. Smith, "Impressions of the Song-Yuan-Ming Transition," 79, 81; Rossabi, "Notes on Mongol Influences on the Ming Dynasty," 201, 203–206.

CHAPTER 1

1. This prohibition was copied directly from the *Tang Code*. During the Tang, "base people" (*jianmin* 賤民) of degraded status were officially referred to as "sundry families" (*zalei zhi jia* 雜類之家). This group included slaves and prostitutes as well as their descendants. Zhang, *Songdai hunyin jiazu*, 2–4.

2. Two poor men would sometimes share a wife, or else a husband would temporarily rent out his wife to another man. In 972, Song Taizu issued an edict prohibiting polyandry. Zhang, *Songdai hunyin jiazu*, 142–143; Zhang, "Liang Song shiqi," 458–459. Polyandry emerged in various societies for different reasons. It is often a pragmatic kinship strategy used to cope with a shortage of resources. Majumdar, *Himalayan Polyandry*, 75; Peter, *A Study of Polyandry*, 54.

3. McKnight, *Law and Order in Sung China*, 76, 401. An exception was made for women convicted of magical poisoning, which was punished by exile.

4. Zhang, *Hunyin yu shehui*, 50–58.

5. In 995, Song Taizong prohibited interethnic marriages. Zhang, *Hunyin yu shehui*, 41.

6. Ebrey, "Conceptions of the Family," 220–221, 232.

7. Li, "Songdai nühu de tedian," 51–52, 54. For Tang dynasty precedents, see Deng, "Women in Turfan," 93; Luo, *Tongju gongcai*, 32, 42–49.

8. Weitz, "Art and Family Identity," 426–428.

9. Zang, "Women and the Transmission of Confucian Culture," 127.

10. Ebrey, "Women, Money, and Class," 13.

11. Knapp, *Selfless Offspring*, 16.

12. Zhang, *Jiating shihua*, 91–93.

13. Weitz, "Art and Family Identity," 427.

14. Ōsawa, "Tō Sō henkaku." Among the fictional families described in the narrative collection *Taiping guangji*, those of officials and literati have an average of 5.2 members that include 2.8 children (1.8 sons and 0.9 daughters). Families of wealthy landowners have 5.6 members, which include 2.3 children (0.6 sons and 1.1 daughters). Commoner families have 3.9 members, which include 1.4 children (1.0 sons and 0.3 daughters). Slave families have 3.6 members, which include 1.6 children (1.0 sons and 0.6 daughters). Peasant families have 4.5 members, which include 1.8 children. Merchant families have 2.4 members, which include 0.7 children. Wang, "Bei Song funü de hunyin," 77, analyzes the information provided in various studies of Northern Song dynasty epitaphs. He finds that among a sample of ninety-two women recorded in epitaphs, those who bore children had an average of 5.5 children each—3.3 boys and 2.2 girls.

15. Ōsawa, "Tō Sō henkaku," 82–83; Ōsawa, *Tō Sō jidai no kazoku*, 173–184. Among the narratives collected in *Yi Jian zhi*, families of literati and officials have 4.7 members on average, which include 2.2 children (1.6 sons and 0.4 daughters). Wealthy families have 4.7 members, which include 2.5 children (2.1 sons and 0.4 daughters). Commoner families have 4.0 members, which include 1.4 children (1.0 boys and 0.2 girls). Families of hired laborers have 4.6 members, which include 2.4 children (2.0 boys and 0.2 girls). Peasant families have 4.9 members, which include 2.2 children. And merchant families have 3.5 members, which include 1.4 children.

16. Dardess, "The Cheng Communal Family," 7–8, 45.

17. Wang, "Songdai jiaci yanjiu," 76–77. Chang, "Theories about the Formation," outlines the various theories of lineage formation that historians in China have put forward. For the distinction between lineage and clan in the Chinese context, see Grafflin, "Social Order," 49.

18. Ebrey, "Early Stages of Descent Group Organization," 22; Bray, *Technology and Gender*, 154.

19. Zurndorfer, "The Hsin-an Ta-tsu-chih," 154.

20. Warner, Lee, and Lee, "Social Organization."

21. Ebrey, "Women, Money, and Class," 36.

22. Watson, "Anthropological Overview," 283.

23. Walton, "Kinship, Marriage and Status," 35–37; Bossler, "A Daughter Is a Daughter," 97–98.

24. Zhang, *Hunyin yu shehui*, 145–161.

25. Liu and Zhang, "Cong 'yi zi qi zhi.'"

26. Bossler, "A Daughter Is a Daughter," 82.

27. Wang, "Bei Song funü," 75–76.

28. Wang, "Bei Song funü," 76–77; Zhang, *Songdai hunyin jiazu*, 39–43; Tian, *Songdai shangren jiating*, 86–88.

29. Ebrey, "Shifts in Marriage Finance," 68–78. Wang, "Tangdai jiazhuang xiaofei kao," describes the rising value of dowries during the Tang.

30. Ebrey, "Conceptions of the Family," 219–220; Walton, "Kinship, Marriage and Status," 68.

31. Huang, "Songdai Xiuzhou wangzu," 118.

32. Bossler, *Powerful Relations*, 82–84.

33. Li, "Songdai Pucheng Wushi."

34. Chang and Saussy, *Women Writers of Traditional China*, 133.

35. Yang, "Zhuangyuan beihou de nüxing."

36. Zhang, *Hunyin yu shehui*, 128–129.

37. Liang, *Sanshan zhi*, 39:632.

38. Sima, *Sima shi shuyi*, 3:33; Yang, "'Fu li' yihuo 'cong su,'" 52.

39. Li, "Songdai Fujian lu," 54–55.

40. Wang, "Bei Song shimen yinqin."

41. Zhang, *Hunyin yu shehui*, 47–50, 96–113.

42. Li, "Songdai ruzhuihun luelun"; Bossler, *Powerful Relations*, 157.

43. Katsuyama, *Chūgoku Sō*, 129.

44. Wang, "Bei Song funü," 75.

45. Song, "Songdai shiren jieceng."

46. Bossler, *Powerful Relations*, 163.

47. Huang, "Songdai Xiuzhou wangzu," 115–116.

48. Wan, *Tangdai nüxing*, 14–15, concludes that women married at an average age of 15.91 *sui* in the early Tang, 16.4 in the mid-Tang, and 17.4 in the dynasty's final phase. Weng, "Tangdai shiren de hunyin yu jiating," 366, argues that the marriage age for women increased more modestly during the Tang, rising from 15.3 to 15.6 *sui*. The marriage age of men rose from 23 to 27 during the same period.

49. Xu, *Songdai shizu funü*, 53.

50. Xue et al., *Liang Song fazhi tonglun*, 311–312. All ages are given in *sui*, which differs somewhat from the Western method of reckoning age. For a description of the ways the Chinese calculated people's ages, see Chen, "Age Inflation and Deflation"; Elvin, "Blood and Statistics," 178–183.

51. Ebrey, *Chu Hsi's* Family Rituals, 45–47; Zheng, "Songdai nannü chuhun nianling," 120.

52. Zhang, *Jiating shihua*, 94; Zheng, "Songdai nannü chuhun nianling," 119.

53. Xu, *Songdai shizu funü*, 56.

54. Wang, "Bei Song funü," 74–75. Of women in this sample of epitaphs, 8.2 percent were from imperial clans, 80.6 percent were from official families, and 11.2 percent were from other backgrounds.

55. Zheng, "Songdai nannü chuhun nianling," 121–122.

56. Wang and Jia, "Jindai jiating renkou shuliang," 99–100.

57. Zheng, "Songdai nannü chuhun nianling," 123.

58. Ebrey, *The Inner Quarters*, 155.

59. Chen, "Songdai nüxing wanhun"; Zheng, "Songdai nannü chuhun nianling," 121–122; Li, "Songdai Fujian lu," 54.

60. Guo et al., "Historical Demography for Late Marriage in China," 116–118.

61. Yang, "'Fu li' yihuo 'cong su,'" 51–52.

62. Ebrey, *Chu Hsi's* Family Rituals, 48–64, gives a detailed description of an idealized marriage ceremony that Zhu believed conformed with the classic rites. De Pee, *The Writing of Weddings*, analyzes the ways that writers described weddings during the Tang and Song.

63. Guo, *Songdai fazhi yanjiu*, 426–431; Xue et al., *Liang Song fazhi tonglun*, 313–314; You, *Songdai minfu*, 11–17. Yang, "Dunhuang chutu," 34, discusses the evolution of terminology in divorce law. For a summary of Tang divorce law, see Guogang, "Family Building in Inner Quarters," 28–35.

64. Yanagita, "Sōdai saiban," 6–9.

65. Chaffee, *Branches of Heaven*, 83.

66. Zang, "Women and the Transmission of Confucian Culture," 131.

67. Guo, *Songdai fazhi yanjiu*, 427–428; Xue et al., *Liang Song fazhi tonglun*, 314; Zhang, *Songdai hunyin jiazu*, 24–25. For medieval precedents, see Liu, "Lun Tangdai de 'yijue.'"

68. McKnight, *Law and Order in Sung China*, 99–100. If a husband killed his wife, this would be treated as an ordinary homicide.

69. Ebrey, *The Inner Quarters*, 158–160.

70. Luo, "Cong fu fu ci," 96–97.
71. Tang, "Nanquan shehui xia de nüxing."
72. Rao and Jianli, "Qing yu li de bianzou," 1–2.
73. Tian, *Songdai shangren jiating*, 112, 129, 131–137.
74. Liu, *Songdai minjian wushu yanjiu*, 153–156. Posthumous weddings were an extremely ancient custom, dating back to the Shang dynasty. Song, *Xia Shang shehui shenghuo shi*, 178.
75. Xu, "Gender and Burial"; Xu, *Crossing the Gate*, 213–260. Empresses were interred near their spouses in the imperial burial ground. Kuhn, *The Age of Confucian Rule*, 156. Although traditional Jurchen burials differed from Chinese procedures, normative Jin practices were based on Chinese precedents combined with Buddhist beliefs. Wang, "Jindai funü sangzang." Tackett, *Origins of the Chinese Nation*, 211–245, compares Song and Khitan mortuary practices.
76. Hou and Goodman, "Rethinking Chinese Kinship."
77. Birge, "Chu Hsi and Women's Education," 347.
78. Xu, *Songdai shizu funü*, 69–70, 81–82.
79. Ebrey, "Women in the Kinship System," 116.
80. Ebrey, "Women in the Kinship System," 120.
81. Bossler, *Powerful Relations*, 161–162. This was not a new custom. During the Tang, men routinely had an extremely close relationship with their maternal uncles. Tackett, *Destruction of the Medieval Chinese Aristocracy*, 131, 136, 174.
82. Liu, "Yuandai muqin chengwei," 74–76, lists the various words for "mother" used during the Yuan dynasty. The terms in common use differed by region and era.
83. Chang and Saussy, *Women Writers of Traditional China*, 128.
84. Zhou and Wang, *Roushun zhi xiang*, 49; Zhang, *Tangdai jiating yu shehui*, 2–5; Yao, *Tangdai funü de shengming licheng*, 326–327, 336; Yao, "Women in Portraits," 167; Yao, "Childbirth and Maternal Mortality"; Zhang, *Jiating shihua*, 70; Guo, Zhao, and Jia, "Tangdai gongzhu zinü kao," 172; Fei, *Tangdai renkou dili*, 79.
85. Fang, "Songdai baoyu wufa shulue," 57–58.
86. Ebrey, "Shifts in Marriage Finance," 77; Zhang, *Hunyin yu shehui*, 98–104; Birge, *Women, Property and Confucian Reaction*, 31–37, gives an overview of Song dowry practices. Mao, *Qingdai jiazhuang yanjiu*, 260–276, argues that dowry and infanticide were closely linked throughout Chinese history.
87. Wang, "Bei Song funü de hunyin," 77. According to a previous study of Song epitaphs, women had an average of 6.5 recorded children. This study of ninety-two epitaphs of women who bore children shows that they bore an average of 5.5 children —3.3 boys and 2.2 girls. (The author's math regarding the relative percentages of boys and girls is wrong. I provide corrected figures in the text.)
88. Wu, "Songdai shiren pingjun siwang nianling," 174–176.
89. Li, "Songdai Fujian lu," 54.
90. Liu, "Guiguai wenhua yu xingbie."
91. Liu, "Cong sunzi huaitai."
92. Liu, "Zuo wei Mengxue."
93. Chaffee, *Branches of Heaven*, 59.

94. Liu, "Cong falü jiufen." For Tang dynasty precedent, see Johnson, *The T'ang Code*, 1:74.

95. Yanagita, "Sōdai saiban," 9–10.

96. McKnight, *Law and Order in Sung China*, 501.

97. Hu and Zhu, "Songdai sifa dui jimu," 101, 103.

98. Ebrey, "Concubines in Song China"; Liu, *Songdai de zongjiao*, 139–262. Xu, "Shixi Yuandai funü," 109–110, discusses Yuan dynasty laws regarding concubines.

99. Ebrey, "Women, Money, and Class," 38.

100. Ebrey, "Concubines in Song China," 44.

101. Liu, *Songdai de zongjiao*, 200–201, 205–209.

102. Yanagita, "Sōdai saiban," 3–5.

103. Guo, "Songdai nüshi zai jiatingzhong."

104. Zhu et al., *Liao Song Xi Xia Jin*, 107–108; Liu, *Songdai de zongjiao*, 162, 164.

105. Ebrey, "Women, Money, and Class," 18, 21.

106. Chaffee, *Branches of Heaven*, 58–59.

107. Ebrey, "Women, Money, and Class," 15.

108. Zhang and Fan, "Cong nügui gushi," 30, 33.

109. Wang, *Shijia dazu*.

110. Zhang, *Liaodai shehuishi*, 131.

111. Holmgren, "Imperial Marriage," 87.

112. Shimada, *Ryōdai shakaishi kenkyū*, 182–198, gives a concise overview of Khitan kinship. Also see Zhang, *Liaodai shehuishi*, 131; Liu and Hu, "Liaodai hunyin zhuangkuang."

113. Qi, "Liaodai Han guan shangceng."

114. Chen and Gao, "Liaodai Qidan jiating."

115. Tuo et al., *Liaoshi*, 10:112.

116. Tuo et al., *Liaoshi*, 23:275.

117. Wu, *Liao Jin shehui*, 38–42.

118. Wang, "Jindai nüxing zhenjieguan," 99.

119. Wu, *Liao Jin shehui*, 288–289; Du, *Liao Jin shi yanjiu*, 263; Wang, "Jindai nüxing zhenjieguan," 99.

120. Tao, *The Jurchen*, 10; Wu, *Liao Jin shehui*, 289; Liu, "Jindai Nüzhen de hunyin," 87–88.

121. Du, *Liao Jin shi yanjiu*, 255.

122. Wang, "Ershi shiji yilai Jindai funü yanjiu."

123. Tao, *The Jurchen*, 95–96, 98.

124. Wang and Jia, "Jindai jiating renkou shuliang," 98, 100. Various estimates range from 5.6 to 6.71 family members.

125. Wang and Jia, "Jindai jiating renkou shuliang," 102.

126. Holmgren, "Observations on Marriage," 135, 137.

127. McMahon, *Celestial Women*, 63.

128. Qiao, "Guanyu Yuandai," 81.

129. Zhang, *Hunyin yu shehui*, 45; Pan, "Yuandai Jiangnan diqu Menggu," 132–134.

130. Zhang, "Yuandai shaoshu minzu."

131. Li, "Luelun Yuandai," 76.

CHAPTER 2

1. Wu, "Yang Miaozhen."

2. Altenburger, *The Sword or the Needle*.

3. Luo, "Lun Songmo nüshiren."

4. Chang and Saussy, *Women Writers of Traditional China*, 391.

5. Davis, *From Warhorses to Ploughshares*, 14–18.

6. Ching-Chung, "Palace Women in the Northern Sung," 81; Ebrey, "Rethinking the Imperial Harem," 187; Ebrey, *Emperor Huizong*, 8.

7. These ages are *sui*. Fan, "Songdai huangzi renshu," 75. The insalubrious conditions of the Song palace were not unique. Ottoman princes also had a high rate of infant mortality in spite of the grandness of their surroundings. Freely, *Inside the Seraglio*, 189. Palaces were often very crowded places, which probably affected standards of hygiene.

8. Liu, "Songdai yueshu houfei," 43–44.

9. Ching-Chung, "Palace Women in the Northern Sung," 91–93. Zhu et al., *Liao Song Xi Xia Jin*, 104–105, lists the titles of Song palace ladies.

10. Ching-Chung, "Palace Women in the Northern Sung," 80–81, 84.

11. Bai, "Qianyi Songdai waimingfu."

12. Cheng, "Jinru Songdai huangshi."

13. Chaffee, *Branches of Heaven*, 35.

14. Chang and Saussy, *Women Writers of Traditional China*, 110.

15. Ebrey, *Emperor Huizong*, 307–308.

16. Ebrey, *Emperor Huizong*, 80.

17. Xie, "Songdai gongting nüshiren zuopin gailan."

18. Xie, "Songdai gongting nüshiren zuopin leibie fenxi."

19. Huang, "Nan Song houfei xinian," gives a detailed chronology of the lives of Southern Song empresses.

20. Han, "Wu Zetian gushi."

21. Zhang, *Hunyin yu shehui*, 132–139; Zhang, *Songdai hunyin jiazu*, 439–458.

22. Liu, "Songdai yueshu houfei," 45.

23. Zhang, *Hunyin yu shehui*, 105, 109; Zhang, *Songdai hunyin jiazu*, 44.

24. Chaffee, "Marriage of Sung Imperial Clanswomen," 139, 145.

25. Chaffee, *Branches of Heaven*, 10–11, 32.

26. McMahon, "Women Rulers in Imperial China," 202. For edicts concerning Song empresses dowager, see Anonymous, *Song da zhaoling ji*, chaps. 11–17; for edicts regarding empresses, chapters 18–20; for lesser imperial consorts, chapters 21–24; for princesses, chapters 36–40.

27. Liu, "Wei Jin yihuan shijia," 33. This criticism had limits. Most people did not blame women for the fall of the Northern Song. They usually condemned the malfeasance of Emperor Huizong and his cronies. Ebrey, *Emperor Huizong*, 313.

28. Qi, "Songdai zhuizun huanghou."

29. McMahon, "Women Rulers in Imperial China," 203; Lee, *Empresses, Art & Agency*, 52–69; McMahon, *Celestial Women*, 32; Hartman, "Cao Xun," 76. Empress Liu was also an enthusiastic patron of the Maitreya cult. Liu, "Empress Liu's 'Icon of Maitreya.'"

30. Social scientists refer to the use of material culture to carry out social strategies as materialization. Earle and Kristiansen, "Introduction," 8, 14.

31. Chang and Saussy, *Women Writers of Traditional China*, 110.

32. Yuan, "Nansong Lin'an Yang," describes archaeological evidence for the mansions of Empress Yang and other Song empresses.

33. Ching-Chung, "Power and Prestige," 99.

34. Lee, *Empresses, Art & Agency*, 18–19.

35. Liu, "Songdai houfei," 429.

36. Holmgren, "Imperial Marriage," 76, 88–89; Lee, *Empresses, Art & Agency*, 232–233.

37. Liu, "Songdai houfei," 432.

38. Chaffee, "The Rise and Regency of Empress Liu"; Luo, "Song Zhangxiao Mingsu Taihou"; McMahon, *Celestial Women*, 10–14.

39. Liu, "Songdai teshu," 103–104.

40. Ebrey, "Empress Xiang," 196.

41. Liu, "Bei Song nüzhu zhengzhi."

42. Tuo et al., *Songshi*, 301:20512.

43. Lee, *Empresses, Art & Agency*, 41, 48–49.

44. Ji, *Politics and Conservatism*, 77–86.

45. Zhang, *Hunyin yu shehui*, 106, provides a table that gives basic information about Tang and Song princesses.

46. Guo, "Tangdai gongzhu de jiating shenghuo."

47. Ebrey, *Emperor Huizong*, 36.

48. Zhang, "Songdai funü de zaijia wenti," 62.

49. Zhuang, "Songdai gongzhu quanli."

50. Holmgren, "Imperial Marriage," 80–81.

51. Zhang, *Liaodai shehuishi*, 131; Wang, *Shijia dazu*, 29–30, 36, 38, 54–55. A chart on pp. 36–37 gives the family backgrounds of Liao dynasty empresses. Shi, *Liaochao houzu*, gives a detailed description of the Liao consort clan and their relations with the imperial clan. Also Shi Fengchun, "Qidan waiqi."

52. Liu and Hu, "Liaodai hunyin zhuangkuang," 142.

53. Holmgren, "Imperial Marriage," 80–81.

54. Sun, "Liaodai guizu lianhun."

55. Huang, *Liaodai wenshi xintan*, 292. A chart on pp. 48–50 of Wang, *Shijia dazu*, gives information regarding the marriages of Liao princesses. Liaoning and Fuxin, "Liaoning Fuxin xian Liaodai Pingyuan Gongzhu," is the site report for the tomb of the Pingyuan 平原 princess. Qing, "Liaodai Chenguo Gongzhu," describes the joint burial of the Chenguo 陳果 princess and her husband. This tomb contained many rich ornaments.

56. Hu, "Liaodai houfei"; Du and Zhao, "Qidan nüxing canzheng"; Wang, "Shixi Liaodai Shulü Hou," 59–61, 65; Wu, "Qidan Xiao Taihou"; Zhang and Zhang, *Qidan jinguo*; Liu, "Liao wangchao Qidanzu." Zhang, "Liaodai waimingfu shilu tanxi," provides a comprehensive list of titles used by elite Liao women, including empresses, consorts, palace concubines, princesses, and the wives of high officials.

57. Wright, "Political and Military Power," 325–326.

58. Li and Li, *Xiao taihou pingzhuan*; Wright, "Political and Military Power," 327.

59. Zheng, "Lun Qidan nüxing"; Kuhn, *The Age of Confucian Rule*, 148. Sun, "Qidanzu de maju yu weilie," describes gear for horseback riding and hunting that archaeologists discovered in the tomb of the Chenguo 陳果 princess of Liao.

60. Wright, "Political and Military Power," 331–332; Liu, "Liaodai jiechu," 56–57.

61. Wang, *Shijia dazu*, 81; Shi, "Rujia sixiang."

62. Zhou, "Qidan Chengtian Taihou."

63. Tao, *The Jurchen*, 95–96.

64. Sang, "Jinshi Wan Yanshi," 272, 286–288; Xia and Zhao, "Liao Jin Qidan Nüzhen"; Xia, *Jindai Qidanren yanjiu*, 131, 138–145. On pp. 132–138 the author discusses Khitan women who became Jin empresses and minor consorts.

65. Song, *Jindai de shehui shenghuo*, 85; Xia and Zhao, "Liao Jin Qidan Nüzhen," 77; Wang, "Jindai fei Nützen," 300–301, 305–312; McMahon, *Celestial Women*, 44–45; Wang, "Ershi shiji yilai Jindai funü yanjiu," 110–121. About 30 percent of Jin empresses were not ethnic Jurchens. They came from other northeastern peoples.

66. Zhang, "Qianxi Jindai houfei."

67. Ebrey, *Emperor Huizong*, 458, 460.

68. Zhang, "Jindai hougong zhidu chutan"; Zhao and Wang, "Jindai pinguan mingfu."

69. Lan, *Jindai jiaoyu yanjiu*, 97–98.

70. Tao, *The Jurchen*, 69–70.

71. Broadbridge, *Women and the Making of the Mongol Empire*, 2–3, 30, 32–35, 94–95, 101–102, 104, 107–108, 137.

72. Barfield, *Perilous Frontier*, 208; Miyawaki-Okada, "The Role of Women," 147.

73. The regency of Töregene Khatun (d. 1246) exemplifies this sort of active female regency. Barfield, *Perilous Frontier*, 214.

74. Weatherford, *Secret History*, 3.

75. Weatherford, *Secret History*, 20, 27–30, 35, 47, 70–72.

76. McMahon, *Celestial Women*, 58; McMahon, "Women Rulers in Imperial China," 211.

77. Holmgren, "Imperial Marriage," 84–86.

78. Xi and Temuer, "Yuandai Gaoli gongnü zhidu."

79. Broadbridge, *Women and the Making of the Mongol Empire*, 237, 239.

80. Holmgren, "Imperial Marriage," 58.

CHAPTER 3

1. Von Glahn, *The Economic History of China*, 269, 275.

2. Japanese scholars have led the debates on the relationship between property ownership and kinship in China. A consensus has yet to be reached. For summaries of these complicated debates, see Shiga, "Family Property," 109–110; Bernhardt, *Women and Property in China*, 9–10. Also see Chen, "Cong jingji guandian"; Xing, *Tang Song fenjia zhidu*, 82. Birge, *Women, Property and Confucian Reaction*, 38–40, 66, contends that women controlled more property during the Song than at any other time in Chinese history.

3. Wang and Zhao, "'Wu si huo' yu 'xu si cai,'" 160.

4. Wang and Zhao, "'Wu si huo' yu 'xu si cai,'" 161, 163.

5. Bossler, *Powerful Relations*, 17–18.

6. Cui, "Songdai nüxing de jingji huodong."

7. Zhu and Chen, "Songdai weirenmu," 111–112.

8. Wang, "Songdai chujianü," 86–88.

9. Bao and Lü, "Funü zhi ren yu waishi," 264–268; Guang, "Songdai funü de cishan houdong"; Zhang, "Songdai funü lianchan," 86.

10. Liu and Ren, "Songdai nüxing shishang xiaofei."

11. Ebrey, *The Inner Quarters*, 85; Wang, "Songdai hunyin zhong," 138; Deng and Gu, "Jinyin shipin."

12. Ebrey, "Shifts in Marriage Finance," 102.

13. Lou, "Nü hede nan zhi ban."

14. Zhang, "Cong Songdai hunyinfa."

15. Ebrey, "Shifts in Marriage Finance," 78–79; Ebrey, *The Inner Quarters*, 103; Ebrey, "Women, Money, and Class," 12–13; Su, "Lun Songdai houlian de yuanyin."

16. The shift from bridewealth to dowry was not unique to China. A similar process occurred in southern Europe, apparently for similar reasons. Hughes, "From Brideprice to Dowry," 288. The similarities of these two cases illuminate the underlying causes for this sort of transition in marriage finance.

17. Lü, "Bridal Dowry Land," 109.

18. Zhu, "Songdai jiazhuang chutan," 119; Mao, *Qingdai jiazhuang*, 11–13, 26–29, 147–158, describes Qing dynasty practices, which are very well documented. During the Qing, dowry customs were extremely varied. Song society seems to have had a similar diversity of practices.

19. Li, "Songdai Fujian lu," 52–53.

20. Lü, "Bridal Dowry Land," 106–124; Zhang, "Songdai funü lianchan," 80–81.

21. Chaffee, "Marriage of Sung Imperial Clanswomen," 142–144.

22. Zhang, "Songdai funü lianchan," 89–92.

23. Ebrey, "Women in the Kinship System," 117–118; Wang and Zhao, "'Wu si huo' yu 'xu si cai,'" 162–163; Zhang, "Songdai funü lianchan," 86.

24. Ebrey, "Women, Money, and Class," 16; Guo, *Songdai minjian falü*, 294–299.

25. Ebrey, "Shifts in Marriage Finance," 75–76; Birge, *Women, Property and Confucian Reaction*, 151, 161; Gao and Zhang, "Muqin shengqian de lianchan quanli," 118–119.

26. Ebrey, "Shifts in Marriage Finance," 77; Ebrey, *The Inner Quarters*, 101; Lü, "Bridal Dowry Land," 106, 111–112; Li, "Songdai Fujian lu," 54.

27. Ebrey, "Women, Money, and Class," 25–27.

28. Mao, *Qingdai jiazhuang*, 260–276, discusses this issue during the Qing, when it was much better documented. The situation during the Song seems to have been very similar.

29. Lou, "Nü hede nan zhi ban," 129, incorrectly argues that rising dowry resulted in a decline in women's inheritance rights.

30. Bernhardt, *Women and Property in China*, 2–3, 12–13; Birge, "Inheritance and Property Law," 852–853.

31. Li, "Shixi jingji zhengce," 890–893, 897; Bernhardt, *Women and Property in China*, 13, 19.

32. Bernhardt, *Women and Property in China*, 2–3.

33. Yang and Yu, "Songdai nüxing caichan," describes the inheritance rights of married women in detail.

34. Lou, "Nü hede nan zhi ban," 128.

35. Yuan, "Songdai nüxing caichanquan shulun," describes the inheritance rights of daughters in great detail. Also see Bernhardt, *Women and Property in China*, 24, 31–33; Birge, "Women and Property in Sung Dynasty China," 105, 120–124; Birge, *Women, Property and Confucian Reaction*, 76, 91, 97–98; Liu, "Nan Song zaishinü fenchan tanyi"; Liu, "Songdai fenchanfa."

36. Bernhardt, *Women and Property in China*, 31–32; Dai, *Songdai fazhi chutan*, 307; Guo, *Songdai falü yu shehui*, 232; Zhang, "Songdai caichan jicheng," 42–43; Takahashi, "Orphaned Daughters," 131, 135.

37. Lou, "Nü hede nan zhi ban," 129.

38. Shi, "Songdai zhuixu."

39. Guo, "Songdai nüer de jiachan"; Takahashi, "Orphaned Daughters," 136.

40. Zhang, *Jiating shihua*, 108; Xue et al., *Liang Song fazhi tonglun*, 320–321.

41. Bernhardt, *Women and Property in China*, 48.

42. Bossler, *Powerful Relations*, 20.

43. Gao, "Songdai funü de caichan," 4–6, documents land sales initiated by widows.

44. Zhang, "Songdai funü lianchan," 83.

45. Cui, "Songdai nüxing de jingji huodong," 128; Bernhardt, *Women and Property in China*, 52–53.

46. Du, "Songdai yilai guafu lisiquan."

47. Guo, *Songdai falü yu shehui*, 243.

48. Ebrey, "Early Stages of Descent Group Organization," 43.

49. Wang and Lü, "Songdai qie zhi caichanquan yanjiu"; Lau, "Changes to Women's Legal Rights," 707.

50. Liu and Yang, "Songdai shangye zhong nüxing jingkuang," 133.

51. Kuhn, *The Age of Confucian Rule*, 179.

52. Chen, *Songdai minfu de shenghuo qingtai*, 96–98.

53. Hinsch, "The Origins of Separation," 598–600.

54. McKnight, *Law and Order in Sung China*, 402–403.

55. Yan and Yang, "Lun Songdai caisangshi," 165.

56. Tajima, "Sōdai no jōnō"; Zhan, "Songdai funü jingji," 98–99; Tian, *Songdai shangren jiating*, 126; Chen, *Songdai minfu*, 98–112.

57. Kuhn, *The Age of Confucian Rule*, 220–221.

58. Tajima, "Sōdai no jōnō," 19–23; Zhan, "Songdai funü jingji," 100; Chen, *Songdai minfu*, 83–95.

59. Xu, *Crossing the Gate*, 95.

60. Tian, *Songdai shangren jiating*, 127.

61. Tian, *Songdai shangren jiating*, 106–109.

62. Goyama, *Ming Qing shidai de nüxing*, 460–465.

63. Ji, "Songdai shibing," 17–18.

64. Liu, "Songdai shangye zhong de nüxing."

65. Cheng, *Songdai diyu wenhua*, 30–32.

66. Quan, "Songdai nüzi zhiye yu shengji"; Zhang, "Songdai nüxing jingshang tanxi."

67. Liu and Yang, "Songdai shangye zhong nüxing jingkuang," 132–135.

68. Liu, "Songdai shangye zhong de nüxing," 102.

69. Katsuyama, *Chūgoku Sō*, 67–73.

70. Wang, "Songdai fuchan yixue"; Liu, "Songdai shangye zhong de nüxing," 103.

71. Cheng, "Songdai rumu."

72. Nomura, "Su Shi 'baomu Yangshi muzhiming' zhi mi."

73. Quan, "Songdai nüzi zhiye yu shengji," 199–204; Yan, *Zhongguo mingji*, 59–60; Yang and Liu, "Songdai guojia"; Bossler, "Floating Sleeves," 1–2.

74. Yang and Liu, "Songdai guojia," 100–103; Guo, "Songdai jiaji zhidu."

75. Jiren, "Lun Zhongguo gudai biaoyan," 48–52; Yan, *Zhongguo mingji*, 52, 61–63. As before, there were also female performers in the palace. Ebrey, *Emperor Huizong*, 294–296.

76. Bossler, "Fantasies of Fidelity," 163.

77. Lin, "Songdai wenxue zuopin," 86.

78. Tian, *Songdai shangren jiating*, 93–102.

79. Chang and Saussy, *Women Writers of Traditional China*, 107.

80. Bossler, "Fantasies of Fidelity," 164–165.

81. Xiong, "Lun Yuan sanqu zhong," 101–102, 104.

82. Chang and Saussy, *Women Writers of Traditional China*, 124.

CHAPTER 4

1. Lu, "Women's Ascetic Practices," 73–82.

2. Lu, "Women's Ascetic Practices," 85–87.

3. Liu, "Song shi yuanxiaojie," 129–130.

4. Fang, *Wu wenhua shiyu*; Fang, "Songdai nüxing chong bing." Besides healing, shamans undertook many other activities as well. See Chen, "Shilun Songdai wuxi." Major, "Characteristics of Late Chu Religion," 136, defines shamanism as it was traditionally practiced within the context of Chinese culture.

5. Hansen, *Changing Gods in Medieval China*, 66; Liu, *Songdai minjian wushu yanjiu*, 77–84.

6. Li, "Wuxi yu Songdai shehui," 38–46, explains how shamanistic lore was transmitted during the Song.

7. Li, "Wuxi yu Songdai shehui," 49–52. Ding, "Songdai jinhui wuwu," gives a detailed chronological analysis of these many prohibitions.

8. Fang, "Songdai nüxing de juwu huodong"; Li, "Songdai jinwu xingyi."

9. Chen, "Yuandai de wuxi yu wushu."

10. Watson, "Standardization of the Gods," 293–294; Hansen, *Changing Gods in Medieval China*, 145–147; Li, "Shilun Yuandai de Mazu chongbai"; Huang, "Yuandai Tianfei chongbai"; Wang, "Yuandai haishang caoyun."

11. Lee, *Empresses, Art & Agency*, 23, 27–30; Li, "Qiyanshan Songdai 'huiying Shengmu.'"

12. Chai, "Shilun Songdai de shuixian wenhua"; Liang, "Songdai wenren dui Hanshui."

13. Fang, "Quanzhen nüguan."

14. Luk, *The Empress and the Heavenly Masters*, 18–24.

15. Jie, "Song shi zhong Gaotang," 156.

16. Liu, "Imagery of Female Daoists," 198–227; Liu, "Songs of Her Spirit."

17. Zhao, "Love, Lust, and Loss."

18. Shao, *Songdai funü de fojiao xinyang*, 68–71.

19. Yü, *Kuan-yin*, 294–296, 303, 311–312, 333; Overmyer, "Values in Chinese Sectarian Literature," 224.

20. Levering, "Lin-chi (Rinzai) Ch'an and Gender," 137–140; Hsieh, "Images of Women," 149, 152–161, 167–171.

21. Levering, "Miao-tao and Her Teacher"; Tsai, "Miaodao."

22. Qin, "Cong muzhi kan Songdai nüzi," 86. The author examined 1,844 epitaphs dating to the Northern and Southern Song eras. Among these inscriptions, 24.6 percent mentioned that the deceased woman had been a Buddhist believer. Shao, "Fojiao xinyang dui Songdai nüxing juchu," 56, estimates that about one-third of epitaphs for Song women mention that they had been Buddhist believers.

23. Sha, "Wudai Song Dunhuang"; Wu, "Cong shike kan Liaodai pingmin," 14; Gao, "Liaodai foxue jiaoyu," 3–4; Peng, "Lun Liaodai pusa jie de liuxing."

24. Jin, "Lun Songdai funü yu fojiao."

25. Shao, *Songdai funü de fojiao xinyang*, 23–50; Jin, "Lun Songdai funü yu fojiao," 397–400; Qin, "Cong muzhi kan Songdai nüzi," 87.

26. Shao, *Songdai funü de fojiao xinyang*, 128–146.

27. Shao, "Fojiao xinyang dui Songdai nüxing juchu," 56–60.

28. Shao and Zhang, "Songdai biqiuni fumian xingxiang"; Luo, "Lun Liang Song fu nici."

29. Hsieh, "Buddhist Nuns in Sung China," 81–82, 89.

30. In the year 1019 there were 15,643 nuns in China. In 1021 there were 61,239 nuns. In 1034 there were 48,740 nuns. In 1042 there were 48,417 nuns. In 1068 there were 34,037 nuns. In 1077 there were 29,692 nuns. Huang, "Songdai funü de ling," 558–559. The number of clerics of each sex fluctuated. In 1019 the ratio of registered

monks to nuns was 14.7:1. In 1021 it was 6.5:1. In 1034, 7.9:1. In 1068, 6.5:1. In 1077, 6.8:1. These numbers include only ordained and registered nuns. Many other women were privately ordained or still novices. Hsieh, "Buddhist Nuns in Sung China," 81. Also see Jin, "Lun Songdai funü yu fojiao," 108. At 66–77, Hsieh describes the ordination of nuns.

31. Huang, "Songdai funü de ling," 573–574.
32. Zhang, "Liang Song shiqi," 457; Liu, *Songdai de zongjiao*, 8–29.
33. Huang, "Songdai funü de ling," 574–577, 587, 644.
34. Hsieh, "Buddhist Nuns in Sung China," 87–88, 92–93.
35. You, "Songdai youguan sengni," 86–88; Shao, *Songdai funü de fojiao xinyang*, 66–76.
36. Shao, *Songdai funü de fojiao xinyang*, 88–126.
37. Shao and Zhang, "Songdai gaoni shiji yanjiu," 18.

CHAPTER 5

1. Ochs and Taylor, "The 'Father Knows Best' Dynamic," 97–98.
2. Lemert, *Social Things*, 81, gives a cogent summary of the sociology of knowledge.
3. Zhou, "Shilun Songdai jiaoyu."
4. Li, *Songdai sixue fazhan*, 9–12.
5. Zurndorfer, "Women in Chinese Learned Culture," 25.
6. Birge, "Chu Hsi and Women's Education," 354–355.
7. Li, "Songdai Donglai Lü," 61–64.
8. Chen and Chen, *Song Yuan shiqi Siming Yuanshi*, 109–110.
9. Ebrey, "Women, Money, and Class," 29–30.
10. Birge, "Chu Hsi and Women's Education," 331, 335–338, 348–351.
11. Lee, *Empresses, Art & Agency*, 19, 160–169.
12. Lee, *Empresses, Art & Agency*, 80–94; Ebrey, *Emperor Huizong*, 126.
13. Fan, "Songdai xiaceng funü."
14. Liu, *Songdai jiaxun yu shehui*, 230–246.
15. Liu, *Songdai jiaxun yu shehui*, 252–254; Liu, "Luelun Songdai jiaxun zhong"; Du and Mann, "Competing Claims on Womanly Virtue," 238.
16. Raphals, *Sharing the Light*, 254–255.
17. Tie, *Songdai shiren jieceng nüxing*, 251.
18. Chang, "Songdai nüxing shufa"; Wang, "Songdai nüxing shujia Guan Kui."
19. Pan, "'Shuhua tongyuan' sixiang," 63.
20. Zhang, "Yuandai de jiazu jiaoyu," 82–84; Zhang, "Lun Yuandai."
21. Shu and Yang, "Wei Jin renxing zijue."
22. Wang, *Songdai wenxue jiazu*, 376.
23. Egan, *The Burden of Female Talent*, 11–13. On pp. 27–43, Egan introduces the most important female poets of the Song.
24. Xie, "Diyu yu minzu shiyu."
25. Hawes, *The Social Circulation of Poetry*, 173, n. 13.

26. Wang, *Songdai wenxue jiazu*, 377, 379.
27. Egan, *The Burden of Female Talent*, 1, 56–59, 64.
28. Egan, *Works of Li Qingzhao*, 193.
29. Chang and Saussy, *Women Writers of Traditional China*, 128.
30. Wang, "Jindai nüxing zuojia."
31. Egan, *The Burden of Female Talent*, 15; Wang, *Songdai wenxue jiazu*, 72–75, 81–94.
32. Zhao, "Songdai nüxing."
33. Zhang, "Communication, Collaboration, and Community," 20–23; Liu, "Songdai nüxing zuojia," 79–82.

CHAPTER 6

1. Chen, *Songdai minfu de shenghuo qingtai*, 35–37.
2. Tian, *Songdai shangren jiating*, 109–112.
3. Xia, "Lun Songdai nüxing."
4. Lu, "Yuanmo nüxing wei yufang shouru," 109–111.
5. Yu, "Yi shenwan wei beiliang."
6. Kuhn, *The Age of Confucian Rule*, 165–166.
7. Tie, "Yulun yu zhixu."
8. Yang, "Cong Songdai funü mingzi."
9. Bossler, "Faithful Wives and Heroic Maidens," 751–753.
10. Wang, "Bei Song funü de hunyin," 76.
11. Liu, Liu, et al., *Songdai Juye Zhaoshi*, 41, 47–48, 52.
12. Zang, "Songdai jiafa de tedian"; He, "Songdai yijiang de jiali shijian"; Shen, "Nansong dao Yuanchao."
13. Zang, "Women and the Transmission of Confucian Culture," 129; Zhu, "Lun Yuan Cai," 83–84.
14. Yan, "Lixuexing jiazu."
15. Ebrey, "Women, Money, and Class," 38; Zhang, *Hunyin yu shehui*, 96; Zhang, "Songdai funü de zaijia wenti," 89; Zhang, *Songdai hunyin jiazu*, 134; Xue et al., *Liang Song fazhi tonglun*, 315.
16. Peng and Wang, "Songdai lixue xingbie"; Tie, *Songdai shiren jieceng nüxing*, 45–85; Wei, "Songdai rujia 'li xia shumin'"; Zheng, "Lixue shengxing," 574–578.
17. Lü, "Lun Zhu Xi shiyezhong," 400.
18. Ebrey, "Education through Ritual," 288, 291; Ebrey, *Chu Hsi's* Family Rituals, xxi; Kuhn, *The Age of Confucian Rule*, 104.
19. Ebrey, "Women, Money, and Class," 12–13, 22, 24–25, 27, 30; Xu, *Songdai shizu funü*, 9–10, 13, 16, 22.
20. Pang-White, "Neo-Confucians and Zhu Xi," 76.
21. However, Zhu Xi wrote epitaphs for women, in which he praised the deceased for various virtues. Birge, "Chu Hsi and Women's Education," 361–367, translates these epitaphs.
22. Li, *Zhuzi yulei*, vol. 8, 136:3245.

23. Chan, *Chu Hsi*, 541–542; Pang-White, "Neo-Confucians and Zhu Xi," 73.

24. Pang-White, "New-Confucians and Zhu Xi," 79.

25. Raphals, *Sharing the Light*, 255–256; Pang-White, "Neo-Confucians and Zhu Xi," 73–74.

26. Birge, "Chu Hsi and Women's Education," 331–333; Lü, "Lun Zhu Xi shiyezhong," 390–417.

27. Birge, "Chu Hsi and Women's Education," 340; Chan, *Chu Hsi*, 538–541.

28. Liu, "Qiantan Songdai funü," 146–148.

29. Cheng, *Yichuan yizhuan*, preface 2a. Liu, "Qiantan Songdai funü," 144; Van Ess, "Cheng Yi and His Ideas about Women."

30. Zhang, *Hunyin yu shehui*, 88–89.

31. Van Norden, *Mengzi*, 153.

32. Ebrey, "Women, Money, and Class," 31.

33. Zhang, *Hunyin yu shehui*, 89–90; Zhang, *Songdai hunyin jiazu*, 169–172.

34. Huang, *Desire and Fictional Narrative*, 23–26, 33; Epstein, "Reflections of Desire," 69–73; Goyama, *Ming Qing shidai de nüxing*, 52.

35. Zhang, *Songdai hunyin jiazu*, 132–133; Huang, *Desire and Fictional Narrative*, 26–27.

36. Deng, "'Neiwai' zhiji yu 'zhixu' geju," 98–100, 105–110; Lei, "Cong haofang dao zhenjing," 54.

37. Ebrey, *Emperor Huizong*, 36.

38. McKnight, *Law and Order in Sung China*, 357, 359.

39. Tie, "Songdai nüxing xinglü fengxian."

40. Li, *Women's Poetry of Late Imperial China*, 40.

41. Allison, "Introduction," 1, 4.

42. Xu, *Crossing the Gate*, 143.

43. Liu, "Song shi yuanxiaojie," 129–133; Tie, "Guiwei zhi wai."

44. Ebrey, *The Inner Quarters*, 26–27.

45. Tao, "Cong Song Yuan"; Ōsawa, *Tō Sō jidai no kazoku*, 54; Zhang, "Anecdotal Writing on Illicit Sex," 256–257.

46. Cheng, *Songdai diyu wenhua*, 22–30, stresses the weakness of ritual orthodoxy in south China.

47. Qi, "Liaodai Hanren muzhi," 614–617. The practice of a woman marrying her dead sister's husband was called *jiexu hun* 接續婚.

48. Song, "Songdai hunyin fangshi." Zhang, *Hunyin yu shehui*, 58–64, describes negative views of levirate.

49. Tao, "Bei Song funü"; Zhang, *Hunyin yu shehui*, 76–82; Zhang, "Songdai funü de zaijia wenti," 77–80; Zhang, *Songdai hunyin jiazu*, 159–167.

50. Zhang, *Hunyin yu shehui*, 67–76, lists the names and details of sixty-one female characters in *Yi Jian zhi* who remarried (fifty-five remarrying once and six remarrying twice) and information about forty-one remarried women mentioned in *Taiping guangji* (thirty-eight remarrying once and three remarrying twice). Also see Zhang, *Songdai hunyin jiazu*, 156–158; Zhang, "Songdai funü de zaijia wenti," 63–71.

51. Qi, "Liaodai Hanren muzhi," 617–618, provides records of remarriage in Liao epitaphs.
52. Chu, "Ye lun Songdai funü."
53. Ebrey, *The Inner Quarters*, 204–216.
54. Wang, "Songdai nüxing shenti."
55. Schlegel, "Status, Property," 719, 724, 730–732.
56. Zhang, "Anecdotal Writings on Illicit Sex," 265–278.
57. Qiu, "Niuqu de jingxiang," 99–102.
58. McKnight, *Law and Order in Sung China*, 103–104.
59. Li, *Women's Poetry of Late Imperial China*, 43–44.
60. Wang and Jia, "Jindai jiating renkou," 101. The sample consisted of 38 inscriptions commemorating deceased women. A larger sample of 407 Jin epitaphs of men yielded an average age at death of 60.7 *sui*. A study of 1,466 Song epitaphs gave a slightly lower number of 56.7 *sui*. Those of higher social status tended to live longer. Wu, "Songdai shiren pingjun siwang nianling," 174, 176. Weng, "Tō Sō bushi kara mita jōsei," 46, notes that Song women were widowed at a wide range of ages. Also see Ebrey, "Women in Liu Kezhuang's Family," 103.
61. Sommer, "The Uses of Chastity," 77.
62. Mann, "Widows," 47–48.
63. Wang, "Yuandai nüxing zaijia."
64. Ebrey, *The Inner Quarters*, 204–216; Yanagita, *Sōdai shomin no onnatachi*, 3–28.
65. Bossler, *Powerful Relations*, 17–18, 21, 24; Liu, "Qiantan Songdai funü," 150–151, 161.
66. Mann, "Widows," 49.
67. Lin, "Lun Songdai shuangfu," 73–74.
68. The fact that widows were rarely in a position to obey their sons disconcerted strict Confucian thinkers. Diao and Wang, "Xiaodao yu wangchang."
69. Such was also the case under the Yuan. Birge, *Marriage and the Law*, 99.
70. Knapp, "The Ru Reinterpretation," 200–202.
71. Holmgren, "Widow Chastity," 170–171.
72. Goyama, *Ming Qing shidai de nüxing*, 198–200.
73. Birge, "Levirate Marriage," 111–113.
74. Chaffee, "Marriage of Sung Imperial Clanswomen," 141.
75. Tie, "Lun Songdai guojia."
76. Mann, "Widows," 51.
77. Mann, "Widows," 45.
78. Zhu, "Identity, Legitimacy, and Chaste Widows," 186.
79. Bossler, "Faithful Wives and Heroic Maidens," 757–760, 765, 769–771.
80. Davis, "Chaste and Filial Women," 213–217.
81. Chong, *Cannibalism in China*, 95–98.
82. Ebrey, "Women, Money, and Class," 27–28.
83. Fang, "Songdai nüxing gegu liaoqin," 210.
84. Yang and Lu, "Songdai zisha nüxing," 70–72.

CHAPTER 7

1. Mann, "Widows," 45; Jing, "Shijing zhong meiren."

2. Lee, *Empresses, Art & Agency*, 18–19; Han, "Wu Zetian gushi"; McMahon, *Celestial Women*, 32.

3. He, "Songdai chuanqi xiaoshuo," 66–67.

4. He, "Songdai chuanqi xiaoshuo," 68–69.

5. Chang and Saussy, *Women Writers of Traditional China*, 98.

6. Blanchard, *Song Dynasty Figures*, 157, 159.

7. Jing, "Shijing zhong meiren," 223–225.

8. Fong, "Images of Women," 22–23.

9. Li, *Women's Poetry*, 37–38; Blanchard, *Song Dynasty Figures*, 68.

10. Huang, *Shinühua de yanjiu yu jifa*, 2–3. In antiquity the term *shinü* referred to depictions of a man and woman together. Northern Song critics reinterpreted this term as referring to paintings of women.

11. Bo, "Physical Beauty and Inner Virtue," 1, 8, 21–22, 40–48; Blanchard, *Song Dynasty Figures*, 2–3.

12. Zheng and Yang, "Tang Song nüxing ticai."

13. Zhang, Hua, and Zhao, "Lun Songdai nüzi."

14. Su, "Jin Yuan shiqi yiliao."

15. Hong, *Hongshi ji yanfang*, 5:59–74, describes medicines considered appropriate for women and children.

16. Cole, *Mothers and Sons*, 203.

17. Sun, "Lixue dui Songdai nüzhuang"; Jing and Feng, "Songdai lixue dui nüxing," 580–581. For a general overview of the clothing of Song women, see Li, *Zhongguo lidai zhuangshi*, 106–134, and Kuhn, *The Age of Confucian Rule*, 264–265.

18. Wang, *Songdai fushi zhidu*, 43–152.

19. Zhang and Feng, "Songdai lixue dui nüxing," 580; Fu and Xu, *Songdai nüxing toushi sheji*.

20. Kehoe, "A Resort to Subtler Contrivances," 24–25, notes that in many cultures the most powerful person deliberately dresses very modestly. For example, when the Blackfoot people perform their sun dance, the most important participant is an old woman dressed in very simple clothing. Mahatma Gandhi famously wore a loincloth as a way to claim moral authority.

21. Fuzhou, *Fuzhou Nan Song Huang Sheng mu*; Bray, *Technology and Gender*, 207–208.

22. Wang, *Songdai fushi zhidu*, 26–42; Zhang, "Shehui jingji shiye," 8, 16; Von Glahn, *The Economic History of China*, 246.

23. Kuhn, *The Age of Confucian Rule*, 260.

24. Qin, "Liaodai Qidan funü."

25. Wang, *Aching for Beauty*, 29–53, gives a concise history of footbinding. Ko, *Cinderella's Sisters*, 109–144, explores the origins of footbinding.

26. Ko, "In Search of Footbinding's Origins," 406–407; Kuhn, *The Age of Confucian Rule*, 253.

CHAPTER 8

1. Holmgren, "Imperial Marriage," 58.
2. Under Tang law, a concubine could not inherit from her master. During the Southern Song, concubines gained the right to inherit from a master's estate and establish an heir for him if he died childless. This right does not appear in Ming or Qing code. Also, in the Northern Song, a daughter inherited half the value of her brother's betrothal gift as her dowry. During the Southern Song, she inherited a sum equal to half the value of her brother's total inheritance. Women lost this right under Ming and Qing law. Lau, "Changes to Women's Legal Rights," 707. Bernhardt, "A Ming-Qing Transition," 29–50, argues that the contraction of women's rights under the Ming and Qing was a culmination of trends that began during the Song.
3. Seol, "Monggol jegug eseo hwangsil."
4. Broadbridge, *Women and the Making of the Mongol Empire*, 2–3.
5. Huang, "Yuandai funü diwei luelun," 162–163, 240; Wang and Liu, "Yuandai funü zhenjie guannian."
6. You, "Cong hunyinfa bijiao."
7. Kuhn, *The Age of Confucian Rule*, 146.
8. Tan, "Yuandai hunyin fagui zhong."
9. Xu, "Liao Jin Yuan," 216, uses statistics from the *Gujin tushu jicheng* encyclopedia to demonstrate the intensification of chastity ideals through the Liao, Jin, and Yuan. The author sees the conquest dynasties as a turning point when chastity ethics became far more stringent than before.
10. Tang, "Liaodai funü zhenjieguan," 33; Wang, "Jindai nüxing zhenjieguan," 98.
11. Rossabi, "Khubilai Khan," 153–154; Näf, "Compared with the Women," 70–71.
12. Women might also earn money from investments, usually managed by merchants on a woman's behalf. Aristocratic women also sometimes received valuable gifts from envoys and the leaders of subject peoples. And after the Mongol Empire established a regular fiscal system, the wives of rulers could receive a share of tax revenues levied on conquered areas. Broadbridge, *Women and the Making of the Mongol Empire*, 23–24.
13. Rossabi, "Khubilai Khan," 155; Tang, "Liaodai funü zhenjieguan," 2–35; Wu, *Liao Jin shehui*, 81, 83, 288–289; Liu and Hu, "Liaodai hunyin zhuangkuang," 142–143.
14. Rossabi, "Khubilai Khan," 154–155; Holmgren, "Observations on Marriage," 145–146; Shimada, *Ryōdai shakaishi kenkyū*, 193–197; Liu and Hu, "Liaodai hunyin zhuangkuang," 143.
15. Qi, "Liaodai Hanren muzhi," 613–168. The replacement of one sister by another was called *jiexu hun* 接續婚.
16. Chen, "Yuandai zaju nüxing xingxiang."
17. Yin and Shen, "Liaodai Qidanzu nüxing wenren."
18. Holmgren, "Imperial Marriage," 84–86; Birge, "Levirate Marriage," 115; Tan, "Yuandai liangzhong hunyin," 35–37; Broadbridge, *Women and the Making of the Mongol Empire*, 10–11, 13–14.

19. McMahon, *Celestial Women*, 58–65.

20. Xin, "Lun Songdai funü gaijia"; Ebrey, "Women, Money, and Class," 10–12.

21. Birge, "Levirate Marriage," 129–130.

22. Chen, *Ming Qing qiyue*, 20–21.

23. Wang, "Jindai nubi laiyuan"; Birge, *Marriage and the Law*, 23.

24. You, "Cong hunyinfa bijiao," 99–162.

25. Riasanovsky, *Fundamental Principles*, 211, 235–236.

26. Riasanovsky, *Fundamental Principles*, 83–84, 86, 199, 242.

27. Birge, *Women, Property and Confucian Reaction*, 229–279; Wu, *Yuandai fa*, 198.

28. Xu, "Shixi Yuandai funü," 104–105, 109–110.

29. Holmgren, "Observations on Marriage," 130–131; Birge, "Levirate Marriage," 132–134; Birge, *Women, Property and Confucian Reaction*, 217, 220–221; Bernhardt, *Women and Property*, 40; You, *Song Yuan zhiji funü*, 258–260; Xu, "Shixi Yuandai funü," 105, 107–108; Zhang, "Songdai funü lianchan," 87–88.

30. Birge, "Levirate Marriage," 135.

31. Holmgren, "Observations on Marriage," 129; Birge, "Levirate Marriage," 114; Song, *Jindai de shehui*, 83.

32. Riasanovsky, *Fundamental Principles*, 239; Weatherford, *Secret History*, 13–14; Wang, "Jindai nüxing zhenjieguan," 99; Liu, "Jindai Nüzhen de hunyin," 89.

33. Cao, "Cong 'Yuan dian zhang,'" 49; Birge, *Marriage and the Law*, 91–92. Chen, *Ming Qing qiyue*, 14, quotes the provisions in two Yuan marriage documents specifying the amount of betrothal gifts.

34. Riasanovsky, *Fundamental Principles*, 241; Wu, *Yuandai fa*, 214; Cao, "Cong 'Yuan dian zhang,'" 52.

35. Birge, *Marriage and the Law*, 157–167, 192. Liao law already stressed the wife's full membership in her husband's family. Zhang, "Liaodai nüxing de fanzui," 8.

36. Birge, *Marriage and the Law*, 198–203.

37. Tan, "Yuandai liangzhong hunyin," 35, 37–39; Xu, "Shixi Yuandai funü," 106; Wang, "Yuandai nüxing zaijia," 63. Some men already practiced *dianqi* during the Song dynasty. In 972, Emperor Song Taizu outlawed the practice. In 972, Taizu prohibited men from renting out their wives and related practices. Zhang, "Liang Song shiqi de xing wenti," 458–459.

38. Wang, "Yuandai nüxing zaijia," 62–63.

39. Riasanovsky, *Fundamental Principles*, 237–238; Liu, "Jindai Nüzhen de hunyin," 90; Birge, *Marriage and the Law*, 23.

40. Riasanovsky, *Fundamental Principles*, 234–235; Liu and Hu, "Liaodai hunyin zhuangkuang," 143; Zhang, *Jinshi lungao*, 145–147; Holmgren, "Observations on Marriage," 153; Wang, "Jindai nüxing zhenjieguan," 99–100; Liu, "Jindai Nüzhen de hunyin," 89; Wang and Jia, "Jindai jiating renkou shuliang," 114; Birge, *Marriage and the Law*, 23–24.

41. Birge, *Marriage and the Law*, 24.

42. Ratchnevsky, "Levirate in the Legislation," 46–47, 58; Birge, "Levirate Marriage," 116, 124; Cao, "Cong 'Yuan dian zhang,'" 51; Birge, *Women, Property and Confucian Reaction*, 206; Birge, *Marriage and the Law*, 216–229, 243.

43. Cao, "Cong 'Yuan dian zhang,'" 49, 51.

44. Zhang, *Liaodai shehuishi*, 131–132.

45. Yang and Meng, "Qidan yinghunzhi kaolue."

46. Kuhn, *The Age of Confucian Rule*, 61–62.

47. Zhang, *Liaodai shehuishi*, 133–134.

48. Kuhn, *The Age of Confucian Rule*, 63.

49. Wang, *Shijia dazu*, 52; Chen and Gao, "Liaodai Qidan jiating," 87–91; Zhang, *Liaodai shehuishi*, 134.

50. Liu and Hu, "Liaodai hunyin zhuangkuang," 142–143.

51. Zhang, "Liaodai Qidan nüxing," 15–16.

52. Zhang and Zhang, *Qidan jinguo*, 162–171.

53. Zhang, "Cong Liaodai shike kan Liaodai shehui"; Zhang, "Liaodai shike zhong suo fanying"; Zhang and Xu, "Cong Liaodai muzhi zhong."

54. Chen, *Ming Qing qiyue*, 17.

55. Sang, "Jinshi Wan Yanshi," 255–288.

56. Du, *Liao Jin shi yanjiu*, 257–258, 261.

57. Tao, *The Jurchen*, 13.

58. Song, *Jindai de shehui shenghuo*, 83–84; Holmgren, "Observations on Marriage," 152; McMahon, *Celestial Women*, 44.

59. Wang, "Jindai Zhenyi Huanghou."

60. Wang, "Jindai nüxing zhenjieguan," 100–101; Lan and Sun, "Jindai Nüzhen jiaoyu zhidu"; Lan, *Jindai jiaoyu yanjiu*.

61. Tuo et al., *Jinshi*, 8:179; An and Jiang, "Jindai de zhongxiao," 67.

62. Xu, "Shixi Yuandai funü," 114–115; Liu, "Yuandai Zhu Xi *Jiali*."

63. Cleaves, "The Eighteenth Chapter"; Li and Liu, "Yuandai tongguo nüxing."

64. Zhang, "Yuandai fei Hanzu funü."

65. Ge, "Yuandai Hanzu funü"; Lam, "A Khotanese Chaste Wife."

66. Li, "Yuandai Bao Gong."

67. Tan, "Yuandai maimai nükou"; Wang, "Yuandai hunyin zhidu gaishuo."

68. Birge, "Levirate Marriage," 114, 137; Chen, *Ming Qing qiyue*, 22; Ge, "Yuandai Hanzu funü," 57–59; He, "Guanyu Yuandai hunyin zhidu," 102–103.

69. Riasanovsky, *Fundamental Principles*, 86.

70. Chen, *Ming Qing qiyue*, 17–19; Zheng, "Guan, min yu fa," 79; Liu, "Cong 'Yuan dian zhang.'"

71. Meijer, *Murder and Adultery*, 39–40; Holmgren, "Observations on Marriage," 155. In this regard, Yuan law adhered to the *Great Yassa*. Riasanovsky, *Fundamental Principles*, 83.

72. Cao, "Cong 'Yuan dian zhang,'" 51.

73. Birge, "Levirate Marriage," 146; Birge, *Women, Property and Confucian Reaction*, 277.

74. Holmgren, "Observations on Marriage," 178.

75. Meijer, *Murder and Adultery*, 40.

76. Zhang and Sun, "Yuandai Xi Xia nüxing," 94–98, use epitaphs to document the influence of Confucian ethics on Tangut women.

77. Bossler, "Fantasies of Fidelity," 158; Xu, "Liao Jin Yuan," 216.

78. Wei and Xu, "Cong 'Yuanshi–Lienüzhuan,'" 101–102; Wei, "Yuandai funü zhenjie." Hang, "Yuanshi lienüzhuan shiyuan tanxi," discusses the composition of the two chapters (chapters 200 and 201) of didactic biographies of women in the *Yuanshi*. Unlike most standard histories, the *Yuanshi* underwent two rounds of editing by two different authors. This unusual textual history explains why there are two chapters of women's biographies instead of just one, as in the earlier standard histories. During each round of editing, the authors relied on different source materials. These narratives were mostly based on contemporary Yuan biographies and posthumous stele inscriptions.

79. Holmgren, "Observations on Marriage," 184–188; Broadbridge, *Women and the Making of the Mongol Empire*, 18.

Bibliography

Allison, Penelope M. "Introduction." In *The Archaeology of Household Activities*, edited by Penelope M. Allison, 1–18. London: Routledge, 1999.

Altenburger, Roland. *The Sword or the Needle: The Female Knight-errant (xia) in Traditional Chinese Narrative*. Bern: Peter Lang, 2009.

An Guichen 安貴臣 and Jiang Weizhong 蔣緯忠. "Jindai de zhongxiao yishi pingxi" 金代的忠孝意識評析. *Zhongyang Minzu Daxue xuebao* 中央民族大學學報 2 (1997): 66–68.

Anonymous. *Song da zhaoling ji* 宋大詔令集. Beijing: Zhonghua shuju, 1962.

Bai Xingrong 白興榮. "Qianyi Songdai waimingfu ji qi jiawu guanli zhineng" 淺議宋代外命婦及其家務管理職能. *Puyang Zhiye Jishu Xueyuan xuebao* 濮陽職業技術學院學報 22, no. 4 (2009): 39–40.

Bailey, Paul J. "Chinese Women Go Global: Discursive and Visual Representations of the Foreign 'Other' in the Early Chinese Women's Press and Media." *Nan Nü* 19 (2017): 213–262.

Bao Jialin 鮑家麟 and Lü Cishan 呂慧慈. "Funü zhi ren yu waishi—Songdai funü he shehui gonggong shiye" 婦女之仁與外事—宋代婦女和社會公共事業. In *Tang Song nüxing yu shehui* 唐宋女性與社會, edited by Deng Xiaonan 鄧小南, vol. 1, 263–274. Shanghai: Shanghai cishu, 2003.

Barfield, Thomas J. *The Perilous Frontier: Nomadic Empires and China, 221 BC to AD 1757*. Cambridge, MA: Blackwell, 1989.

Bernhardt, Kathryn. "A Ming-Qing Transition in Chinese Women's History? The Perspective from Law." In *The History and Theory of Legal Practice in China: Toward a Historical-Social Jurisprudence*, edited by Philip C. C. Huang and Kathryn Bernhardt, 29–50. Leiden: Brill, 2014.

———. *Women and Property in China, 960–1949*. Stanford, CA: Stanford University Press, 1999.

Biran, Michal. "Introduction: Nomadic Culture." In *Nomads as Agents of Cultural Change: The Mongols and their Eurasian Predecessors*, edited by Reuven Amitai and Michal Biran, 1–9. Honolulu: University of Hawaii Press, 2014.

————. "Periods of Non-Han Rule." In *A Companion to Chinese History*, edited by Michael Szonyi, 129–142. Chichester, UK: Wiley Blackwell, 2017.

Birge, Bettine. "Chu Hsi and Women's Education." In *Neo-Confucian Education: The Formative Stage*, edited by William Theodore de Bary and John Chaffee, 325–367. Berkeley: University of California Press, 1989.

————. "Inheritance and Property Law from Tang to Song: The Move away from Patrilineality." In *Tang Song nüxing yu shehui* 唐宋女性與社會, edited by Deng Xiaonan 鄧小南, vol. 2, 849–866. Shanghai: Shanghai cishu, 2003.

————. "Levirate Marriage and the Revival of Widow Chastity in Yuan China." *Asia Major*, 3rd ser., 8, no. 2 (1995): 107–146.

————. *Marriage and the Law in the Age of Khubilai Khan: Cases from the* Yuan Dianzhang. Cambridge, MA: Harvard University Press, 2017.

————. "Women and Property in Sung Dynasty China (960–1279): Neo-Confucianism and Social Change in Chien-chou, Fukien." PhD diss., Columbia University, 1992.

————. *Women, Property and Confucian Reaction in Sung and Yüan China (960–1368)*. Cambridge: Cambridge University Press, 2002.

Blanchard, Laura C. W. *Song Dynasty Figures of Longing and Desire: Gender and Interiority in Chinese Painting and Poetry*. Leiden: Brill, 2018.

Bossler, Beverly J. *Courtesans, Concubines, and the Cult of Female Fidelity: Gender and Social Change in China, 1000–1400*. Cambridge, MA: Harvard Asia Center, 2012.

————. "A Daughter Is a Daughter All Her Life: Affinal Relations and Women's Networks in Song and Late Imperial China." *Late Imperial China* 21, no. 1 (2000): 77–106.

————. "Faithful Wives and Heroic Maidens: Politics, Virtue, and Gender in Song China." In *Tang Song nüxing yu shehui* 唐宋女性與社會, edited by Deng Xiaonan 鄧小南, vol. 2, 751–784. Shanghai: Shanghai cishu, 2003.

————. "Fantasies of Fidelity: Loyal Courtesans to Faithful Wives." In *Beyond Exemplar Tales: Women's Biography in Chinese History*, edited by Joan Judge and Hu Ying, 158–174. Berkeley: University of California Press, 2011.

————. "Floating Sleeves, Willow Waists, and Dreams of Spring: Entertainment and Its Enemies in Song History and Historiography." In *Senses of the City: Perceptions of Hangzhou & Southern Song China, 1127–1279*, edited by Joseph S. C. Lam et al., 1–24. Hong Kong: Chinese University Press, 2017.

————. *Powerful Relations: Kinship, Status, & the State in Sung China (960–1279)*. Cambridge, MA: Council on East Asian Studies, Harvard University, 1998.

Bray, Francesca. *Technology and Gender: Fabrics of Power in Late Imperial China*. Berkeley: University of California Press, 1997.

Broadbridge, Anne F. *Women and the Making of the Mongol Empire*. Cambridge: Cambridge University Press, 2018.

Cao Tingting 曹婷婷. "Cong 'Yuan dian zhang' kan Yuandai funü hunyin wenti" 從 '元典章' 看元代婦女婚姻問題. *Shijiazhuang Xueyuan xuebao* 石家莊學院學報 18, no. 5 (2016): 49–53.

Chaffee, John W. *Branches of Heaven: A History of the Imperial Clan of Sung China*. Cambridge, MA: Harvard University Asia Center, 1999.

————. "The Marriage of Sung Imperial Clanswomen." In *Marriage and Inequality in Chinese Society*, edited by Rubie S. Watson and Patricia Buckley Ebrey, 133–169. Berkeley and Los Angeles: University of California Press, 1991.

————. "The Rise and Regency of Empress Liu." *Journal of Song-Yuan Studies* 31 (2001): 1–25.

Chai Jihong 柴繼紅. "Shilun Songdai de shuixian wenhua" 試論宋代的水仙文化. *Mingzuo xinshang* 名作欣賞 10 (2010): 38–40.

Chan, Wing-tsit. *Chu Hsi: New Studies*. Honolulu: University of Hawaii Press, 1989.

Chang Chun 常春. "Songdai nüxing shufa wenhua tanlue" 宋代女性書法文化探略. *Lilun daokan* 理論導刊 1 (2012): 98–100.

Chang Jianhua. "Theories about the Formation of Lineage System since the Song and Ming Dynasties." *Frontiers of History in China* 3, no. 1 (2008): 41–77.

Chang, Kang-I Sun, and Haun Saussy, eds. *Women Writers of Traditional China: An Anthology of Poetry and Criticism*. Stanford, CA: Stanford University Press, 1999.

Chen Gaohua 陳高華. "Yuandai de wuxi yu wushu" 元代的巫覡與巫術. *Zhejiang shehui kexue* 浙江社會科學 2 (2000): 119–123.

Chen Jianhua 陳建華. "Yuandai zaju nüxing xingxiang de pingminhua secai" 元代雜劇女性形象的平民化色彩. *Zhonghua Nüzi Xueyuan Shandong fenyuan xuebao* 中華女子學院山東分院學報 2 (2002): 25–26.

Chen Liping 陳莉萍 and Chen Xiaoliang 陳小亮. *Song Yuan shiqi Siming Yuanshi zongzu yanjiu* 宋元時期四明袁氏宗族研究. Hangzhou: Zhejiang Daxue, 2012.

Chen Peng 陳鵬 and Gao Yunsong 高雲松. "Liaodai Qidan jiating qianlun—yi Hanwen shike ziliao wei zhongxin" 遼代契丹家庭淺論—以漢文石刻資料為中心. *Heilongjiang minzu congkan* 黑龍江民族叢刊 4 (2016): 87–91.

Chen, Sanping. "'Age Inflation and Deflation' in Medieval China." *Journal of the American Oriental Society* 133, no. 3 (2013): 527–533.

Chen Weiqing 陳偉慶. "Shilun Songdai wuxi dui nongye shengchan de yingxiang" 試論宋代巫覡對農業生產的影響. *Huaihua Xueyuan xuebao* 懷化學院學報 33, no. 4 (2014): 1–4.

————. *Songdai minfu de shenghuo qingtai* 宋代民婦的生活情態. New Taipei: Hua Mulan wenhua, 2015.

————. "Songdai nüxing wanhun yuanyin tanxi" 宋代女性晚婚原因探析. *Gansu shehui kexue* 甘肅社會科學 6 (2014): 95–98.

Chen Yingxun 陳瑛珣. "Cong jingji guandian kan Tang zhi Bei Song de funüquanyi" 從經濟觀點看唐至北宋的婦女權益. *Guoli Kongzhong Daxue shehui kexue xuebao* 國立空中大學社會科學系社會科學學報 6 (1998): 161–181.

————. *Ming Qing qiyue wenshu zhong de funü jingji huodong* 明清契約文書中的婦女經濟活動. Taipei: Taiming wenhua, 2001.

Cheng Minsheng 程民生. *Songdai diyu wenhua* 宋代地域文化. Kaifeng: Henan Daxue, 1997.

Cheng Yi 程頤. *Yichuan yizhuan* 伊川易傳. Taipei: Xinwenfeng, 1997.

Cheng Yu 程郁. "Jinru Songdai huangshi de rumu yu gongting zhengzhi douzheng" 進入宋代皇室的乳母與宮廷政治鬥爭. *Zhonghua wenshi luncong* 中華文史論叢 3 (2015): 125–161.

———. "Songdai rumu yu qie de qubie ji lianxi" 宋代乳母與妾的區別及聯繫. *Shanghai Shifan Daxue xuebao* 上海師範大學學報 6 (2016): 133–145.

Ching-Chung, Priscilla. "Palace Women in the Northern Sung: Their Social Organization." *Bulletin of Sung Yuan Studies* 15 (1979): 79–97.

———. "Power and Prestige: Palace Women in the Northern Sung (960–1126)." In *Women in China: Current Directions in Historical Scholarship*, edited by Richard W. Guisso and Stanley Johannesen, 99–112. Youngstown, NY: Philo Press, 1981.

Chong, Key Ray. *Cannibalism in China*. Wakefield, NH: Longwood Academic, 1990.

Chu Chunying 初春英. "Ye lun Songdai funü de lihun, zaijia ji qi diwei" 也論宋代婦女的離婚、再嫁及其地位, *Heilongjiang Jiaoyu Xueyuan xuebao* 黑龍江教育學院學報 21, no. 3 (2002): 87–89.

Cleaves, Francis Woodman. "The Eighteenth Chapter of an Early Mongolian Version of the Hsiao Ching." *Harvard Journal of Asiatic Studies* 45, no. 1 (1985): 225–254.

Cole, Alan. *Mothers and Sons in Chinese Buddhism*. Stanford, CA: Stanford University Press, 1998.

Cui Biru 崔碧茹. "Songdai nüxing de jingji huodong: Yi dichan maimai yu qiyue wei zhongxin" 宋代女性的經濟活動: 以地產買賣與契約為中心. *Zhongguo jingjishi yanjiu* 中國經濟史研究 3 (2010): 123–133.

Dai Jianguo 戴建國. *Songdai fazhi chutan* 宋代法制初探. Harbin: Heilongjiang renmin, 2000.

Dardess, John W. "The Cheng Communal Family: Social Organization and Neo-Confucianism in Yüan and Ming China." *Harvard Journal of Asiatic Studies* 34 (1974): 7–52.

Davis, Richard L. "Chaste and Filial Women in Chinese Historical Writings of the Eleventh Century." *Journal of the American Oriental Society* 121, no. 2 (2001): 204–218.

———. *From Warhorses to Ploughshares: The Later Tang Reign of Emperor Mingzong*. Hong Kong: Hong Kong University Press, 2014.

de Pee, Christian. *The Writing of Weddings in Middle-Period China: Text and Ritual Practice in the Eighth through Fourteenth Centuries*. Albany: State University of New York Press, 2007.

Deng Lili 鄧莉麗 and Gu Ping 顧平. "Jinyin shipin yu Songdai chengshi hunyin lisu" 金銀飾品與宋代城市婚姻禮俗. *Meishu yanjiu* 美術研究 4 (2012): 112–114.

Deng Xiaonan 鄧小南. "'Neiwai' zhiji yu 'zhixu' geju: Jiantan Songdai shidaifu duiyu 'Zhouyi jiaren' de chanfa" '內外' 之際與 '秩序' 格局: 兼談宋代士大夫對於 '周易・家人' 的闡發. In *Tang Song nüixing yu shehui* 唐宋女性與社會, edited by Deng Xiaonan 鄧小南, vol. 1, 97–123. Shanghai: Shanghai cishu, 2003.

———. "Women in Turfan during the Sixth to Eighth Centuries: A Look at Their Activities Outside the Home." *Journal of Asian Studies* 58, no. 1 (1999): 85–103.

Diao Peijun 刁培俊 and Wang Yijie 王藝潔. "Xiaodao yu wangchang de boni: Bei Song nüzi 'fu si cong zi' guifan de jianxing" 孝道與網常的悖逆: 北宋女子 '夫死從子' 規範的踐行. *Xueshu yanjiu* 學術研究 11 (2014): 107–113.

Ding Shumei 丁淑梅. "Songdai jinhui wuwu 'yin' xi ziliao biannian jizhu" 宋代禁毀
巫舞 '淫' 戲資料編年輯注. *Zhonghua xiqu* 中華戲曲 38, no. 2 (2008): 262–293.

Du, Fangqin, and Susan Mann. "Competing Claims on Womanly Virtue in Late
Imperial China." In *Women and Confucian Cultures in Premodern China, Korea,
and Japan*, edited by Dorothy Ko, JaHyun Kim Haboush, and Joan R. Piggott,
219–247. Berkeley: University of California Press, 2003.

Du Guangzhi 都光智. *Liao Jin shi yanjiu* 遼金史研究. Beijing: Renmin, 2004.

Du Xingzhi 都興智 and Zhao Hao 趙浩. "Qidan nüxing canzheng ji qi yuanyin ji-
anxi" 契丹女性參政及其原因淺析. *Wenhua xuekan* 文化學刊 6 (2010): 165–169.

Du Zhengzhen 杜正貞. "Songdai yilai guafu lisiquan wenti de zai yanjiu—ji yu
fadian, pandu he dang'an deng shiliao de fansi" 宋代以來寡婦立嗣權問題 的再
研究一基於法典，判讀和檔案等史料的反思. *Wenshi* 文史 2 (2014): 175–193.

Duan Tali 段塔麗. *Tangdai funü diwei yanjiu* 唐代婦女地位研究. Beijing: Renmin,
2000.

Earle, Timothy, and Kristian Kristiansen. "Introduction: Theory and Practice in the
Late Prehistory of Europe." In *Organizing Bronze Age Societies: The Mediterra-
nean, Central Europe, and Scandinavia Compared*, edited by Timothy Earle and
Kristian Kristiansen, 1–33. Cambridge: Cambridge University Press, 2010.

Ebrey, Patricia Buckley. *Chu Hsi's* Family Rituals*: A Twelfth-Century Chinese Man-
ual for the Performance of Cappings, Weddings, Funerals, and Ancestral Rites*.
Princeton, NJ: Princeton University Press, 1990.

———. "Conceptions of the Family in the Sung Dynasty." *Journal of Asian Studies*
43, no. 2 (1984): 219–245.

———. "Concubines in Song China." In *Women and the Family in Chinese History*,
edited by Patricia Buckley Ebrey, 39–61. London: Routledge, 2003.

———. "Early Stages of Descent Group Organization." In *Kinship Organization in
Late Imperial China, 1000–1940*, edited by Patricia Buckley Ebrey and James L.
Watson, 16–61. Berkeley and Los Angeles: University of California Press, 1986.

———. "Education through Ritual: Efforts to Formulate Family Rituals during
the Sung Period." In *Neo-Confucian Education: The Formative Stage*, edited by
William Theodore de Bary and John Chaffee, 277–306. Berkeley: University of
California Press, 1989.

———. *Emperor Huizong*. Cambridge, MA: Harvard University Press, 2014.

———. "Empress Xiang (1046–1101) and Biographical Sources beyond Formal
Biographies." In *Beyond Exemplar Tales: Women's Biography in Chinese History*,
edited by Joan Judge and Hu Ying, 193–211. Berkeley: University of California
Press, 2011.

———. *The Inner Quarters: Marriage and the Lives of Chinese Women in the Sung
Period*. Berkeley: University of California Press, 1993.

———. "Rethinking the Imperial Harem: Why Were There So Many Palace
Women?" In *Women and the Family in Chinese History*, edited by Patricia Buckley
Ebrey, 177–193. London: Routledge, 2003.

————. "Shifts in Marriage Finance from the Sixth to the Thirteenth Century." In *Women and the Family in Chinese History*, edited by Patricia Buckley Ebrey, 62–88. London: Routledge, 2003.

————. "Women in the Kinship System of the Southern Song Upper Class." In *Women in China: Current Directions in Historical Scholarship*, edited by Richard W. Guisso and Stanley Johannesen, 113–128. Youngstown, NY: Philo Press, 1981.

————. "The Women in Liu Kezhuang's Family." In *Women and the Family in Chinese History*, edited by Patricia Buckley Ebrey, 89–106. London: Routledge, 2003.

————. "Women, Money, and Class: Sima Guang and Song Neo-Confucian Views on Women." In *Women and the Family in Chinese History*, edited by Patricia Buckley Ebrey, 10–38. London: Routledge, 2003.

Egan, Ronald C. *The Burden of Female Talent: The Poet Li Qingzhao and Her History in China*. Cambridge, MA: Harvard University Art Center, 2014.

————, trans. *The Works of Li Qingzhao*. Boston and Berlin: Walter de Gruyter, 2019.

Elvin, Mark. "Blood and Statistics: Reconstructing the Population Dynamics of Late Imperial China from the Biographies of Virtuous Women in Local Gazateers." In *Chinese Women in the Imperial Past: New Perspectives*, edited by Harriet Zurndorfer, 135–222. Leiden: Brill, 1999.

Epstein, Maram. "Reflections of Desire: The Poetics of Gender in *Dream of the Red Chamber*." *Nan Nü* 1, no. 1 (1999): 64–106.

Fan Meng 范夢. "Songdai xiaceng funü de shehui shenghuo" 宋代下層婦女的社會生活. *Xinan Nongye Daxue xuebao* 西南農業大學學報 8, no. 5 (2010): 110–113.

Fan Shuai 范帥. "Songdai huangzi renshu ji shouming kao" 宋代皇子人數及壽命考. *Kunming Xueyuan xuebao* 昆明學院學報 37, no. 1 (2015): 72–77.

Fang Yan 方燕. "Songdai baoyu wufa shulue" 宋代保育巫法述略. *Sichuan Jiaoyu Xueyuan xuebao* 四川教育學院學報 6 (2008): 57–59.

————. "Songdai nüxing chong bing de minjian liaofa—yi *Yi jian zhi* wei zhongxin" 宋代女性崇病的民間療法—以夷堅志為中心. *Zongjiaoxue yanjiu* 宗教學研究 4 (2008): 90–94.

————. "Songdai nüxing de juwu huodong" 宋代女性的拒巫活動. *Hebei Daxue xuebao* 河北大學學報 32, no. 3 (2007): 120–124.

————. "Songdai nüxing gegu liaoqin wenti shixi" 宋代女性割股療親問題試析. *Qiusuo* 求索 11 (2007): 210–212.

————. *Wu wenhua shiyu xia de Songdai nüxing—lizu yu nüxing shengchan, jibing de kaocha* 巫文化視域下的宋代女性—立足於女性生育, 疾病的考察. Beijing: Zhonghua, 2008.

Fei Sheng 費省. *Tangdai renkou dili* 唐代人口地理. Xi'an: Xibei Daxue chubanshe, 1996.

Fogel, Joshua A. *Politics and Sinology: The Case of Naitō Konan, 1866–1934*. Cambridge, MA: Harvard University Press, 1984.

Fong, Mary H. "Images of Women in Traditional Chinese Painting." *Women's Art Journal* 17, no. 1 (1996): 22–27.

Freely, John. *Inside the Seraglio: Private Lives of the Sultans in Istanbul*. London: Tauris Parke, 2016.

Fu Liming 付黎明 and Xu Jing 許靜. *Songdai nüxing toushi sheji: Yishu tanze ji qi wenhua suoyin* 宋代女性頭飾設計: 藝術探賾及其文化索隱. Jilin: Jilin Daxue, 2014.

Fuzhou Sheng Bowuguan 福州省博物館. *Fuzhou Nan Song Huang Sheng mu* 福州南宋黃昇墓. Beijing: Wenwu, 1982.

Gao Fushun 高福順. "Liaodai foxue jiaoyu de shehui yingxiang shulun" 遼代佛學教育的社會影響述論. *Liaoning Gongcheng Jishu Daxue xuebao* 遼寧工程技術大學學報 19, no. 1 (2017): 1–8.

Gao Nan 高楠 and Zhang Po 張波. "Muqin shengqian de lianchan quanli—yi Song-dai wei zhongxin" 母親生前的奩產權利—以宋代為中心, *Yunnan shehui kexue* 雲南社會科學 5 (2007): 118–121.

Gao Yuling 高玉玲. "Songdai funü de caichan chufenquan neng yu maimai qiyue xiaoli" 宋代婦女的財產處分權能與買賣契約效力. *Huainan Shifan Xueyuan xuebao* 淮南師範學院學報 17, no. 1 (2015): 1–6.

Ge Renkao 葛仁考. "Yuandai Hanzu funü shoujie wenti chutan" 元代漢族婦女守節問題初探. *Nei Menggu shehui kexue (Hanwen ban)* 內蒙古社會科學 (漢文版) 24, no. 3 (2003): 57–59.

Goyama Kiwamu 合山究. *Ming Qing shidai de nüxing yu wenxue* 明清時代的女性與文學. Translated by Xiao Yanwan 蕭燕婉. Taipei: Lianjing, 2016.

Grafflin, Dennis. "Social Order in the Early Southern Dynasties: The Formation of Eastern Chin." PhD diss., Harvard University, 1980.

Guang Xiaoxia 光曉霞. "Songdai funü de cishan houdong—yi muzhi wei zhongxin" 宋代婦女的慈善活動—以墓誌為中心. *Leshan Shifan Xueyuan xuebao* 樂山師範學院學報 26, no. 4 (2011): 80–85.

Guo, Chao, Lihua Pang, Lei Zhang, and Xiaoying Zheng. "Historical Demography for Late Marriage in China: A Verification Study." *Journal of Family History* 40, no. 1 (2015): 111–125.

Guo Dongxu 郭東旭. *Songdai falü yu shehui* 宋代法律與社會. Beijing: Renmin, 2008.

———. *Songdai fazhi yanjiu* 宋代法制研究. Baoding: Hebei Daxue, 2000.

———. *Songdai minjian falü shenghuo yanjiu* 宋代民間法律生活研究. Beijing: Renmin, 2012.

Guo Feng 郭鋒. "Songdai jiaji zhidu ji qi dui Songci yahua de zuoyong" 宋代家妓制度及其對宋詞雅化的作用. *Jiangxi shehui kexue* 江西社會科學 4 (2011): 98–102.

Guo Haiwen 郭海文. "Tangdai gongzhu de jiating shenghuo" 唐代公主的家庭生活. *Shaanxi Shifan Daxue xuebao* 陝西師範大學學報 40, no. 2 (2011): 71–78.

Guo Haiwen 郭海文, Zhao Wenduo 趙文朵, and Jia Qiangqiang 賈強強. "Tangdai gongzhu zinü kao" 唐代公主子女考. *Beilin jikan* 碑林集刊 20 (2014): 172–189.

Guo Libing 郭麗冰. "Songdai nüer de jiachan jichengquan tantao" 宋代女兒的家產繼承權探討. *Hanshan Shifan Xueyuan xuebao* 韓山師範學院學報 2 (2008): 38–40.

Guo Lin 郭琳. "Songdai nüshi zai jiatingzhong de diwei—yi *Minggong shupan qin-gmingji* wei zhongxin de kaocha" 宋代女使在家庭中的地位—以 '名公書 判清

明集' 為中心的考察. *Puyang zhiye jishu xueyuan xuebao* 濮陽職業技術學院學報 23, no. 2 (2010): 60–63.

Han Lin 韓林. "Wu Zetian gushi de wenben yanbian yu wenhua neihan" 武則天故事的文本演變與文化內涵. PhD diss., Nankai University, 2012.

Hang Sujing 杭素婧. "Yuanshi lienüzhuan shiyuan tanxi—yi Yuanshi Lienüzhuan yu Yuanren wenji xiangguan jizai de guanxi wei zhongxin" 元史列女傳史源探析—以元史列女傳與元人文集相關記載的關係為中心. *Yuanshi ji minzu yu bianjiang yanjiu jikan* 元史及民族與邊疆研究集刊 28 (2014): 179–185.

Hansen, Valerie. *Changing Gods in Medieval China, 1127–1276*. Princeton, NJ: Princeton University Press, 1990.

Hartman, Charles. "Cao Xun and the Legend of Emperor Taizu's Oath." In *State Power in China, 900–1325*, edited by Patricia Buckley Ebrey and Paul Jakov Smith, 62–98. Seattle: University of Washington Press, 2016.

Hawes, Colin S. C. *The Social Circulation of Poetry in the Mid–Northern Song: Emotional Energy and Literati Self-Cultivation*. Albany: State University of New York Press, 2005.

He Deting 何德廷. "Guanyu Yuandai hunyin zhidu de dutexing yu jibuxing de ruogan sikao" 關於元代婚姻制度的獨特性與進步性的若干思考. *Zhengfa xuekan* 政法學刊 21, no. 3 (2004): 102–104.

He Siqin 何斯琴. "Songdai yijiang de jiali shijian yu xiangcun lisu chongjian" 宋代以降的家禮實踐與鄉村禮俗重建. *Shehui zhili* 社會治理 5 (2016): 126–131.

He Xinling 何新岭. "Songdai chuanqi xiaoshuo nüxing xingxiang de yanbian" 宋代傳奇小說女性形象的演變. *Shaanxi Ligong Xueyuan xuebao* 陝西理工學院學報 2 (2009): 66–70.

Hinsch, Bret. "The Origins of Separation of the Sexes in China." *Journal of the American Oriental Society* 123, no. 3 (2003): 595–616.

Holmgren, Jennifer. "Imperial Marriage in the Native Chinese and Non-Han State, Han to Ming." In *Marriage and Inequality in Chinese Society*, edited by Rubie S. Watson and Patricia Buckley Ebrey, 58–96. Berkeley: University of California Press, 1991.

———. "Observations on Marriage and Inheritance Practices in Early Mongol and Yuan Society, with Particular Reference to the Levirate." *Journal of Asian History* 20, no. 2 (1986): 127–192.

———. "Widow Chastity in the Northern Dynasties: The Lieh-nu Biographies in the Wei-shu." *Papers on Far Eastern History* 23 (1981): 165–186.

Hong Zun 洪遵. *Hongshi ji yanfang* 洪氏集驗方. Shanghai: Shanghai kexue jishu, 2003.

Hou Xudong and Howard Goodman. "Rethinking Chinese Kinship in the Han and the Six Dynasties: A Preliminary Observation." *Asia Major* 23, no. 1 (2010): 29–63.

Hsieh, Ding-hwa. "Buddhist Nuns in Sung China (960–1279)." *Journal of Sung–Yuan Studies* 30 (2000): 63–96.

———. "Images of Women in Ch'an Buddhist Literature of the Sung Period." In *Buddhism in the Sung*, edited by Peter N. Gregory and Daniel A. Getz Jr., 148–187. Honolulu: University of Hawaii Press, 1999.

Hu Xiaowen 胡曉文 and Zhu Siyuan 朱思遠. "Songdai sifa dui jimu jiating neibu fanzui de chayixing guiding" 宋代司法對繼母家庭內部犯罪的差異性規定. *Hengshui Xueyuan xuebao* 衡水學院學報 17, no. 2 (2015): 101–104.

Hu Xingdong 胡興東. "Liaodai houfei yu Liaodai zhengzhi" 遼代后妃與遼代政治. *Beifang wenwu* 北方文物 2 (2003): 68–72.

Huang Jinjun 黃錦君. "Nan Song houfei xinian" 南宋后妃繫年. In *Songdai wenhua yanjiu* 7 宋代文化研究, edited by Sichuan Daxue guji zhengli yanjiusuo, 170–198. Chengdu: Bashu, 1998.

Huang Jun 黃均. *Shinühua de yanjiu yu jifa* 仕女畫的研究與技法. Beijing: Beijing gongyi meishu, 1995.

Huang Junjie 黃軍杰. "Songdai Xiuzhou wangzu hunhuan shulun" 宋代秀州望族婚宦述論. *Hengshui Xueyuan xuebao* 衡水學院學報 17, no. 3 (2015): 115–120.

Huang, Martin W. *Desire and Fictional Narrative in Late Imperial China*. Cambridge, MA: Harvard University Asia Center, 2001.

Huang Minzhi 黃敏枝. "Songdai funü de ling yi cemian—guanyu Songdai de biqiuni" 宋代婦女的另一側面—關於宋代的比丘尼. In *Tang Song nüxing yu shehui* 唐宋女性與社會, edited by Deng Xiaonan 鄧小南, vol. 2, 567–655. Shanghai: Shanghai cishu, 2003.

Huang Taiyong 黃太勇. "Yuandai Tianfei chongbai de sange wenti xintan" 元代天妃崇拜的三個問題新探. *Zhongguo haiyang daxue* 中國海洋大學 6 (2014): 64–68.

Huang Zhenyun 黃震雲. *Liaodai wenshi xintan* 遼代文史新探. Beijing: Zhongguo shehui kexue, 1999.

Huang Zongkai 黃宗凱. "Yuandai funü diwei luelun" 元代婦女地位略論. *Guangxi Minzu Xueyuan xuebao* 廣西民族學院學報 12 (2001): 162–163, 240.

Hughes, Diane Owen. "From Brideprice to Dowry in Mediterranean Europe." *Journal of Family History* 3, no. 3 (1978): 262–298.

Isay, Gad C. "To Regain Self-Affirmation: Qian Mu and His Exile." *East Asian History* 39 (2014): 103–116.

Ji, Xiao-bin. *Politics and Conservatism in Northern Song China: The Career and Thought of Sima Guang (A.D. 1019–1086)*. Hong Kong: Chinese University Press, 2005.

Ji Yong 籍勇. "Songdai shibing qizi shengcun zhuangtai yanjiu" 宋代士兵妻子生存狀態研究. *Lantai shijie* 蘭台世界 6 (2012): 17–18.

Jie Tingting 解婷婷. "Song shi zhong Gaotang shennü yixiang de zhuanbian ji qi yuanyin fenxi" 宋詩中高唐神女意象的轉變及其原因分析. *Xueshujie* 學術界 2 (2012): 155–165.

Jin Jianfeng 金建鋒. "Lun Songdai funü yu fojiao" 論宋代婦女與佛教. *Songdai yanjiu luncong* 宋代研究論叢 13 (2012): 389–403.

Jing Jing 井精. "Shijing zhong meiren guannian dui Zhongguo shinühua de yingxiang" 詩經中美人觀念對中國仕女畫的影響. *Yishu baijia* 藝術百家 7 (2011): 223–225.

Johnson, Wallace. *The T'ang Code*. Vol. 1, *General Principles*. Princeton, NJ: Princeton University Press, 1979.

Katsuyama Minoru 騰山稔. *Chūgoku Sō—Min dai ni okeru konin no gakusaiteki kenkyū* 中国宋—明代における婚姻の学際的研究. Tokyo: Tōhoku Daigaku shuppankai, 2007.

Kehoe, Alice B. "A Resort to Subtler Contrivances." In *Manifesting Power: Gender and the Interpretation of Power in Archaeology*, edited by Tracy L. Sweely, 17–29. London: Routledge, 1999.

Knapp, Keith. "The Ru Reinterpretation of Xiao." *Early China* 20 (1995): 195–222.

———. *Selfless Offspring: Filial Children and Social Order in Early Medieval China*. Honolulu: University of Hawaii Press, 2005.

Ko, Dorothy. *Cinderella's Sisters: A Revisionist History of Footbinding*. Berkeley: University of California Press, 2005.

———. "In Search Footbinding's Origins." In *Tang Song nüxing yu shehui* 唐宋女性與社會, edited by Deng Xiaonan 鄧小南, vol. 1, 375–414. Shanghai: Shanghai cishu, 2003.

Kuhn, Dieter. *The Age of Confucian Rule: The Song Transformation of China*. Cambridge, MA: Belknap Press of Harvard University Press, 2009.

Lam, Yuan-chu. "A Khotanese Chaste Wife and Her Biographer in Yuan China." In *The Role of Women in the Altaic World*, edited by Veronica Veit, 123–130. Wiesbaden: Harrassowitz Verlag, 2007.

Lan Ting 蘭婷. *Jindai jiaoyu yanjiu* 金代教育研究. Changchun: Jilin Daxue, 2009.

Lan Ting 蘭婷 and Sun Yunlai 孫運來. "Jindai Nüzhen jiaoyu zhidu" 金代女真教育制度. *Heilongjiang minzu congkan* 黑龍江民族叢刊 6 (2005): 75–80.

Lau Nap-yin. "Changes to Women's Legal Rights in the Family from the Song to the Ming." In *Modern Chinese Religion*, vol. 1, *Song–Liao–Jin–Yuan (960–1368 AD)*, edited by John Lagerwey and Pierre Marsone, 643–717. Leiden: Brill, 2015.

Lee, Hui-shu. *Empresses, Art & Agency in Song Dynasty China*. Seattle: University of Washington Press, 2010.

Lei Yanping 雷艶平. "Cong haofang dao zhenjing—lun wenhua zhuanxing hou de Songdai guige nüjiao" 從豪放到貞靜—論文化轉型後的宋代閨閣女教. *Lanzhou xuekan* 蘭州學刊 3 (2013): 52–56.

Lemert, Charles. *Social Things: An Introduction to the Sociological Life*. 4th ed. Lanham, MD: Rowman & Littlefield, 2008.

Levering, Miriam. "Lin-chi (Rinzai) Ch'an and Gender." In *Buddhism, Sexuality and Gender*, edited by Jose Ignacio Cabezon, 137–156. Albany: State University of New York Press, 1992.

———. "Miao-tao and Her Teacher Ta-hui." In *Buddhism in the Sung*, edited by Peter N. Gregory and Daniel A. Getz Jr., 188–219. Honolulu: University of Hawaii Press, 1999.

Li Caiyun 李彩雲. "Yuandai Bao Gong xi zhong fangdang tongjian nüxing xingxiang lunxi" 元代包公戲中放蕩通姦女性形象論析. *Mudanjiang Daxue xuebao* 牡丹江大學學報 24, no. 4 (2015): 45–47.

Li Danlin 李丹林 and Li Jingzhan 李景屏. *Xiao taihou pingzhuan* 蕭太后評傳. Chengdu: Sichuan Daxue, 2000.

Li Hong 李宏. *Songdai sixue fazhan luelun* 宋代私學發展略論. Beijing: Zhongyang bianyi, 2014.

Li Jingde 黎靖德. *Zhuzi yulei* 朱子語類. Beijing: Zhonghua shuju, 1986.

Li Junhong 李俊紅 and Liu Jun 劉軍. "Yuandai tongguo nüxing xianxiao wenhua xianxiang tanxi" 元代通過女性顯孝文化現象探析. *Nei Menggu Shifan Daxue xuebao* 內蒙古師範大學學報 7 (2016): 114–117.

Li Peilin 李培林. "Qiyanshan Songdai 'huiying Shengmu' xinyang de yuanliu yanbian" 七岩山宋代 '惠應聖母' 信仰的源流演變. *Wutaishan* 五臺山 2 (2017): 74–80.

Li Peng 李鵬. "Songdai Donglai Lü shi jiazu mujiao tanwei" 宋代東萊呂氏家族母教探微. *Baoding Xueyuan xuebao* 保定學院學報 25, no. 5 (2012): 61–64.

Li Qing 李倩. "Shilun Yuandai de Mazu chongbai" 試論元代的媽祖崇拜. *Zhongnan Minzu Daxue xuebao* 中南民族大學學報 6 (2005): 128–131.

Li Sha 李莎. "Luelun Yuandai jiayang de renkou zhuangkuang" 略論元代家庭的人口狀況. *Heilongjiang shizhi* 黑龍江史志 12 (2012): 76–78.

Li Xiaohong 李小紅. "Wuxi yu Songdai shehui" 巫覡與宋代社會. PhD diss., Zhejiang University, 2004.

Li, Xiaorong. *Women's Poetry of Late Imperial China*. Seattle: University of Washington Press, 2012.

Li Ya 李芽. *Zhongguo lidai zhuangshi* 中國歷代妝飾. Beijing: Zhongguo fangzhi, 2004.

Li Yungen 李雲根. "Songdai Fujian lu de caihun xianxiang" 宋代福建路的財婚現象. *Putian Xueyuan xuebao* 莆田學院學報 19, no. 4 (2012): 52–56.

———. "Songdai Pucheng Wushi jiazu ji qi hunqin kaolun" 宋代浦城吳氏家族及其婚親考論. *Wuyi Xueyuan xuebao* 武夷學院學報 35, no. 4 (2016): 7–11.

———. "Songdai ruzhuihun luelun" 宋代入贅婚略論. *Jiangxi shehui kexue* 江西社會科學 8 (2012): 108–112.

Li Yuqing 李玉清. "Songdai jinwu xingyi yuanyin zhi fenxi" 宋代禁巫興醫原因之分析. *Yixueshi yanjiu* 醫學史研究 12 (2008): 58–59.

Li Zhiping 李智萍. "Songdai nühu de tedian" 宋代女戶的特點. *Funü yanjiu luncong* 婦女研究論叢 6 (2009): 51–56.

Li Zhisheng 李志生. "Shixi jingji zhengce dui Zhongguo gudai funü zhenjie de yingxiang—jian tan Tang houqi funü zhenjie bianhua de yiyi" 試析經濟政策對中國古代婦女貞節的影響—兼談唐後期婦女貞節變化的意義. In *Tang Song nüxing yu shehui* 唐宋女性與社會. Edited by Deng Xiaonan 鄧小南, vol. 2, 884–904. Shanghai: Shanghai cishu, 2003.

Liang Kejia 梁克家. *Sanshan zhi* 三山志. Fuzhou: Haifeng chubanshe, 2000.

Liang Zhongxiao 梁中效. "Songdai wenren dui Hanshui nüshen wenhua de kaituo" 宋代文人對漢水女神文化的開拓. *Jingchu xuekan* 荊楚學刊 16, no. 6 (2015): 16–21.

Liaoning Sheng Wenwu Kaogu Yanjiusuo 遼寧省文物考古研究所 and Fuxin Shi Kaogudui 阜新市考古隊. "Liaoning Fuxin xian Liaodai Pingyuan Gongzhu mu yu tizi miao 4 hao mu" 遼寧阜新縣遼代平原公主墓與梯子廟4號墓. *Kaogu* 考古 8 (2011): 46–65.

Lin Hong 林紅. "Lun Songdai shuangfu de falü diwei" 論宋代孀婦的法律地位. *Yanshan Daxue xuebao* 燕山大學學報 9, no. 2 (2008): 73–76.

Lin Na 林娜. "Songdai wenxue zuopin zhong de nüxing yishi chutan" 宋代文學作品中的女性意識初探. *Taiyuan Shifan Xueyuan xuebao* 太原師範學院學報 10, no. 4 (2011): 86–88.

Liu, Bo. "Physical Beauty and Inner Virtue: 'Shinü tu' in the Song Dynasty." *Journal of Song–Yuan Studies* 45 (2015): 1–57.

Liu Fang 劉舫. "Yuandai Zhu Xi *Jiali* lunlue" 元代朱熹 '家禮' 論略. *Lishi jiaoxue wenti* 歷史教學問題 2 (2017): 49–55.

Liu Guangfeng 劉廣豐. "Bei Song nüzhu zhengzhi Hong de nüxing yizhi—yi due Liu Taihou de kaocha wei zhongxin" 北宋女主政治中的女性意識一以對劉太后的考察為中心. *Funü yanjiu luncong* 婦女研究論叢 6 (2014): 72–78.

———. "Songdai houfei yu diwei chuancheng" 宋代后妃與帝位傳承. *Wuhan Daxue xuebao* 武漢大學學報 4 (2009): 429–433.

———. "Songdai teshu zhengzhi shili yu nüzhu quanli de hudong—yi Liu Taihou tongzhi shiqi wei zhongxin" 宋代特殊政治勢力與女主權力的互動一以劉太后統治時期為中心. *Jianghan luntan* 江漢論壇 10 (2015): 98–105.

Liu Heng 劉姮. "Cong 'Yuan dian zhang' kan Yuandai pingmin nüxing zaoshou de jiating baoli wenti" 從 '元典章' 看元代平民女性遭受的家庭暴力問題. *Huaibei Zhiye Jishu Xueyuan xuebao* 淮北職業技術學院學報 14, no. 5 (2015): 139–141.

Liu, Heping. "Empress Liu's 'Icon of Maitreya': Portraiture and Privacy at the Early Song Court." *Artibus Asiae* 63, no. 2 (2003): 129–190.

Liu Huanyang 劉煥陽 and Liu Jingchen 劉京臣 et al. *Songdai Juye Zhaoshi jiazu wenhua yanjiu* 宋代巨野晁氏家族文化研究. Beijing: Zhonghua, 2013.

Liu Jingzhen 劉靜貞. "Cong sunzi huaitai de baoying chuanshuo kan Songdai funü de shengyu wenti" 從損子壞胎的報應傳說看宋代婦女的生育問題. *Dalu zazhi* 大陸雜誌 90, no. 1 (1995): 25–39.

Liu Jinqin 劉金勤. "Yuandai muqin chengwei de gongsi yu lishi kaocha" 元代母親稱謂的共時與歷時考察. *Changjiang Daxue xuebao* 長江大學學報 35, no. 12 (2012): 74–76.

Liu Jinzhu 劉金柱 and Zhang Yongcui 張永翠. "Cong 'yi zi qi zhi' dao 'pang xia zhuo xu'—Songdai zexu hunyin tanxi" 從 '以子妻之' 到 '榜下捉婿'一宋代擇婿婚姻探析. *Hebei Daxue xuebao* 河北大學學報 4 (2010): 93–97.

Liu, Joanna Yang. "Songs of Her Spirit: Poetic Musings of a Song Daoist Nun." *Journal of Song Yuan Studies* 44 (2014): 175–201.

Liu Liming 劉黎明. *Songdai minjian wushu yanjiu* 宋代民間巫術研究. Chengdu: Sichuan chubanshe, 2004.

Liu Liyan 柳立言. "Cong falü jiufen kan Songdai de fuquan jiazhangzhi—fumu jiugu yu zinü xixu xiangzheng" 從法律糾紛看宋代的父權家長制一父母舅姑與子女媳婿相爭. *Zhongyang Yanjiuyuan Lishi Yuyan Yanjiusuo jikan* 中央研究院歷史語言研究所集刊 69, no. 3 (1998): 483–556.

———. "Nan Song zaishinü fenchan tanyi—shiliao jiedu ji yanjiu fangfa" 南宋在室女分產權探疑一史料解讀及研究方法. *Zhongyang Yangjiuyuan Lishi Yuyan Yanjiusuo jikan* 中央研究院歷史語言研究所集刊 83, no. 3 (2012): 445–505.

————. "Qiantan Songdai funü de shoujie yu zaijia" 淺談宋代婦女的守節與再嫁. In *Songshi yanjiuji* 25 宋史研究集, edited by Songshi Zuotanhui 宋史座談會, 143–183. Taipei: Guoli Bianyiguan, 1995.

————. *Songdai de zongjiao, shenfen yu sifa* 宋代的宗教, 身分與司法. Beijing: Zhonghua, 2012.

————. "Songdai fenchanfa 'zaishinü de nan zhi ban' xintan (xia)" 宋代分產法 '在室女得男之半' 新探 (下). *Fazhishi yanjiu* 法制史研究 6 (2004): 41–97.

Liu Miaofen 呂妙芬. "Zuo wei Mengxue yu nüjiao duben de X*iaojing*—jian lun qi webben dingwei de lishi bianhua" 做為蒙學與女教讀本的 '孝經'—兼論其文 本 定位的歷史變化. *Taida lishi xuebao* 台大歷史學報 6 (2008): 1–64.

Liu Min 劉敏. "Song shi yuanxiaojie zhong de nüxing minsu" 宋時元宵節中的女性 民俗. *Fuyang Shifan Xueyuan xuebao* 阜陽師範學院學報 3 (2016): 129–133.

Liu Pujiang 劉浦江. "Jindai hukou yanjiu" 金代戶口研究. *Zhongguoshi yanjiu* 中國史研究 2 (1994): 86–96.

Liu Qiugen 劉秋根 and Ren Huanhuan 任歡歡. "Songdai nüxing shishang xiaofei" 宋代女性時尚消費. *Hebei xuekan* 河北學刊 31, no. 3 (2011): 71–77.

Liu Shuangqin 劉雙琴. "Songdai nüxing zuojia tibi chuangzuo lunxi" 宋代女性作家題壁創作論析. *Jinggangshan Daxue xuebao* 靜岡山大學學報 37, no. 6 (2016): 79–85.

Liu Suyong 劉肅勇. "Liao wangchao Qidanzu nüjie Chengtian Taihou Xiao Chuo" 遼王朝契丹族女傑承天太后蕭綽. *Liao Jin lishi yu kaogu* 遼金歷史與考古 8 (2017): 118–127.

Liu Xin 劉欣. "Luelun Songdai jiaxun zhong de 'nüjiao'" 略論宋代家訓中的 '女教.' *Zhonghua Nüzi Xueyuan xuebao* 中華女子學院學報 21, no. 5 (2009): 91–95.

————. *Songdai jiaxun yu shehui zhenghe yanjiu* 宋代家訓與社會整合研究. Kunming: Yunnan Daxue, 2015.

Liu Xinjun 劉馨珺. "Guiguai wenhua yu xingbie: Cong Songdai duotai shaying tanqi" 鬼怪文化與性別: 從宋代墮胎殺嬰談起. *Xueshu yanjiu* 學術研究 3 (2013): 114–122.

Liu, Yang. "Imagery of Female Daoists in Tang and Song Poetry." PhD diss., University of British Columbia, 2011.

Liu Yongcong 劉詠聰. "Wei Jin yihuan shijia dui houfei zhuzheng zhi fumian pingjia" 魏晉以還史家對后妃主政之負面評價. In *Zhongguo funüshi lunji sanji* 中國婦女史論集三集, edited by Bao Jialin 鮑家麟, 29–40. Taipei: Daoxiang, 1993.

Liu Yuchun 柳雨春. "Songdai shangye zhong de nüxing" 宋代商業中的女性. *Baoding Shifan Zhuanke Xuexiao xuebao* 保定師範專科學校學報 20, no. 4 (2007): 102–104.

Liu Yuchun 柳雨春 and Yang Guo 楊果. "Songdai shangye zhong nüxing jingkuang fenxi" 宋代商業中女性境況分析. *Beijing Ligong Daxue xuebao* 北京理工大學學報 13, no. 1 (2011): 132–135.

Liu Yutang 劉玉堂. "Lun Tangdai de 'yijue' zhidu ji qi falü houguo" 論唐代的 '義絕' 制度及其法律後果. *Zhongguo Minzu Daxue xuebao* 中國民族大學學報 6 (2005): 113–117.

Liu Zhengping 劉正萍. "Songdai yueshu houfei guizhi shuping" 宋代約束后妃規制述評. *Yancheng Shifan Xueyuan xuebao* 鹽城師範學院學報 5 (2010): 43–47.

Liu Zhengzheng 劉箏箏. "Jindai Nüzhen de hunyin xingshi he xisu" 金代女真的婚姻形式和習俗. *Manzu yanjiu* 滿族研究 1 (2009): 87–90.

Liu Zi 劉梓. "Liaodai jiechu de houmu (huang taihou) shezheng" 遼代傑出的后母 (皇太后) 攝政. *Liao Jin lishi yu kaosu* 遼金歷史與考古 2 (2010): 56–60.

Liu Zi 劉梓 and Hu Jian 胡健. "Liaodai hunyin zhuangkuang qianxi—yi huangzu Yelüshi yu houzu Xiaoshi wei zhongxin" 遼代婚姻狀況淺析—以皇族耶律氏與后族蕭氏為中心. *Liao Jin lishi yu kaogu* 遼金歷史與考古 6 (2015): 140–144.

Lou Jingjing 樓菁晶. "'Nü hede nan zhi ban'—cong *Ming gong shu pan qingming ji* kan Nansong de nüfenfa" '女合得男之半'—從名公書判清明集看南宋的女 分法. *Zhejiang shehui kexue* 浙江社會科學 10 (2011): 128–132.

Lü Bianting 呂變庭. "Lun Zhu Xi shiyezhong de Songdai 'jiating funü'—yi Zhu Xi de 'Nüjie' tiwang wei li" 論朱熹視野中的宋代 '家庭婦女'—以朱熹的 '女戒' 提網為例. *Songshi yanjiu luncong* 宋史研究論叢 15 (2014): 390–417.

Lü, Bianting. "Bridal Dowry Land and the Economic Status of Women from Wealthy Families in the Song Dynasty." Translated by Austin Dean and Jinxu Yang. *Frontiers of History in China* 5, no. 1 (2010): 106–124.

Lu, Huitzu. "Women's Ascetic Practices during the Song." *Asia Major* 15, no. 1 (2002): 73–108.

Lu Jianrong 盧建榮. "Yuanmo nüxing wei yufang shouru er zisha shijian de xingsi—xugou dangan hu, yidai youse yanjing kan wushi hu?" 元末女性為預防受辱而自殺事件的省思—虛構檔案乎, 抑戴有色眼睛看物事乎？ In *Jindai bainian chengshi shenghuo de xingbie yu quanli* 近代百年城市生活的性別 與權利, edited by Lu Jianrong 盧建榮, 79–114. Taipei: Xin gaodi, 2019.

Luk, Yu-ping. *The Empress and the Heavenly Masters: A Study of the Ordination Scroll of Empress Zhang (1493).* Hong Kong: Chinese University Press, 2016.

Luo Ling 羅凌. "Song Zhangxiao Mingsu Taihou yu Dangyang Yuquansi guanxi zhi shishi bianzheng" 宋章獻明肅太后與當陽玉泉寺關係之史實辨正. *Sanxia luntan* 三峽論壇 1 (2013): 22–25.

Luo Tonghua 羅彤華. *Tongju gongcai: Tangdai jiating yanjiu* 同居共財: 唐代家庭研究. Taipei: Zhengda, 2015.

Luo Xinquan 駱新泉. "Cong fu fu ci jiedu Songdai jiating zhong qizi de kuqing yu huanqing" 從賦夫詞解讀宋代家庭中妻子的苦情與歡情. *Nanyang Shifan Xueyuan xuebao* 南陽師範學院學報 10, no. 10 (2011): 95–100.

———. "Lun Liang Song fu nici de yanqing tezhi" 論兩宋賦尼詞的豔情特質. *Nanyang Shifan Xueyuan xuebao* 南陽師範學院學報 13, no. 4 (2014): 38–42.

———. "Lun Songmo nüshiren Zhang Yuniang de aiqing qinghuai" 論宋末女詩人張玉娘的愛情情懷. *Nanyang Ligong Xueyuan xuebao* 南陽理工學院學報 6, no. 5 (2014): 55–59.

Major, John S. "Characteristics of Late Chu Religion." In *Defining Chu: Image and Reality in Ancient China*, edited by Constance A. Cooke and John S. Major, 121–143. Honolulu: University of Hawaii Press, 1999.

Majumdar, D. N. *Himalayan Polyandry: Structure, Functioning and Cultural Change; A Field-Study of Jaunsar-Bawar.* Bombay: Asia Publishing House, 1960.

Mann, Susan. "Widows in the Kinship, Class, and Community Structures of Qing Dynasty China." *Journal of Asian Studies* 46, no. 1 (1987): 37–56.

Mao Liping 毛立平. *Qingdai jiazhuang yanjiu* 清代嫁妝研究. Beijing: Renmin Daxue, 2007.

McKnight, Brian E. *Law and Order in Sung China*. Cambridge: Cambridge University Press.

McMahon, Keith. *Celestial Women: Imperial Wives and Concubines in China from Song to Qing*. Lanham, MD: Rowman & Littlefield, 2016.

———. "Women Rulers in Imperial China." *Nan Nü* 15, no. 2 (2013): 179–218.

Meijer, M. J. *Murder and Adultery in Late Imperial China: A Study of Law and Morality*. Leiden: Brill, 1991.

Miyakawa, Hisayuki. "An Outline of the Naito Hypothesis and Its Effect on Japanese Studies of China." *Far Eastern Quarterly* 14, no. 4 (1955): 533–552.

Miyawaki-Okada, Junko. "The Role of Women in the Imperial Succession of the Nomadic Empire." In *The Role of Women in the Altaic World*, edited by Veronica Veit, 57–68. Wiesbaden: Harrassowitz Verlag, 2007.

Näf, Barbara Frey. "Compared with the Women the . . . Menfolk Have Little Business of Their Own—Gender Division of Labour in the History of the Mongols." In *The Role of Women in the Altaic World*, edited by Veronica Veit, 57–68. Wiesbaden: Harrassowitz Verlag, 2007.

Ni Wenjie 倪文杰 et al. *Zuijia nüxing miaoxie cidian* 最佳女性描寫辭典. Beijing: Zhongguo guoji guangbo, 1990.

Nomura Ayuko 野村鮎子. "Su Shi 'baomu Yangshi muzhiming' zhi mi" 蘇軾 '保母 楊氏墓誌銘' 之謎. In *Songdai wenhua yanjiu* 12 宋代文化研究, edited by Sichuan Daxue gejij zhengli zhongxin 四川大學古籍整理研究中心, 102–115. Beijing: Qianzhuang, 2003.

Ochs, Elinor, and Carolyn Taylor. "The 'Father Knows Best' Dynamic in Dinnertime Narratives." In *Gender Articulate: Language and the Socially Constructed Self*, edited by Kira Hall and Mary Bucholtz, 67–120. New York: Routledge, 1995.

Ōsawa Masāki 大澤正昭. "Tō Sō henkaku no kazoku kibo to kōsei—shōsetsu shiryō ni yoru bunseki" 唐宋變革期の家族規模と構成—小說史料による分析. *Tōdaishi kenkyū* 唐代史研究 6 (2003): 59–90.

———. *Tō Sō jidai no kazoku, konin, josei—tsuma wa tsuyoku* 唐宋時代の家族, 婚姻, 女性—婦は強く. Tokyo: Akashi, 2005.

Overmyer, Daniel L. "Values in Chinese Sectarian Literature: Ming and Ch'ing *Pao-chüan*." In *Popular Culture in Late Imperial China*, edited by David Johnson et al., 219–254. Berkeley and Los Angeles: University of California Press, 1985.

Pan Qing 潘清. "Yuandai Jiangnan diqu Menggu, Semu qiaoyu renhu hunyin zhuangtai de fenxi" 元代江南地區蒙古, 色目僑寓人戶婚姻狀態的分析. *Xuehai* 學海 3 (2002): 132–136.

Pan Wenting 潘文婷. "'Shuhua tongyuan' sixiang dui Yuandai nühuajia Guan Daosheng de yingxiang" 書畫同源思想對元代女畫家管道升的影響. *Meishu daguan* 美術大觀 10 (2013): 63.

Pang-White, Ann A. "Neo-Confucians and Zhu Xi in Family and Women: Challenges and Potentials." In *The Bloomsbury Research Handbook of Chinese Philosophy and Gender*, edited by Ann A. Pang-White, 69–87. New York: Bloomsbury Publishing, 2016.

Peng Hua 彭華 and Wang Lifang 王黎芳. "Songdai lixue xingbie yishi tanwei" 宋代理學性別意識探微. *Chuanshan xuekan* 船山學刊 3 (2010): 107–109.

Peng Ruihua 彭瑞花. "Lun Liaodai pusa jie de liuxing" 論遼代菩薩戒的流行. *Zongjiaoxue yanjiu* 宗教學研究 1 (2018): 90–95.

Peter, Prince of Greece and Denmark. *A Study of Polyandry*. The Hague: Mouton, 1963.

Qi Hongwei 祁紅偉. "Songdai zhuizun huanghou fumiao kaolun" 宋代追尊皇后祔廟考論. *Henan Keji Daxue xuebao* 河南科技大學學報 35, no. 3 (2017): 23–29.

Qi Wei 齊偉. "Liaodai Han guan shangceng hunyin guanxi de jianrongxing—yi Han Zhigu, Han Yanhui jiazu wei li" 遼代漢官上層婚姻關係的兼容性—以韓知古，韓延徽家族為例. *Liaoning Sheng Bowuguan guankan* 遼寧省博物館館刊 (2009): 428–439.

———. "Liaodai Hanren muzhi zhong tixian de Qidan hunsu tezheng" 遼代漢人墓誌中體現的契丹婚俗特徵. *Songshi yanjiu luncong* 宋史研究論叢 12 (2011–2012): 612–620.

Qi Xia 漆俠. *Songdai jingjishi* 宋代經濟史. Beijing: Zhonghua, 2009.

Qiao Zhiyong 喬志勇. "Guanyu Yuandai liangjian tonghun de shenfen wenti—jian tan liangjian tongjian suosheng zinü de shenfen" 關於元代良賤通婚的身分問題—兼談良賤通姦所生子女的身分. *Jinan shixue* 濟南史學 2 (2015): 81–88.

Qin Bo 秦博. "Liaodai Qidan funü de 'fozhuang'" 遼代契丹婦女的 '佛妝.' *Neimenggu Minzu Daxue xuebao* 內蒙古民族大學學報 42, no. 2 (2016): 63–66.

Qin Yan 秦艷. "Cong muzhi kan Songdai nüzi de fojiao xinyang" 從墓誌看宋代女性的佛教信仰. *Jinyang xuekan* 晉陽學刊 6 (2009): 86–91.

Qiu Aili 仇愛麗. "Niuqu de jingxiang—Yuandai shuihuxi nüxing xingxiang shixi" 扭曲的鏡像—元代水滸戲女性形象試析. *Wenxue qianyan* 文學前沿 2 (2008): 95–104.

Quan Hansheng 全漢昇. "Songdai nüzi zhiye yu shengji" 宋代女子職業與生計. In *Zhongguo funüshi lunji* 中國婦女史論集, edited by Bao Jialin 鮑家麟, 193–204. Taipei: Daoxiang, 1979.

Rao Daoqing 饒道慶 and Ye Jianli 葉堅麗. "Qing yu li de bianzou—Yuandai aiqing hunyin zaju zhong—Yuandai aiqing hunyin zaju zhong 'qiang' yixiang de wenhua toushi" 情與禮的變奏—元代愛情婚姻雜劇中 '牆' 意象的文化透視. *Xiqu yanjiu* 戲曲研究 3 (2002): 1–16.

Raphals, Lisa. *Sharing the Light: Representations of Women and Virtue in Early China*. Albany: State University of New York Press, 1998.

Ratchnevsky, Paul. "The Levirate in the Legislation of the Yuan Dynasty." In *Tamura hakuse shouju tōyōshi ronsō* 田村博士頌壽東洋史論叢, edited by Tamura hakuse taikan kinen jigyō kai 田村博士退官紀念事業會, 45–62. Kyoto: n.p., 1968.

Riasanovsky, Valentin A. *Fundamental Principles of Mongol Law*. Tientsin, 1937; reprint, The Hague: Mouton and Indiana University, 1965.

Rossabi, Morris. "Khubilai Khan and the Women in His Family." In *Studia Sino-Mongolica, Festschrift für Herbert Franke*, edited by Wolfgang Bauer, 153–180. Wiesbaden: Franz Steiner Verlag, 1979.

———. "Notes on Mongol Influences on the Ming Dynasty." In *Eurasian Influences on Yuan China*, edited by Morris Rossabi, 200–223. Singapore: ISEAS, 2013.

Sang Xiuyun 桑秀雲. "Jinshi Wan Yanshi hunyin zhi shishi" 金室完顏氏婚姻之試釋. *Zhongyang Yanjiuyuan Lishi Yuyan Yanjiusuo jikan* 中央研究院歷史語言研究所集刊 39, no. 1 (1969): 255–288.

Schlegel, Alice. "Status, Property, and the Value on Virginity." *American Ethnologist* 18, no. 4 (1991): 719–734.

Seol Baehwan 설배환. "Monggol jegug eseo hwangsil yeoseongui wisang byeonhwa" 몽골제국에서 황실 여성의 位相 변화. *Yeoksa hakhoe* 역사학회 228 (2015): 317–350.

Sha Wutian 沙武田. "Wudai Song Dunhuang shiku Huihu zhuang nü gongyang xiang yu Cao shi guiyijun de minzu texing" 五代宋敦煌石窟回鶻裝女供養像與曹氏歸義軍的民族特性. *Dunhuang yanjiu* 敦煌研究 2 (2013): 74–83.

Shao Yuxin 邵育欣. "Fojiao xinyang dui Songdai nüxing juchu kongjian de yingxiang" 佛教信仰對宋代女性居處空間的影響. *Shandong Nüzi Xueyuan xuebao* 山東女子學院學報 3 (2015): 56–60.

———. *Songdai funü de fojiao xinyang yu shenghuo kongjian* 宋代婦女的佛教信仰與生活空間. Beijing: Zhongguo shehui kexue chubanshe, 2015.

Shao Yuxin 邵育欣 and Zhang Fuhai 張付海. "Songdai biqiuni fumian xingxiang yanjiu" 宋代比丘尼負面形象研究. *Chifeng Xueyuan xuebao* 赤峰學院學報 35, no. 11 (2014): 22–23.

———. "Songdai gaoni shiji yanjiu" 宋代高尼事跡研究. *Heilongjiang shizhi* 黑龍江史志 15 (2014): 18–19.

Shen Wanli 申萬里. "Nansong dao Yuanchao de shehui bianqian: Yi jiazu guannian wei zhongxin de kaocha" 南宋到元朝的社會變遷: 以家族觀念為中心的考察. *Zhongyuan wenhua yanjiu* 中原文化研究 4 (2016): 116–122.

Shi Fan 石璠. "Songdai zhuixu de caichan jicheng quanli" 宋代贅婿的財產繼承權利. *Shehui zongheng* 社會縱橫 30, no. 8 (2015): 112–116.

Shi Fengchun 史風春. *Liaochao houzu zhu wenti yanjiu* 遼朝后族諸問題研究. Beijing: Renmin, 2017.

———. "Qidan waiqi shufang shici kao" 契丹外戚屬房世次考. *Nei Menggu shehui kexue* 內蒙古社會科學 32, no. 6 (2011): 68–72.

Shi Jinmin 石金民. "Rujia sixiang dui Liaodai qidan nüxing de yingxiang" 儒家思想對遼代契丹女性的影響. *Beifang wenwu* 北方文物 3 (2009): 67–70.

Shiga, Shūzō. "Family Property and the Law of Inheritance in Traditional China." In *Chinese Family Law and Social Change in Historical and Comparative Perspective*, edited by David C. Buxbaum, 109–150. Seattle: University of Washington Press, 1978.

Shimada Masao 島田正郎. *Ryōdai shakaishi kenkyū* 遼代社會史研究. Tokyo: Iwanandō, 1977.

Shu Hongxia 舒紅霞 and Yang Dongxia 楊東霞. "Wei Jin renxing zijue dui Songdai nüzuojia de yingxiang" 魏晉人性自覺對宋代女作家的影響. *Dalian Daxue xuebao* 大連大學學報 1 (2006): 30–33.

Sima Guang 司馬光. *Sima shi shuyi* 司馬氏書儀. Beijing: Zhonghua shuju, 1985.

Smith, Paul Jakov. "Impressions of the Song-Yuan-Ming Transition: The Evidence from *Biji* Memoirs." In *The Song-Yuan-Ming Transition in Chinese History*, edited by Paul Jakov Smith and Richard von Glahn, 71–110. Cambridge, MA: Harvard Asia Center, 2003.

Sommer, Matthew H. "The Uses of Chastity: Sex, Law, and the Property of Widows in Qing China." *Late Imperial China* 17, no. 2 (1996): 77–130.

Song Dejin 宋德金. *Jindai de shehui shenghuo* 金代的社會生活. Xi'an: Shaanxi renmin, 1988.

Song Dongxia 宋冬霞. "Songdai hunyin fangshi zhi jie wang mei xu tanxi" 宋代婚姻方式之姊亡妹續探析. *Guizhou Shifan Xueyuan xuebao* 貴州師範學院學 報 5 (2010): 31–34.

———. "Songdai shiren jieceng fengbi hunyinquan tanxi" 宋代士人階層封閉婚姻圈探析. *Nanfang lunkan* 南方論刊 6 (2015): 61–63, 36.

Song Zhenhao 宋鎮豪. *Xia Shang shehui shenghuo shi* 夏商社會生活史. Beijing: Zhongguo shehui kexue, 1994.

Su Qingwen 蘇倩雯. "Lun Songdai houlian de yuanyin" 論宋代厚奩的原因. *Haiyang Redai Haiyang Xueyuan xuebao* 海南熱帶海洋學院學報 23, no. 6 (2016): 92–96.

Su Wanling 蘇婉綾, "Jin Yuan shiqi yiliao wenhua zhong de xingbie yanjiu" 金元 時期醫療文化中的性別研究. MA thesis, Fo Guang University, 2019.

Sun Jianhua 孫建華. "Qidanzu de maju yu weilie—cong Chenguo Gongzhu chutu wenwu tanqi" 契丹族的馬具與圍獵—從陳果公主墓出土文化談起. *Nei Menggu wenwu kaogu* 內蒙古文物考古 1 (2002): 22–25.

Sun Keli 孫科麗. "Liaodai guizu lianhun guanxi shulun" 遼代貴族聯婚關係述論. *Neimenggu shehui kexue* 內蒙古社會科學 3 (2008): 38–41.

Sun Yang 孫陽. "Lixue dui Songdai nüzhuang de yingxiang" 理學對宋代女裝的影響. *Yishu sheji yuekan* 藝術設計月刊 5 (2007): 90–91.

Tackett, Nicolas. *The Destruction of the Medieval Chinese Aristocracy*. Cambridge, MA: Harvard University Asia Center, 2014.

———. "Great Clansmen, Bureaucrats, and Local Magnates: The Structure and Circulation of the Elite in Late-Tang China." *Asia Major* 21, no. 2 (2008): 101–152.

———. *The Origins of the Chinese Nation: Song China and the Forging of an East Asian World Order*. Cambridge: Cambridge University Press, 2017.

Tajima Miki 田嶋美喜. "Sōdai no jōnō keiei ni okeru josei rōdō" 宋代の小農經營における女性勞動. In *Ronshū: Chūgoku joseishi* 論集: 中國女性史, edited by Chūgoku joseishi kenkyūkai 中國女性史研究會, 19–36. Tokyo: Yoshikawa Kōbun kan, 1999.

Takahashi, Yoshirō. "Orphaned Daughters: On the So-Called Property Rights of Daughters in the Southern Song Period." Translated by Matthew Raleigh. *International Journal of Asian Studies* 12, no. 2 (2015): 131–165.

Tan Xiaolin 譚曉琳. "Yuandai hunyin fagui zhong de funü wenti zaitan" 元代婚姻法規中的婦女問題再探. *Nei Menggu Daxue xuebao* 內蒙古大學學報 32 (2000): 17–21.

Tan Xiaoling 譚曉玲. "Yuandai liangzhong hunyin xingtai de tantao" 元代兩種婚姻型態的探討. *Nei Menggu Daxue xuebao* 內蒙古大學學報 5 (2007): 35–39.

———. "Yuandai maimai nükou xianxiang chutan" 元代買賣女口現象初探. *Zhongyang Minzu Daxue xuebao* 中央民族大學學報 4 (2003): 96–99.

Tang Yu 楊玉. "Nanquan shehui xia de nüxing yishi—cong Tang Song hunlian chuanqi de xiqu gaibian zhong tanxun" 男權社會下的女性意識—從唐宋婚戀傳奇的戲曲改編中探尋. *Zhejiang yishu zhiye xueyuan xuebao* 浙江藝術職業學院學報 15, no. 2 (2017): 70–74.

Tang Yuping 唐玉萍. "Liaodai funü zhenjieguan danhua weiyi" 遼代婦女貞節觀淡化微議. *Zhaowuda Mengzu Shizhuan xuebao* 昭烏達蒙族師專學報 17, no. 4 (1996): 2–35, 24.

Tao Jianrong 陶建榮. "Cong Song Yuan huaben kan Songdai funü hunyin zhuang-kuang" 從宋元話本看宋代婦女婚姻狀況. *Suzhou Jiaoyu Xueyuan xuebao* 宿州教育學院學報 6, no. 1 (2003): 35–37.

Tao, Jing-shen. *The Jurchen in Twelfth Century China: A Study of Sinicization.* Seattle: University of Washington Press, 1976.

Tao Jinsheng 陶晉生. "Bei Song funü de zaijia yu gaijia" 北宋婦女的再嫁與改嫁. *Xin shixue* 新史學 9 (1995): 1–28.

Tian Xin 田欣. *Songdai shangren jiating* 宋代商人家庭. Beijing: Shehui kexue wenxian, 2013.

Tie Aihua 鐵愛花. "Guiwei zhi wai: Songdai nüxing youlan huodong tanxi" 閨闈之外: 宋代女性遊覽活動探析. *Jiangxi shehui kexue* 江西社會科學 8 (2017): 119–125.

———. "Lun Songdai guojia dui nüxing de jingbiao" 論宋代國家對女性的旌表. *Lishi jiaoxue* 歷史教學 12 (2008): 5–9.

———. "Songdai nüxing xinglü fengxian wenti tanxi—yi nüxing xinglü yujie wei zhongxin" 宋代女性行旅風險問題探析—以女性行旅遇劫為中心. *Zhejiang xuekan* 浙江學刊 1 (2015): 58–66.

———. *Songdai shiren jieceng nüxing yanjiu* 宋代士人階層女性研究. Beijing: Renmin, 2011.

———. "Yulun yu zhixu: Songdai xiangping dui nüxing de guifan ji qi yingxiang." 輿論與秩序: 宋代鄉評對女性的規範及其影響. *Shilin* 史林 2 (2012): 51–61.

Tsai, Katheryn A. "Miaodao." In *Biographical Dictionary of Chinese Women*, vol. 2, *Tang through Ming, 618–1644*, edited by Lily Xiao Hong Lee and Sue Wiles, 291–292. London: Routledge, 2015.

Tuo Tuo 脫脫 et al. *Jinshi* 金史. Taipei: Dingwen shuju, 1980.

———. *Liaoshi* 遼史. Taipei: Dingwen shuju, 1980.

———. *Songshi* 宋史. Beijing: Zhonghua shuju, 1977.

Van Ess, Hans. "Cheng Yi and His Ideas about Women as Revealed in His Commentary to the *Yijing*." *Oriens Extremus* 49 (2010): 63–77.

Van Norden, Bryan W., trans. *Mengzi: With Selections from Traditional Commentaries.* Indianapolis: Hackett, 2008.

Von Glahn, Richard. *The Economic History of China: From Antiquity to the Nineteenth Century.* Cambridge: Cambridge University Press, 2016.

Walton, Linda. "Kinship, Marriage and Status in Song China: A Study of the Lou Lineage of Ningbo, c. 1050–1250." *Journal of Asian History* 18, no. 1 (1984): 35–77.

Wan Junjie 萬軍杰. *Tangdai nüxing de shengqian yu zuhou: Weirao muzhi ziliao zhankai de ruogan tantao* 唐代女性的生前與卒後: 圍繞墓誌資料展開的若干探討. Tianjin: Tianjin guji, 2010.

Wang Chao 汪超. "Bei Song shimen yinqin guanxi yu wenxue chuancheng" 北宋師門姻親關係與文學傳承. *Hunan Keji Daxue xuebao* 湖南科技大學學報 17, no. 6 (2014): 133–139.

Wang Chunhua 王春花. "Songdai hunyin zhong de caili xiaokao—yi Dunhuang wenxian 'Deng jia caili mu' wei zhongxin" 宋代婚姻中的財禮小考—以敦煌文獻 '鄧家財禮目' 為中心. *Sheke zongheng* 社科縱橫 8 (2007): 138–139, 157.

Wang Cui 王翠. "Songdai chujianü yu benjia de jingji guanxi" 宋代出嫁女與本家的經濟關係. *Xuchang Xueyuan xuebao* 許昌學院學報 1 (2013): 86–90.

Wang Depeng 王德朋. "Jindai Zhenyi Huanghou chujia yuanyin xinyi" 金代貞懿皇后出家原因新議. *Liaoning Daxue xuebao* 遼寧大學學報 42, no. 3 (2014): 145–148.

Wang Haidong 王海冬. "Yuandai haishang caoyun yu Mazu xinyang de fazhan" 元代海上漕運與媽祖信仰的發展. *Putian Xueyuan xuexiao* 莆田學院學校 23, no. 4 (2016): 1–5.

Wang Heming 王鶴鳴. "Songdai jiaci yanjiu" 宋代家祠研究. *Anhui shixue* 安徽史學 3 (2013): 75–83.

Wang Jianhong 王劍虹. "Yuandai hunyin zhidu gaishuo" 元代婚姻制度概說. *Xingtai Xueyuan xuebao* 邢台學院學報 1 (2003): 43–46.

Wang Lianlian 王連連. "Shixi Liaodai Shulü Hou de houquan he muquan" 試析遼代述律后的后權和母權. *Jiangsu Gongye Xueyuan xuebao* 江蘇工業學院學報 1 (2010): 59–61, 65.

Wang Ping. *Aching for Beauty: Footbinding in China*. Minneapolis: University of Minnesota Press, 2000.

Wang Shanjun 王善軍. *Shijia dazu yu Liaodai shehui* 世家大族與遼代社會. Beijing: Renmin, 2008.

Wang Shilian 王世蓮. "Jindai fei Nützen houfei chuyi" 金代非女真族后妃芻議. In *Liao Jin shi lunji 6* 遼金史論集 6, edited by Zhang Changgeng 張暢耕 et al., 300–318. Beijing: Shehui kexue wenxian, 2001.

Wang Xiao 王曉. "Tangdai jiazhuang xiaofei kao" 唐代嫁妝消費考. *Yibin Xueyuan xuebao* 宜賓學院學報 14, no. 4 (2014): 56–61.

Wang Xin 王昕. "Jindai nüxing zhenjieguan de bianyi" 金代女性貞節觀的變異. *Wenshi zhishi* 文史知識 2 (2007): 98–101.

Wang Xingchen 王星晨 and Liu Hanlun 劉翰倫. "Yuandai funü zhenjie guannian danbo yuanyin tanwei" 元代婦女貞節觀念淡薄原因探微. *Qianyan* 前沿 17 (2012): 194–196.

Wang Xinli 王新利. "Songdai nüxing shujia Guan Kui" 宋代女性書家管窺. *Zhongguo shufa* 中國書法 3 (2017): 177–181.

Wang Xinying 王新英 and Jia Shurong 賈淑榮. "Jindai jiating renkou shuliang kaolue—yi Jindai shike wenxian wei zhongxin" 金代家庭人口數量考慮—以金代時刻文獻為中心. *Heilongjiang minzu congkan* 黑龍江民族叢刊 6 (2014): 98–103.

Wang Xue 王雪. "Songdai fuchan yixue de fazhan yu congye renqun fenxi" 宋代婦產醫學的發展與從業人群分析. *Heilongjiang shizhi* 黑龍江史志 5 (2014): 29–31.

———. "Songdai nüxing shenti shufu yu cuican" 宋代女性身體束縛與摧殘. *Haerbin Xueyuan xuebao* 哈爾濱學院學報 36, no. 4 (2015): 87–92.

Wang Xueli 王雪莉. *Songdai fushi zhidu yanjiu* 宋代服飾制度研究. Hangzhou: Hangzhou, 2007.

Wang Yi 王毅. *Songdai wenxue jiazu* 宋代文學家族. Changsha: Hunan Shifa Daxue chubanshe, 2008.

Wang Yijie 王藝潔. "Yuandai nüxing zaijia hou de jiating xiaodao lunchang" 元代女性再嫁後的家庭孝道倫常. *Xibei Shida xuebao* 西北師大學報 55, no. 2 (2018): 60–65.

Wang Yiming 王禕茗 and Zhao Xiaogeng 趙曉耕. "'Wu si huo' yu 'xu si cai'—Songdai nüxing jiazhuang quanli de yizhong jiedu" '無私貨' 與 '蓄私財'—宋代女性嫁妝權利的一種解讀. *Jiangsu shehui kexue* 江蘇社會科學 2 (2013): 160–165.

Wang Yonggen 王永根 and Lü Yong 呂永. "Songdai qie zhi caichanquan yanjiu" 宋代妾之財產權研究. *Yichun Xueyuan xuebao* 宜春學院學報 2 (2010): 98–100.

Wang Yue 汪悅. "Bei Song funü de hunyin yu shengyu—yi muzhiming wei yanjiu yangben" 北宋婦女的婚姻與生育—以墓誌銘為研究樣本. *Chongqing Ligong Daxue xuebao* 重慶理工大學學報 26, no. 4 (2012): 74–78.

Wang Zhu 王姝. "20 shiji yilai Jindai funü yanjiu zongshu" 世紀以來金代婦女研究綜述. *Funü yanjiu luncong* 婦女研究論叢 3 (2016): 110–121.

———. "Ershi shiji yilai Jindai funü yanjiu zongshu" 20 世紀以來金代婦女研究綜述. Funü yanjiu luncong 婦女研究論叢 3 (2016): 110–121.

———. "Jindai funü sangzang lisu kaolun—yi fufu hezang lisu wei yanjiu zhongxin" 金代婦女喪葬禮俗考論—以夫婦合葬禮俗為研究中心. *Shehui kexue zhanxian* 社會科學戰線 10 (2016): 120–127.

———. "Jindai nubi laiyuan yu diwei" 金代奴婢來源與地位. *Liaoning Gongcheng Jishu Daxue xuebao* 遼寧工程技術大學學報 18, no. 6 (2016): 798–813.

———. "Jindai nüxing zuojia ji qi shizuo kaolue" 金代女性作家及其詩作略. *Tonghua Shifan Xueyuan xuebao* 通化師範學院學報 6 (2016): 139–144.

Warner, Rebecca L., Gary R. Lee, and Janet Lee. "Social Organization, Spousal Resources, and Marital Power: A Cross-Cultural Study," *Journal of Marriage and Family* 48, no. 1 (1986): 121–128.

Watson, James L. "Anthropological Overview: The Development of Chinese Descent Groups." In *Kinship Organization in Late Imperial China, 1000–1940,* edited by Patricia Buckley Ebrey and James L. Watson, 274–292. Berkeley: University of California Press, 1986.

———. "Standardization of the Gods: The Promotion of T'ien You ('Empress of Heaven') along the South China Coast, 960–1960." In *Popular Culture in Late Imperial China,* edited by David Johnson et al., 292–324. Berkeley and Los Angeles: University of California Press, 1985.

Weatherford, Jack. *The Secret History of the Mongol Queens: How the Daughters of Genghis Khan Rescued His Empire.* New York: Broadway Books, 2010.

Wei Xueyan 位雪艷. "Yuandai funü zhenjie wenti zaitan" 元代婦女貞節問題再探. *Hebei Shifan Daxue xuebao* 河北師範大學學報 3 (2007): 109–112.

Wei Xueyan 位雪燕 and Xu Kuoduan 徐适端. "Cong 'Yuanshi–Lienüzhuan' xi Yuandai funü de zhenjieguan" 從 '元史‧列女傳' 析元代婦女的貞節觀. *Nei Menggu Shifan Daxue xuebao* 內蒙古師範大學學報 3 (2007): 101–105.

Wei Zhiyuan 魏志遠. "Songdai rujia 'li xia shumin' sixiang de xingqi yu shijian" 宋代儒家 '禮下庶民' 思想的興起與實踐. *Pingdingshan Xueyuan xuebao* 平頂山學院學報 29, no. 4 (2014): 14–18.

Weitz, Ankeney. "Art and Family Identity during the Yuan Dynasty: The Zhao Family of Wuxing." In *The Family Model in Chinese Art and Culture*, edited by Jerome Silbergeld and Dora C. Y. Ching, 423–458. Princeton, NJ: P. Y. and Kinmay Tang Center for East Asian Art and Department of Art and Archaeology, Princeton University, 2013.

Weng Yuxuan 翁育瑄. "Tangdai shiren de hunyin yu jiating—yi qiqie wenti wei zhongxin" 唐代士人的婚姻與家庭—以妻妾問題為中心. In *Zhongguo zhonggu shehui yu guojia* 中國中古社會與國家, edited by Song Dexi 宋德熹, 355–376. Banqiao: Daoxiang, 2009.

———. "Tō Sō bushi kara mita jōsei no shusetsu to saika ni tsuite—mibōjin no sentaku to sono seikatsu" 唐宋墓誌から見た女性の守節と再嫁について―未亡人の選擇とその生活. *Tōdaishi kenkyū* 唐代史研究 6 (2003): 41–58.

Wright, David C. "The Political and Military Power of Khitan Empress Dowagers." In *The Role of Women in the Altaic World*, edited by Veronica Veit, 325–334. Wiesbaden: Harrassowitz Verlag, 2007.

Wu Haihang 吳海航. *Yuandai fa wenhua yanjiu* 元代法文化研究. Beijing: Beijing Shifan Daxue, 2000.

Wu Hongli 武宏麗. "Qidan Xiao Taihou chuanshuo yanjiu" 契丹蕭太后傳說研究. *Dongbei shilun* 東北史論 1 (2013): 72–75.

Wu, Pei-yi. "Yang Miaozhen: A Woman Warrior in Thirteenth Century China." *Nan Nü* 4, no. 2 (2002): 137–169.

Wu Qiong 吳瓊. "Cong shike kan Liaodai pingmin jieji nüxing chongfo qingkkuang" 從石刻看遼代平民階級女性崇佛情況. *Chifeng Xueyuan xuebao* 赤峰學院學報 37, no. 7 (2016): 14–16.

Wu Yuhuan 武玉環. *Liao Jin shehui yu wenhua yanjiu* 遼金社會與文化研究. Beijing: Zhongguo shehui kexue, 2014.

Wu Zhihao 吳志浩. "Songdai shiren pingjun siwang nianling kao" 宋代士人平均死亡年齡考. *Zhejiang xuekan* 浙江學刊 4 (2017): 170–181.

Xi Lei 喜蕾 and Temuer Bagena 特木爾巴格那. "Yuandai Gaoli gongnü zhidu yu qi zhengzhi wenhua beijing" 元代高麗貢女制度與其政治文化背景. *Nei Menggu shehui kexue* 內蒙古社會科學 5 (2003): 5–9.

Xia Tao 夏濤. "Lun Songdai nüxing jingji fanzui wenti" 論宋代女性經濟犯罪問題. *Hebei Daxue xuebao* 河北大學學報 40, no. 5 (2015): 44–49.

Xia Yuxu 夏宇旭. *Jindai Qidanren yanjiu* 金代契丹人研究. Beijing: Zhongguo shehui kexue chubanshe, 2014.

Xia Yuxu 夏宇旭 and Zhao Weibin 趙瑋彬. "Liao Jin Qidan Nüzhen hunzhi hunsu zhi bijiao" 遼金契丹女真婚制婚俗之比較. *Jilin Shifan Daxue xuebao* 吉林師範大學學報 3 (2007): 76–78.

Xie Jingwen 謝靜雯. "Songdai gongting nüshiren zuopin gailan" 宋代宮廷女詩人作品概覽. *Shehuixue lun* 社會學論 4 (2015): 134–135.

———. "Songdai gongting nüshiren zuopin leibie fenxi" 宋代宮廷女詩人作品類別分析. *Anhui wenxue* 安徽文學 6 (2015): 8–11.

Xie Yue 謝玥. "Diyu yu minzu shiyu xia de Yuandai nüxing shiren qunti" 地域與民族視域下的元代女性詩人群體. *Xiandai yuyan* 現代語言 4 (2015): 37–39.

Xin Gengru 辛更儒. "Lun Songdai funü gaijia bushou yulun feiyi" 論宋代婦女改嫁不受輿論非議. *Funü yanjiu luncong* 婦女研究論叢 3 (1999): 31–35.

Xing Tie 邢鐵. *Tang Song fenjia zhidu* 唐宋分家制度. Beijing: Shangwu, 2010.

Xiong Du 熊篤. "Lun Yuan sanqu zhong de qinglou ci jian lun Yuandai jinü tedian" 論元散曲中的青樓詞兼論元代妓女特點. *Chongqing Gongshang Daxue xuebao* 重慶工商大學學報 24, no. 5 (2007): 99–104.

Xu Bingyu 徐秉愉. "Liao Jin Yuan sandai funü jielie shiji yu zhenjie guannian zhi fazhan" 遼金元三代婦女節烈事跡與貞節觀念之發展. In *Zhongguo Funüshi lunji xuji* 中國婦女史論集續集, edited by Bao Jialin 鮑家麟, 215–240. Taipei: Daoxiang chubanshe, 1991.

Xu Kuoduan 徐适端. "Shixi Yuandai funü zai falü zhong de diwei" 試析元代婦女在法律中的地位. *Zhongguo shi yanjiu* 中國史研究 4 (2000): 104–116.

Xu, Man. *Crossing the Gate: Everyday Lives of Women in Song Fujian (960–1279)*. Albany: State University of New York Press, 2016.

———. "Gender and Burial in Imperial China: An Investigation of Women's Space in Fujian Tombs of the Song Era (960–1279)." *Nan Nü* 13, no. 1 (2011): 1–51.

Xu Xiufang 徐秀芳. *Songdai shizu funü de hunyin shenghuo—yi renji guanxi wei zhongxin* 宋代士族婦女的婚姻生活—以人際關係為中心. New Taipei: Hua Mulan wenhua, 2011.

Xue Meiqing 薛梅卿 et al. *Liang Song fazhi tonglun* 兩宋法制通論. Beijing: Falü, 2002.

Yan Ming 嚴明. *Zhongguo mingji yishu shi* 中國名妓藝術史. Taipei: Wenjin, 1992.

Yan Xurui 閻續瑞 and Yang Maowen 楊茂文. "Lun Songdai caisangshi de nongshi zhuti" 論宋代採桑詩的農事主題. *Wenyi pinglun* 文藝評論 10 (2012): 165–168.

Yan Zuozhi 嚴佐之. "Lixuexing jiazu, nüxing zunzhang, qijia zhi dao—Song Yuzhao Boshan Hushi zongzu 'Mo tai furen jiaxun' jiedu" 理學型家族, 女性尊長, 齊家之道—宋餘姚柏山胡氏宗族 '莫太夫人家訓' 解讀. *Lishi wenxian* 歷史文獻 19 (2016): 308–366.

Yanagita Setsuko 柳田節子. "Sōdai saiban ni okeru josei no soshō" 宋代裁判における女性の訴訟. In *Ronshū: Chūgoku joseishi* 論集: 中國女性史, edited by Chūgoku joseishi kenkyūkai 中國女性史研究會, 2–17. Tokyo: Yoshikawa Kōbunkan, 1999.

———. *Sōdai shomin no onnatachi* 宋代庶民の女たち. Tokyo: Kyuko shoin, 2003.

Yang, Binbin. "A Pictorial Autobiography by Zeng Jifen (1852–1942) and the Use of the 'Exemplary' in China's Modern Transformation." *Nan Nü* 19 (2017): 263–315.

Yang Da 陽達. "Zhuangyuan beihou de nüxing—yi Song Yuan keju xi zhong de qizi juese wei li" 狀元背後的女性—以宋元科舉戲中的妻子角色為例. *Lanzhou xuekan* 蘭州學刊 4 (2017): 130–138.

Yang Fuxue 楊富學 and Meng Fanyun 孟凡雲. "Qidan yinghunzhi kaolue" 契丹媵婚制考略. *Heilongjiang minzu congkan* 黑龍江民族叢刊 4 (2001): 94–98.

Yang Guo 楊果. "Cong Songdai funü mingzi kan shehui xingbie wenhua jiangou yi Songren biji wei zhongxin" 從宋代婦女名字看社會性別文化建構—以宋人筆記為中心. *Wuhan Daxue xuebao* 武漢大學學報 67, no. 1 (2014): 112–126.

Yang Guo 楊果 and Liu Yuchun 柳雨春. "Songdai guojia dui guanyuan suchang de guanli" 宋代國家對官員宿娼的管理. *Wuhan Daxue xuebao* 武漢大學學 報 1 (2011): 98–104.

Yang Guo 楊果 and Lu Xi 陸溪. "Songdai zisha nüxing shenhou zhi shi" 宋代自殺女性身後之事. *Henan Daxue xuebao* 河南大學學報 52, no. 2 (2012): 69–73.

Yang Jiping 楊祭平. "Dunhuang chutu de fangqi shu suoyi" 敦煌出土的放妻書瑣議. *Ximen Daxue xuebao* 西門大學學報 4 (1999): 34–41.

Yang Tianbao 楊天保 and Yu Hui 于輝. "Songdai nüxing caichan jichengquan de shixian chengdu—jiyu chujianü songan de lishi kaocha" 宋代女性財產繼承權的實現程度—基於出嫁女訟案的歷史考察. *Gaige yu zhanlue* 改革與戰略 5 (2013): 24–29.

Yang Yi 楊逸. "'Fu li' yihuo 'cong su': Lun Songdai jiali zhong de hunli" '復禮' 抑或 '從俗': 論宋代家禮中的婚禮. *Minsu yanjiu* 民俗研究 2 (2016): 51–58.

Yao Ping 姚平. *Tangdai funü de shengming licheng* 唐代婦女的生命歷程. Shanghai: Shanghai guji chubanshe, 2004.

Yao, Ping. "Childbirth and Maternal Mortality in Tang China." *Chinese Historical Review* 12, no. 2 (2005): 263–286.

———. "Women in Portraits: An Overview of Epitaphs from Early and Medieval China." In *Overt and Covert Treasures: Essays on the Sources for Chinese Women's History*, edited by Clara Wing-Chung Ho, 157–183. Hong Kong: City University Press, 2012.

Yi Jo-lan. "Social Status, Gender Division and Institutions: Sources Relating to Women in Chinese Standard Histories." In *Overt and Covert Treasures: Essays on the Sources for Chinese Women's History*, edited by Clara Wing-Chung Ho, 131–155. Hong Kong: City University Press, 2012.

Yin Xiaolin 尹曉琳 and Shen Ling 沈玲. "Liaodai Qidanzu nüxing wenren chuangzuo de zhengzhi yishi" 遼代契丹族女性文人創作的政治意識. *Changchun Ligong Daxue xuebao* 長春理工大學學報 30, no. 5 (2017): 141–144.

You Biao 游彪. "Songdai youguan sengni de fatiao chutan" 宋代有關僧尼的法條初探. *Henan Daxue xuebao* 河南大學學報 53, no. 3 (2013): 86–91.

You Huiyuan 游惠遠. "Cong hunyinfa bijiao Song Jin funü diwei de chayi" 從婚姻法比較宋金婦女地位的差異. *Zhongguo lishi xuehui jikan* 中國歷史學會史學集刊 7 (2001): 99–162.

———. *Song Yuan zhiji funü diwei de bianqian* 宋元之際婦女地位的變遷. Taipei: Xin wenfeng, 2003.

———. *Songdai minfu de jiaose yu diwei* 宋代民婦的角色與地位. Taipei: Xinwenfeng, 1998.

Yü, Chün-fang. *Kuan-yin: The Chinese Transformations of Avalokiteśvara*. New York: Columbia University Press, 2001.

Yu Huijuan 郁慧娟. "Yi shenwan wei beiliang—Songmo nüxing shici de aiyin fenzhi" 以深婉為悲涼—宋末女性詩詞的哀音憤志. *Yangshan xuekan* 陽山學刊 2 (2011): 38–41.

Yuan Li 袁俐. "Songdai nüxing caichanquan shulun" 宋代女性財產權述論. In *Zhongguo Funüshi lunji xuji* 中國婦女史論集續集, edited by Bao Jialin 鮑家麟, 173–213. Taipei: Daoxiang chubanshe, 1991.

Yuan Yiya 袁怡雅. "Nansong Lin'an Yang huanghou zhai yizhi kao" 南宋臨安楊皇后宅遺址考. *Hangzhou wenbo* 杭州文博 1 (2017): 106–120.

Zang Jian 臧健. "Songdai jiafa de tedian ji qi dui jiazu zhong nannü xingbie jiaose de rending" 宋代家法的特點及其對家族中男女性別角色的認定. In *Tang Song nüxing yu shehui* 唐宋女性與社會, edited by Deng Xiaonan 鄧小南, vol. 1, 275–298. Shanghai: Shanghai cishu, 2003.

Zang, Jian. "Women and the Transmission of Confucian Culture in Song China." In *Women and Confucian Cultures in Premodern China, Korea, and Japan*, edited by Dorothy Ko, JaHyun Kim Haboush, and Joan R. Piggott, 123–141. Berkeley: University of California Press, 2003.

Zhan Xiumei 戰秀梅. "Songdai funü jingji huodong tanxi" 宋代婦女經濟活動探析. *Zhongguo shehui jingji shi yanjiu* 中國社會經濟史研究 1 (2010): 98–103.

Zhang Bangwei 張邦煒. *Hunyin yu shehui (Songdai)* 婚姻與社會 (宋代). Chengdu: Sichuan renmin chubanshe, 1989.

———. "Liang Song shiqi de xing wenti" 兩宋時期的性問題. In *Tang Song nüxing yu shehui* 唐宋女性與社會, edited by Deng Xiaonan 鄧小南, vol. 1, 447–464. Shanghai: Shanghai cishu, 2003.

———. "Songdai funü de zaijia wenti he shehui diwei" 宋代婦女的再嫁問題和社會地位. In *Zhongguo funüshi lunji sanji* 中國婦女史論集三集, edited by Bao Jialin 鮑家麟, 61–95. Taipei: Daoxiang, 1993.

———. *Songdai hunyin jiazu shilun* 宋代婚姻家族史論. Beijing: Renmin, 2003.

Zhang Beibei 張蓓蓓. "Shehui jingji shiye xia de Songdai feshi xiaofei wenhua yanjiu" 社會經濟視野下的宋代服飾消費文化研究. *Zhongguo shehui jingji shi yanjiu* 中國社會經濟史研究 3 (2015): 8–18.

Zhang Benshun 張本順. "Cong Songdai hunyinfa zhong caihunzhi kan Songdai de jinshihua zhuanxing" 從宋代婚姻法中財婚制看宋代的近世化轉型. *Zhoukou Shifan Xueyuan xuebao* 周口師範學院學報 28, no. 6 (2011): 74–80.

———. "Songdai funü lianchan suoyouquan tanxi ji qi yiyi" 宋代婦女奩產所有權探析及其意義. *Fazhi yu shehui fazhan* 法制與社會發展 5 (2011): 79–95.

Zhang Boquan 張博泉. *Jinshi lungao* 金史論稿. Jilin: Jilin wenzhe, 1986.

Zhang, Cong Ellen. "Anecdotal Writing on Illicit Sex in Song China (960–1279)." *Journal of the History of Sexuality* 22, no. 2 (2013): 253–280.

———. "Communication, Collaboration, and Community: Inn-Wall Writing during the Song (960–1279)." *Journal of Song–Yuan Studies* 35 (2005): 1–27.

Zhang Fang 張方. "Quanzhen nüguan yu Yuandai shehui" 全真女冠與元代社會. *Zongjiaoxue yanjiu* 宗教學研究 1 (2011): 64–68.

Zhang Feiyi 張斐怡. "Yuandai fei Hanzu funü xingxiang de Hanhua—Menggu, Semu nüzi beichuan shiliao de fenxi" 元代非漢族婦女形象的漢化一蒙古，色目女子碑傳史料的分析. In *Songshi yanjiuji* 36 宋史研究集, edited by Songshi Zuotanhui 宋史座談會, 505–558. Taipei: Xin wenfeng, 2006.

Zhang Guogang 張國剛. "'Family Building in Inner Quarters': Conjugal Relationships in Tang Families." Translated by Yipeng Lai. *Frontiers of History in China* 4, no. 1 (2009): 1–38.

———. *Jiating shihua* 家庭史話. Beijing: Shehui kexue wenxian, 2012.

———. *Tangdai jiating yu shehui* 唐代家庭與社會. Beijing: Zhonghua, 2014.

Zhang Guoqing 張國慶. *Liaodai shehuishi yanjiu* 遼代社會史研究. Beijing: Zhongguo shehui kexue, 2006.

Zhang Guowang 張國旺. "Lun Yuandai de nütong jiaoyu yu nüjiaoshu" 論元代的女童教育與女教書. *Xiamen Daxue xuebao* 廈門大學學報 2 (2018): 46–52.

Zhang Hong 張宏. "Jindai hougong zhidu chutan" 金代後宮制度初探. *Shehui kexue zhanxian* 社會科學戰線 7 (2012): 105–110.

———. "Qianxi Jindai houfei de xuanna tujing" 淺析金代后妃的選納途徑. *Lantai shijie* 蘭台世界 10 (2012): 48–49.

Zhang Jianwei 張建偉. "Yuandai de jiazu jiaoyu yu minzu wenhua de 'hanhua'" 元代的家族教育與民族文化的 '涵化.' *Minzu jiaoyu yanjiu* 民族教育研究 26, no. 6 (2015): 82–86.

Zhang Jing 張靜 and Feng Weiyi 馮偉一. "Songdai lixue dui nüxing xingxiang de yingxiang" 宋代理學對女性形象的影響. *Xi'an Gongcheng Daxue xuebao* 西安工程大學學報 5 (2008): 579–582.

Zhang Jingwei 張經緯. "Songdai caichan jicheng zhidu tanjiu" 宋代財產繼承制度探究. *Chifeng Xueyuan xuebao* 赤峰學院學報 35, no. 1 (2014): 40–44.

Zhang Jinhua 張金花. "Songdai nüxing jingshang tanxi" 宋代女性經商探析. *Zhongguoshi yanjiu* 中國史研究 6, no. 4 (2006): 1–10.

Zhang Min 張敏. "Cong Liaodai shike kan Liaodai shehui zhong de xianfuguan" 從遼代石刻看遼代社會中的賢婦觀. *Chifeng Xueyuan xuebao* 赤峰學院學報 35, no. 4 (2014): 10–12.

———. "Liaodai nüxing de fanzui wenti yanjiu" 遼代女性的犯罪問題研究. *Chifeng Xueyuan xuebao* 赤峰學院學報 34, no. 8 (2016): 7–9.

———. "Liaodai Qidan nüxing de jiaoyu wenti tanxi" 遼代契丹女性的教育問題探析. *Chifeng Xueyuan xuebao* 赤峰學院學報 34, no. 12 (2013): 15–17.

———. "Liaodai shike zhong suo fanying de Liaochao muyi guifan" 遼代石刻中所反應的遼朝母儀規範. *Tianshui Shifan Xueyuan xuebao* 天水師範學院學報 34, no. 5 (2014): 81–84.

———. "Liaodai waimingfu shilu tanxi" 遼代外命婦制度探析. *Neimenggu Minzu Daxue xuebao* 內蒙古民族大學學報 4 (2012): 8–9.

Zhang Min 張敏 and Xu Liying 徐麗穎. "Cong Liaodai muzhi zhong de nüxing dianfan kan Liaodai shehui de nüxingguan" 從遼代墓誌中的女性典範看遼代社會的女性觀. *Baicheng Shifan Xueyuan xuebao* 百城師範學院學報 29, no. 1 (2015): 28–31.

Zhang Peizhi 張沛之. "Yuandai shaoshu minzu guanliao jiazu hunyin chutan" 元代少數民族官僚家族婚姻初探. *Henan Shifan Daxue xuebao* 河南師範大學學報 1 (2004): 114–116.

Zhang Qing 張倩. "Liaodai Chenguo Gongzhu fuma hezangmu chutu de shoushi ji qi wenhua neihan" 遼代陳國公主駙馬合葬墓出土的首飾及其文化內涵. *Hulunbeier Xueyuan xuebao* 呼倫貝爾學院學報 22, no. 3 (2014): 45–49.

Zhang Ting 張婷, Hua Jingmei 華景梅, and Zhao Yang 趙揚. "Lun Songdai nüzi de xiangpu yundong" 論宋代女子的相撲運動. *Song Liao Jin shi* 宋遼金史 6 (2015): 76–77.

Zhang Wen 張文 and Fan Meng 范夢. "Cong nügui gushi kan Songdai qiebi de renjian shenghuo—Songdai qiebi guanxi yanjiu" 從女鬼故事看宋代妾婢的人間生活—宋代妻妾關係研究. *Anhui Shifan Daxue xuebao* 安徽師範大學學報 1 (2011): 29–34.

Zhang Yanling 張琰玲 and Sun Yinghui 孫穎慧. "Yuandai Xi Xia nüxing yimin renwu shiliao zhengli yu yanjiu" 元代西夏女性遺民人物史料整理與研究. *Tushuguan lilun yu shijian* 圖書館理論與實踐 10 (2013): 94–98.

Zhang Ye 張鄴 and 張敏 Zhang Min. *Qidan jinguo: Liaodai Qidanzu nüxing yanjiu* 契丹巾幗: 遼代契丹族女性研究. Beijing: Minzu chubanshe, 2014.

Zhao Qingfang 趙慶芳. "Songdai nüxing ci de yuyan tese" 宋代女性詞的語言特色. *Sichuan Wenli Xueyuan xuebao* 四川文理學院學報 4 (2007): 55–56.

Zhao, Xiaohuan. "Love, Lust, and Loss in the Daoist Nunnery as Presented in Yuan Drama." *T'oung Pao* 100, nos. 1–3 (2014): 80–119.

Zhao Yongchun 趙永春 and Wang Zhu 王姝. "Jindai pinguan mingfu huo feng zeng tujing yanjiu" 金代品官命婦獲封贈途徑研究. *Xinan Daxue xuebao* 西南大學學報 3 (2014): 163–169.

Zheng Liping 鄭麗萍. "Songdai nannü chuhun nianling tanxi" 宋代男女初婚年齡探析. *Huadong Shifan Daxue xuebao* 華東師範大學學報 3 (2010): 118–124.

Zheng Peng 鄭鵬. "Guan, min yu fa—Yuandai panjue lihun de zhidu yu shijian" 官民與法—元代判決離婚的制度與實踐. *Gudai wenming* 古代文明 9, no. 4 (2015): 78–90.

Zheng Xiaoqiang 鄭小強 and Yang Qianqian 楊茜茜. "Tang Song nüxing ticai huihua bijiao" 唐宋女性題材繪畫比較. *Lincang Shifan Gaodeng Zhuanke Xuexiao xuebao* 臨滄師範高等專科學校學報 20, no. 4 (2010): 102–104.

Zheng Yawen 鄭雅文. "Lixue shengxing xia de funü diwei—tan Li Qingzhao, Zhu Shuzhen hunyin shenghuo zhong de nüquan yishi" 理學盛行下的婦女地位—談李清照，朱淑真婚姻生活中的女權意識. *Songdai wenhua yanjiu* 宋代文化研究 17 (2009): 572–593.

Zheng Yushu 鄭玉書. "Lun Qidan nüxing de minzu yishi yu junshi fengmao" 論契丹女性的民族意識和軍事風貌. *Liaoning Gongcheng Jishu Daxue xuebao* 遼寧工程技術大學學報 3 (1999): 64–67.

Zhou Baorong 周寶榮. "Qidan Chengtian Taihou de ruhua zhanlue" 契丹承天太后的儒化戰略. *Shixue yuekan* 史學月刊 7 (2003): 32–35.

———. "Shilun Songdai jiaoyu de 'pingminhua'" 試論宋代教育的 '平民化.' *Henan Shifan Daxue xuebao* 河南師範大學學報 4 (2009): 134–137.

Zhou Jiren 周繼仁. "Lun Zhongguo gudai biaoyan yishu de shangpinhua wenti" 論中國古代表演藝術的商品化問題. *Zhongguoshi yanjiu* 中國史研究 15, no. 4 (1993): 44–57.

Zhou Xiaowei 周曉薇 and Wang Qiyi 王其禕. *Roushun zhi xiang: Suidai nüxing yu shehui* 柔順之象: 隋代女性與社會. Beijing: Zhongguo shehui kexue chubanshe, 2012.

Zhu Hailin 朱海琳 and Chen Xu 陳旭. "Songdai weirenmu de minshi falü diwei" 宋代為人母的民事法律地位. *Zhonghua Nüzi Xueyuan xuebao* 中華女子學院學報 20, no. 2 (2008): 110–113.

Zhu Junling 朱均靈. "Lun Yuan Cai de nuxingguan" 論袁采的女性觀. *Zhangzhou Shifan Xueyuan xuebao* 漳州師範學院學報 4 (2010): 83–87.

Zhu, Rui. "Identity, Legitimacy, and Chaste Widows." *Asian Philosophy* 26, no. 2 (2016): 182–192.

Zhu Ruixi 朱瑞熙 et al. *Liao Song Xi Xia Jin shehui shenghuo shi* 遼宋西夏金社會生活史. Beijing: Zhongguo shehui kexue, 1998.

Zhu Yunrong 朱運榮. "Songdai jiazhuang chutan" 宋代嫁妝初探. *Anhui Guangbo Dianshi Daxue xuebao* 安徽廣播電視大學學報 4 (2009): 118–123.

Zhuang Guorui 庄國瑞. "Songdai gongzhu quanli pangluo yuanyin tanxi—yi Song Renzong nü Yanguo gongzhu wei li" 宋代公主權利旁落原因探析—以宋仁宗女兗國公主為例. *Henan Keji Daxue xuebao* 河南科技大學學報 33, no. 5 (2015): 14–20.

Zurndorfer, Harriet T. "The Hsin-an Ta-tsu-chih and the Development of the Chinese Gentry Society, 800–1600." *T'oung Pao* 67, nos. 3–5 (1981): 154–215.

———. "Women in Chinese Learned Culture: Complexities, Exclusivities and Connecting Narratives." *Gender & History* 16, no. 1 (2014): 23–35.

Index

Hidden Horrors: Japanese War Crimes in World War II, Second Edition
    by Yuki Tanaka
Zen Terror: The Death of Democracy in Prewar Japan
    by Brian A. Victoria
No Time for Dreams: Living in Burma under Military Rule
    by Carolyn Wakeman and San San Tin
A Thousand Miles of Dreams: The Journeys of Two Chinese Sisters
    by Sasha Su-Ling Welland
Dancing in Shadows: Sihanouk, the Khmer Rouge, and the United Nations in Cambodia
    by Benny Widyono
Voices Carry: Behind Bars and Backstage during China's Revolution and Reform
    by Ying Ruocheng and Claire Conceison